JOURNAL FOR THE STUDY OF THE NEW TESTAMENT
SUPPLEMENT SERIES
296

Editor
Mark Goodacre

Women and Marriage in Paul and his Early Interpreters

Gillian Beattie

t&t clark

Published by T&T Clark International
an imprint of Continuum

The Tower Building,
11 York Road,
London SE1 7NX

15 East 26th Street,
Suite 1703,
New York, NY 10010

www.tandtclark.com

British Library Cataloguing-in-Publication Data
A catalogue record for this book is available from the British Library.

ISBN 0–567–03050–4 (hardback)

Typeset by RefineCatch Ltd, Bungay, Suffolk
Printed on acid-free paper in Great Britain by Antony Rowe Ltd, Chippenham, Wiltshire

CONTENTS

PREFACE

This book had its origins in a Ph.D. thesis submitted to the University of Manchester in September 2003. Since then, I have forsaken my student life and become acquainted with the benefits and constraints of full-time employment; so while the work has been revised and refined, it does remain to a large extent the product of a particular time and place. That it should be read as such is entirely in keeping with the theory which it is intended to advance. Indeed, it is specifically not my desire that this volume should be regarded as making any kind of attempt to have the 'final word' on the texts and ideas with which it deals; on the contrary, it is offered as a partial contribution to an ongoing discussion in which many voices are to be heard. If some readers are encouraged or provoked by what they find here to participate in the debate themselves, then the book will have achieved its goal.

ACKNOWLEDGMENTS

The process of academic research and writing is often thought of as a solitary enterprise. In one sense this is true; but throughout the times I was working on the original thesis and revising it for publication, I benefited from the support and encouragement of many individuals and groups, my gratitude to whom I wish to record here.

I should mention first the Arts and Humanities Research Board, whose financial support, in the form of a Postgraduate Studentship Award, made it possible for me to carry out this research. My supervisor, Dr Todd Klutz, has been constructive in his criticism and unstinting in his encouragement through the entire process, while the whole Department of Religions and Theology at the University of Manchester offered a stimulating and supportive environment in which to work. The empathetic friendship of my fellow postgraduate students provided a genuine sense of community and kept any feelings of isolation firmly at bay.

Valuable feedback on my work came from a number of sources. I am grateful to the members of the Ehrhardt seminar at the University of Manchester for their insightful and challenging responses to the papers I presented to them as a doctoral student; I also benefited from similar experiences at the Manchester–Lausanne Colloquium on Canon held in Lausanne and Geneva in June 2000, and in the Paul Seminar at the British New Testament Conference held in Manchester in September 2001. Particular thanks are due to my examiners, Professor George Brooke and Dr Edward Adams, for their thorough and rigorous engagement with my doctoral thesis; any errors or omissions which remain in the present volume are mine alone.

With particular regard to the publication of this work, I am grateful to Rebecca Mulhearn and Rebecca Vaughan Williams at T&T Clark International for their encouragement and their prompt and helpful advice.

Finally, on a personal note, I want to acknowledge my parents, Dale and Mary Beattie, who have been unfailingly tolerant and supportive of their daughter's strange obsession with books and academic study. Last but not least, I thank David, for enabling me to see a great many things differently, and for making the years during which my doctoral work was completed and revised such happy ones.

ABBREVIATIONS

Ancient texts

Ad Uxor.	Tertullian, *Ad uxorem*
Adv. Haer.	Irenaeus, *Adversus haereses*
Adv. Val.	Tertullian, *Adversus Valentinianos*
Apion.	Josephus, *Contra Apionem*
Apoc. John	*Apocryphon of John*
Apol.	Tertullian, *Apologia*
De Bap.	Tertullian, *De baptismo*
De Exhor. Cast.	Tertullian, *De exhortatione castitatis*
Deus Imm.	Philo, *Quod Deus sit immutabilis*
Ex. Soul	*Exegesis on the Soul*
Fug.	Philo, *De fuga et inventione*
Gos. Phil.	*Gospel of Philip*
Gos. Thom.	*Gospel of Thomas*
Hyp. Arch.	*Hypostasis of the Archons*
LXX	Septuagint
Praem. Poen.	Philo, *De praemiis et poenis*
Praescr.	Tertullian, *De praescriptione haereticorum*
Quaest. in Gen.	Philo, *Quaestiones in Genesin*
Ref.	Hippolytus, *Refutatio omnium haeresium*
Spec. Leg.	Philo, *De specialibus legibus*
Test. Naph.	*Testament of Naphthali*
Vit. Cont.	Philo, *De vita contemplativa*
Vit. Mos.	Philo, *De vita Mosis*

Modern sources

AB	Anchor Bible
ANRW	Hildegard Temporini and Wolfgang Haase (eds), *Aufstieg und Niedergang der römischen Welt: Geschichte und Kultur Roms im Spiegel der neueren Forschung* (Berlin: W. de Gruyter, 1972–)
BDF	Friedrich Blass, A. Debrunner and Robert W. Funk, *A*

	Greek Grammar of the New Testament and Other Early Christian Literature (Cambridge: Cambridge University Press, 1961)
BTB	*Biblical Theological Bulletin*
CBQ	*Catholic Biblical Quarterly*
CH	*Church History*
EvQ	*Evangelical Quarterly*
HDR	Harvard Dissertations in Religion
HR	*History of Religions*
HTR	*Harvard Theological Review*
JBL	*Journal of Biblical Literature*
JECS	*Journal of Early Christian Studies*
JSNT	*Journal for the Study of the New Testament*
JSNTSup	*Journal for the Study of the New Testament* Supplement Series
JSOTSup	*Journal for the Study of the Old Testament* Supplement Series
NCB	New Century Bible
NICNT	New International Commentary on the New Testament
NIGTC	New International Greek Testament Commentary
NovT	*Novum Testamentum*
NRSV	New Revised Standard Version
NTS	*New Testament Studies*
RB	*Revue Biblique*
SBLDS	Society of Biblical Literature Dissertation Series
SNTSMS	Society for New Testament Studies Monograph Series
TDNT	Gerhard Kittel and Gerhard Friedrich (eds), *Theological Dictionary of the New Testament*, tr. Geoffrey W. Bromiley, 10 vols (Grand Rapids: Eerdmans, 1964–)
VC	*Vigiliae christianae*

Introduction

WOMEN AND MARRIAGE IN PAUL AND HIS EARLY INTERPRETERS

> . . . of course she realized one could make a fetish of the scriptures.
>
> Muriel Spark, *The Mandelbaum Gate*

The form which this volume now takes is rather different from the one I originally had in mind when, several years ago, I began working on the doctoral thesis upon which the book is based. While some factors – the biblical texts to be examined; the topical focus on women and marriage – remained constant, others – most notably my theoretical perspective and with it the project's overall aim – changed considerably as my research progressed. It therefore seems to me important to explain in this Introduction what exactly I am (and am not) trying to do in the pages that follow, and to set out the methodology that underpins my endeavours, as well as to give some account of how I came to adopt it.

It is perhaps easiest to explain each element of the title in order. To begin with the first (and perhaps simplest) question: why women and marriage? From a purely practical point of view, when engaging in a comparative exercise such as this, some such topical focus is a helpful device to confine the work to manageable proportions. My initial decision to concentrate on these subjects in particular was guided in part by a feminist sensibility and desire to subject to the strongest possible scrutiny certain New Testament passages whose impact on women's lives is still in evidence today. What individual readers will choose to make of these passages in the light of such scrutiny is, of course, a matter for them; but I believe this choice of topic was a good one for other reasons as well. In every part of this volume, the various authors' treatments of women and marriage throw into especially sharp relief the complex and fascinating question of the relationship between text and (cultural) context, so that one is never able to escape awareness of these authors' situatedness. Other topics could no doubt have been chosen for a study such as this (baptism, the Lord's Supper, the idea of resurrection all spring to mind); women and marriage simply happens to have been the most interesting and the most useful to me.

Secondly, then: why Paul? Perhaps because, on both a personal and professional level, he loomed so large in my field of vision as to appear unavoidable, and it seemed preferable to confront him head on. I decided to focus here on his first letter to the Corinthians, since it is there that his most expansive treatment of my chosen topic is to be found; as Daniel Boyarin puts it, 1 Corinthians is the Pauline text that 'most manifests ... fleshly concerns'.[1] The complexity and ambivalence which seem to characterize Paul's teachings on both women and marriage, and the difficulties encountered by me and others in making sense of them, gave rise to the question of what might have been made of those teachings by the generations of readers who immediately followed him. Thus I conceived the original aim of the thesis: to pursue the uses to which Paul's writings on these subjects were put by a variety of his ancient interpreters.

But whom to include in this group of interpreters? The deutero-Pauline letters (Colossians, Ephesians, the Pastoral Epistles) seemed to be obvious candidates, their interest in Paul's name and tradition being so great that they sought to take on his identity by means of the device of pseudonymity.[2] Intriguing though these texts are, however, their appropriation of Paul could be said to be a little one-sided; as I shall show in Part II, their endorsement of marriage and constriction of women's roles draw on one aspect of Paul's teaching while completely neglecting others. Where might one look to find an alternative view? The pro-women and anti-marriage reputation of the 'gnostic'[3] texts of Nag Hammadi led me to suppose that they would provide a ready solution,[4] and furthermore, their interest in Paul was also well documented.[5]

As I began to explore these 'gnostic' writings, however, it quickly became apparent that these authors' readings of Paul had earned them some highly unfavourable reviews. Irenaeus, for example, assesses them in the following terms:

---

1. Daniel Boyarin, *A Radical Jew: Paul and the Politics of Identity* (Berkeley: University of California Press, 1994), p. 185.

2. It is assumed throughout this book that all these letters are pseudonymous. A thorough justification for this assumption will be presented in the relevant chapters for each document in turn.

3. This use of inverted commas will be explained presently.

4. It is not my intention to explore how, or even to suggest that, the 'gnostics' influenced Paul rather than the other way round. In this way my approach is in marked contrast to that of Walter Schmithals in his *Gnosticism in Corinth: An Investigation of the Letters to the Corinthians*, tr. John E. Steely (Nashville and New York: Abingdon, 1971). Although it may be possible to see in Paul's opponents in Corinth 'the first tentative beginnings of what was later to develop into full-scale Gnosticism' (R. McL. Wilson, 'How Gnostic Were the Corinthians?', *NTS* 19 [1972/73], pp. 65–74 [74]), it is not my purpose to address the vexed question of the historical origins of this phenomenon. The point to which I do want to draw attention at this juncture is that, as Wilson observes elsewhere, later 'gnostic' appeal to Paul does not make Paul himself a 'gnostic' ('Gnosis at Corinth', in M.D. Hooker and S.G. Wilson [eds], *Paul and Paulinism: Essays in Honour of C.K. Barrett* [London: SPCK, 1982], pp. 102–14 [109]).

5. See for example Elaine Pagels, *The Gnostic Paul: Gnostic Exegesis of the Pauline Letters* (Philadelphia: Trinity Press International, 1975).

> It is necessary to subjoin ... the doctrine of Paul ... to examine the
> opinion of this man, and expound the apostle, and to explain whatsoever
> [passages] have received other interpretations from the heretics, who have
> altogether misunderstood what Paul has spoken, and to point out the
> folly of their mad opinions; and to demonstrate from that same Paul,
> from whose [writings] they press questions upon us, that they are indeed
> utterers of falsehood, but that the apostle was a preacher of the truth,
> and that he taught all things agreeable to the preaching of the truth.[6]

Similarly Tertullian, while noting how very great is the use these people
make of Paul in respect of all manner of questions, disparages the interpretations they make and opines, 'let them believe without the Scriptures, if
their object is to believe contrary to the Scriptures'.[7] In fact, these negative
assessments of 'gnostic' readings of Paul are just one component of a thoroughgoing attack mounted by the heresiologists on those they regarded as
their opponents. Moreover, it is the writings of these thoroughly biased
observers which provide the primary source for the modern category of
'gnosticism',[8] the category from which my initial impressions of a proto-
feminist, ascetic movement were derived, but which, in relation to the Nag
Hammadi texts themselves, proves (as I shall demonstrate in Part III) to be
inaccurate, misleading and ultimately unsustainable.

My aim for the project thus became twofold: to explore a variety of
readings of Paul, as before (while bearing in mind that such readings take
place in a highly charged atmosphere in which a great deal is at stake); but
also to subject the category of 'gnosticism' to a thoroughgoing interroga-
tion, with the goal of reinstating the texts classified under its rubric as valid
interpretations of Paul worthy of serious consideration. One's understanding of the category affects one's understanding of the texts it is used to
describe; and one's engagement with these texts can and should, I believe,
have an impact on one's engagement with the more familiar canonical
documents, so that all the writings treated in this study can be seen in a new
light at the end of it. Hence my use of inverted commas with the terms
'gnostic' and 'gnosticism': these words frequently serve as useful shorthand
for referring to particular texts or phenomena, but I would not wish my
employment of them to be taken for an endorsement of a category I believe
to be unsustainable. The reasons why I find it to be so will be outlined below
in the section 'Redescribing "Gnosticism" '; but first it is necessary for me to
discuss in rather more detail the theoretical perspective that motivates and
governs the book.

---

6. Irenaeus, *Adv. Haer.* 4.41.4.

7. Tertullian, *Praescr.* 23.

8. This category is masterfully deconstructed by Michael Williams in *Rethinking 'Gnosticism': An Argument for Dismantling a Dubious Category* (Princeton: Princeton University
Press, 1996).

Theoretical Perspective: 'The Pragmatist's Progress'

The philosophical outlook I now embrace is the result of a lengthy process of reflection, the catalyst for which was a few throwaway remarks made at the start of a seminar paper given some eighteen months into my research, on the nature of meaning and the role of the author. I began my paper with the title of Jeffrey Stout's article, 'What is the Meaning of a Text?', before proceeding to note with some disappointment that Stout's own stated aim in this piece was 'to undermine the widespread assumption that this question either requires or deserves an answer'.[9] I went on to refer to his notion that 'good commentary is whatever suits our interests and purposes' with what was at the time genuinely felt alarm.[10]

In search of a secure refuge from this unsettling relativism, I turned to the work of E.D. Hirsch, a writer who appeared to be quite happy actually to answer the question of what meaning might be, and who did so in the following definition: '*Meaning* is that which is represented by a text; it is what the author meant by his use of a particular sign sequence; it is what the signs represent. *Significance*, on the other hand, names a relationship between that meaning and a person, or a conception, or a situation, or indeed anything imaginable.'[11] While acknowledging that the author's meaning can never be known with certainty, Hirsch cautions that '[i]t is a logical mistake to confuse the impossibility of certainty in understanding with the impossibility of understanding'.[12] In fact, believing that consensus rather than certainty should be the goal of interpretation, he privileges the author's meaning as 'the only compelling normative principle that could lend validity to an interpretation'.[13]

While I was encouraged to find that my attempts to discover what Paul may have actually meant in 1 Corinthians need not be utterly futile, at the same time I found myself forced to acknowledge certain difficulties with Hirsch's position. First of all, with regard to the distinction he draws between meaning and significance, under what circumstances could one ever conceive of meaning which does not have some relation to a context? As is

---

9. Jeffrey Stout, 'What is the Meaning of a Text?', *New Literary History* 14 (1982), pp. 1–12 (1).

10. Stout, 'What is the Meaning of a Text?', p. 6.

11. E.D. Hirsch, *Validity in Interpretation* (New Haven and London: Yale University Press, 1967), p. 8; emphasis in original. This distinction is still more or less in place in Hirsch's later work, *The Aims of Interpretation* (Chicago and London: University of Chicago Press, 1976), pp. 2–3: 'the term "meaning" refers to the whole verbal meaning of a text, and "significance" to textual meaning in relation to a larger context, i.e. another mind, another era, a wider subject matter, an alien system of values, and so on. In other words, "significance" is textual meaning as related to some context, any context, beyond itself.'

12. Hirsch, *Validity in Interpretation*, pp. 16–17.

13. Hirsch, *Validity in Interpretation*, p. 10.

obviously the case for all of the documents I shall examine here, texts are never produced in a vacuum, and the context in which they are written must be taken into account if one is to appreciate them fully. An attentive reading of the Pastoral Epistles or the *Gospel of Philip*, for example, reveals that while they both interact with ideas presented in Paul's Corinthian correspondence, neither is particularly interested in what Paul might originally have meant when he wrote those letters. Am I therefore to dismiss their readings of Paul as invalid? The answer must surely be no, for an interpretation that is 'valid' in Hirsch's terms would have been of little use or relevance in the new sets of circumstances in which these later texts were produced.

A recognition of the importance of context, therefore, effectively removes the author's intended meaning from its position of privilege. This is not to say, however, that I go so far as to subscribe to what Richard Rorty archly describes as 'the weird Barthian view that language works all by itself'.[14] To allow Barthes to make his case in his own words: 'writing is the destruction of every voice, of every point of origin. Writing is that neutral, composite, oblique space where our subject slips away, the negative where all identity is lost, starting with the very identity of the body writing.'[15] In my opinion, this report of the author's death has not only been rather exaggerated; it is also more than a little disingenuous. To borrow Hirsch's words once again, 'Whenever meaning is attached to a sequence of words, it is impossible to escape an author'[16] of that meaning, whether that author be the person who wrote the words whose meaning a reader sets out to rediscover, or the reader herself consciously makes meanings of her own regardless of the writer's original intention. However far-reaching language's 'complexities and web-like traps'[17] might be, texts are both written and read by human beings in concrete circumstances, with particular ends in view; they neither compose nor interpret themselves.

It was thus that I came to embrace Richard Rorty's concept of contingency as central to my project. Discussing the work of Donald Davidson, Rorty rejects the idea (implicit in Hirsch's definition of meaning quoted above) that language can be a medium either for expression of the self or for representation of the 'real world', since neither the self nor reality has an intrinsic nature which can be expressed or represented.[18] Contrary to what the

---

14. Richard Rorty, *Contingency, Irony, and Solidarity* (Cambridge: Cambridge University Press, 1989), p. 167.

15. Roland Barthes, 'The Death of the Author', in David Lodge (ed.), *Modern Criticism and Theory: A Reader* (London and New York: Longman, 1988), pp. 167–72 (168).

16. Hirsch, *Validity in Interpretation*, p. 5.

17. John D. Caputo, *More Radical Hermeneutics: On Not Knowing Who We Are* (Bloomington and Indianapolis: Indiana University Press, 2000), p. 103.

18. Rorty, *Contingency, Irony, and Solidarity*, p. 11.

popular science-fiction show *The X-Files* would have us believe, the truth, Rorty insists, is *not* out there: 'the world is out there, but descriptions of the world are not'.[19] The ways in which people talk about the world, the vocabularies they use to describe it, are not dictated to them by the world itself, but are instead guided by what people want to do in given situations and by what will be useful to them in achieving their purposes. I want to suggest here that the same is true for texts. While texts, unlike the physical world, are already linguistic entities, they also do not command the terms of their interpretation, but can be read in ways as diverse and numerous as the goals of their interpreters.

A little sheepishly, perhaps, I therefore now find myself in basic agreement with that assertion of Stout's which once alarmed me so much, that 'good commentary is whatever suits our interests and purposes'. But does not this leave me open to the same charge that I once levelled against him, the charge of relativism, the idea that 'anything goes'? Stanley Fish comes to my defence at this point, observing that a pragmatist position such as the one I have just set out does not mean that 'anything goes'; it means rather that 'anything that can be made to go goes'.[20] This is an important distinction. Fish notes elsewhere that 'while relativism is a position one can entertain, it is not a position one can occupy'.[21] In other words, while one can believe that no one way of describing the world or interpreting a text is inherently more apt than, or necessarily superior to, all the others, this does not mean that one operates without adhering to a certain set of criteria or principles, a particular way of seeing the world which Rorty calls a 'final vocabulary'.[22] Although contingent and subject to change, such vocabularies nonetheless *feel* final; as Fish observes, 'no one is indifferent to the norms and values that enable his consciousness'.[23] It is on the level of these norms and values, the level where interpretative interests, aims and motivations are formed, that debates and disagreements must now be worked out.[24]

Looking back over the process of my development, it might be said that the position I now embrace is the consequence of my encounters (some by chance) with a variety of texts, which, taken together, have produced a

19.   Rorty, *Contingency, Irony, and Solidarity*, p. 5.

20.   Stanley Fish, *The Trouble with Principle* (Cambridge, Mass. and London: Harvard University Press, 1999), p. 307.

21.   Stanley Fish, *Is There a Text in This Class? The Authority of Interpretive Communities* (Cambridge, Mass. and London: Harvard University Press, 1980), p. 319.

22.   Rorty, *Contingency, Irony, and Solidarity*, p. 73.

23.   Fish, *Is There a Text in This Class?*, p. 319.

24.   Stephen Fowl, 'The Ethics of Interpretation, or What's Left Over after the Elimination of Meaning', in David J.A. Clines, Stephen E. Fowl and Stanley E. Porter (eds), *The Bible in Three Dimensions: Essays in Celebration of Forty Years of Biblical Studies in the University of Sheffield* (Sheffield: JSOT Press, 1990), pp. 379–98 (385–86). This is not to say, of course, that any such 'working out' will be an easy or straightforward matter; rather the opposite, in fact.

certain result. This is a process that Rorty playfully refers to as the 'Pragmatist's Progress'[25] – a process which can never be regarded as complete. His description of this phenomenon might serve as a useful summary of what is happening in this volume: '[r]eading texts is a matter of reading them in the light of other texts, people, obsessions, bits of information, or what have you, and then seeing what happens'.[26] By examining Paul alongside and in relation to some of his early interpreters, all the texts involved come to be seen in a new light. Readers of this book will find that it is not only scholarly authors who assist me in this examination; from time to time I draw on the insights of certain writers of fiction as well. This, perhaps, reflects one or two of my own personal 'obsessions', as well as being an acknowledgment (wry though it may be in such a piece of work as this) of Rorty's suggestion that 'novels are a safer medium than theory for expressing one's recognition of the relativity and contingency of authority figures'.[27]

Redescribing 'Gnosticism'

Before embarking on the main part of the book, it is necessary to say a little more about the category 'gnosticism' and why it is so unhelpful to anyone wishing to engage with the Nag Hammadi texts. Some of the main elements of the category, namely its caricatured portrayals of 'gnostic' morality and methods of biblical interpretation, will be considered in detail in Chapters 5 and 6, so I shall discuss it here only in general terms. Michael Williams offers the following summary of 'gnosticism' as traditionally understood:

> 'gnostics' had an 'attitude.' They had an attitude of 'protest' or of 'revolt,' an 'anti-cosmic attitude.' This attitude allegedly showed up in the way 'gnostics' treated scripture (they are alleged to have reversed all its values), viewed the material cosmos (they are supposed to have rejected it), took an interest in society at large (they didn't, we are told), felt about their own bodies (they hated them). These revolutionaries are supposed to have lacked any serious ethical concern, and to have been driven instead by their attitude toward their cosmic environment to one of two characteristically 'gnostic' forms of behavior: fanatical ascetic renunciation of sex and other bodily comforts and pleasures, or the exact opposite, unbridled debauchery and lawbreaking. 'Gnostics,' it is asserted, had no worries about their own ultimate salvation, since they understood themselves to be automatically saved because of their inner divine nature. With salvation predetermined, ethics were irrelevant to them.[28]

25. Richard Rorty, *Philosophy and Social Hope* (Harmondsworth: Penguin, 1999), p. 133.
26. Rorty, *Philosophy and Social Hope*, p. 144.
27. Rorty, *Contingency, Irony, and Solidarity*, p. 107.
28. Williams, *Rethinking 'Gnosticism'*, p. 5.

Williams' book as a whole offers a systematic debunking of this stereotype. He notes that it has almost no basis in the self-designation of the groups described,[29] and that as a typological construct, it has failed not only to achieve clarity in classification, but also to help readers understand the texts it purports to explain.[30]

The phenomena and texts that have been referred to by the designations 'gnosticism' and 'gnostic' therefore seem more than ready to undergo a process of redescription. The concept of redescription, also derived from Rorty's work, is almost as important for my purposes in this volume as that of contingency. Since the truth about the world is not out there waiting to be found, changes in understanding take place not by 'discovering' something new, but rather by talking about things in new ways. Hence, as Rorty puts it, 'anything can be made to look good or bad by being redescribed'.[31] As Rorty shows in his analysis of Marcel Proust's *Remembrance of Things Past*, the process of redescription is a particularly useful way to reconfigure the relationship of the oppressed, excluded or misrepresented to those who have dominated them by claiming the right to define who and what they are. Such a process is not one of simple reversal whereby the underdog becomes the master, but rather one in which the underdog recognizes and exposes the contingency and finitude of *all* powers.[32] Applying this to the field of early Christianity, my aim in redescribing 'gnosticism' and the Nag Hammadi texts is not simply to reverse the polar opposition of 'orthodoxy' and 'heresy' so that the latter term comes to be seen as superior and preferred. This opposition is itself a description of the state of affairs from only one viewpoint – the 'orthodox' viewpoint – and there are other, quite possibly more fruitful, ways to talk about the complexities of this situation.[33] For this reason, 'orthodoxy' and 'heresy' too will be accompanied by inverted commas throughout the rest of the book.

That descriptions of 'gnosticism' should have derived in large part from the evidence of the 'orthodox' heresiological authors is to some extent understandable, given that the Nag Hammadi library was not unearthed until 1945. However, even though the evidence of the so-called 'gnostic' documents themselves is now freely available, some scholars still prefer to rely on the more familiar sources. Michel Desjardins' work on Valentinianism may be extended to apply to the category of 'gnosticism' as a whole. He insists that it is not justified to give the Nag Hammadi texts priority over the heresiologists because it is only on the basis of the secondary patristic

---

29. Williams, *Rethinking 'Gnosticism'*, p. 42.
30. Williams, *Rethinking 'Gnosticism'*, p. 49.
31. Rorty, *Contingency, Irony, and Solidarity*, p. 73.
32. Rorty, *Contingency, Irony, and Solidarity*, pp. 102–103.
33. Of course, I am far from being the first to make this suggestion. See, for example, Walter Bauer, *Orthodoxy and Heresy in Earliest Christianity* (London: SCM Press, 1972 [1934]).

sources that one can designate the primary texts as 'Valentinian' at all.[34] But with all due recognition of the dangers of arguments from silence, surely the lack of explicit 'Valentinian' (or 'gnostic') self-designations in the Nag Hammadi texts themselves should cause the interpreter to question not their reliability but rather that of the heresiologists. I find it impossible to escape the impression that if one's primary interest is in the Nag Hammadi documents themselves, one might do better to leave the category aside and read the texts on their own terms.

More satisfactory explanations of the disparity between 'orthodox' and 'heretical' sources may be found when one is less prepared to take Irenaeus and his colleagues at their word. Pheme Perkins, for example, draws attention to the rhetorical character of *Adversus Haereses*, noting that rhetorical models 'dictate the form and content of many of [Irenaeus'] assertions, which must, therefore, be understood as meeting rhetorical expectations and not as factual reports'.[35] When Irenaeus accuses his opponents of obscurity, inconsistency, and dubious morals, his primary aim is to discredit them, not to give a measured and accurate account.

This hypothesis makes a good deal of sense when one bears in mind what the relationship between many of the so-called 'gnostic' heretics and the 'orthodox' church may in fact have been.[36] Consider Tertullian's account of one 'gnostic' leader: 'Valentinus had expected to become a bishop, because he was an able man both in genius and eloquence. Being indignant, however, that another obtained the dignity by reason of a claim which confessorship had given him, he broke with the church of the true faith.'[37] Tertullian goes on to assert that Valentinus went in search of revenge and 'applied himself with all his might to exterminate the truth', but it seems clear that the emerging conflict had more to do with authority than doctrine; as Frederik Wisse puts it, 'Heresy at this point was not teaching which conflicted with official doctrine, but rather the distinctive teaching of persons who were no longer in communion with the church.'[38] Valentinus and others like him were

34. Michel Desjardins, *Sin in Valentinianism*, SBLDS 108 (Atlanta: Scholars Press, 1990), pp. 8–10.

35. Pheme Perkins, 'Irenaeus and the Gnostics: Rhetoric and Composition in *Adversus Haereses* Book One', *VC* 30 (1976), pp. 193–200 (197).

36. This should not be taken to indicate that I see the phenomenon known as 'gnosticism' as a purely Christian phenomenon. (For an example of one who does take this view, see Simone Pétrement, *A Separate God: The Christian Origins of Gnosticism*, tr. Carol Harrison [New York: HarperCollins, 1990].) It is true that I am primarily interested in the 'gnostic' texts as they relate to other early documents that are indubitably Christian; but to answer the question of the actual historical origins of 'gnosticism' is beyond the scope of the present work.

37. Tertullian, *Adv. Val.* 4.

38. Frederik Wisse, 'Prolegomena to the Study of the New Testament and Gnosis', in A.H.B. Logan and A.J.M. Wedderburn (eds), *The New Testament and Gnosis: Essays in Honour of Robert McL. Wilson* (Edinburgh: T. & T. Clark, 1983), pp. 138–45 (140).

a threat to the 'orthodox' church not because they were outrageously different from it in their teachings, but because they were in many respects so
similar.

As will be seen in Part III, the heresiologists devote considerable energies
to discrediting their opponents' moral behaviour and ways of reading scripture. These were not their only targets. Irenaeus, '[w]ith characteristic concern for veracity' as Morton Smith bitingly observes,[39] also seeks to discredit
his opponents by means of spurious genealogies, tracing their origins back
not to the apostles to whom they appeal, but rather to the arch-enemy of the
apostles, Simon Magus.[40] One can imagine the persuasive potential of such a
strategy in a society in which ascribed (dis)honour was an important concept.[41] The genealogies, showing ever-multiplying branches of gnostic sects
splitting off from one another, served to discredit Irenaeus' opponents in
another way, allowing him to contrast the disarray and diversity of these
groups with the unified teaching of the church. 'Numbers of them – indeed,
we may say all – desire themselves to be teachers, and to break off from the
particular heresy in which they have been involved. . . . [T]hey insist upon
teaching something new'.[42] Wisse may be correct that this picture of 'system-
building' could be the result of Irenaeus' failure properly to comprehend the
nature of the 'gnostic' teachings which he encountered,[43] but his claim to
unity is also a rhetorical strategy. It is thus not surprising to find that unity is
similarly prized in 'gnostic' works like the *Gospel of Truth* (24.25–25.24).

The Selection of Nag Hammadi Texts

Given the (over)abundance of material in the Nag Hammadi library, a final
word is necessary on how and why I selected which texts to include in this
study. I thought at first I might restrict myself to the output of one particular branch of 'gnosticism', such as Valentinianism, since Williams seems
open, almost surprisingly so, to the retention of smaller abstractions such as
this:

> It still makes sense . . . to speak of something called 'Valentinianism,' as a
> subtradition within the broader early Christian tradition. There will be
> debates about the degree to which this or that document is really 'Valen-

39. Morton Smith, 'The History of the Term Gnostikos', in Bentley Layton (ed.), *Sethian
Gnosticism* (Leiden: E.J. Brill, 1981), pp. 796–807 (805).

40. Perkins, 'Irenaeus and the Gnostics', p. 198.

41. Bruce J. Malina, *The New Testament World: Insights from Cultural Anthropology*, revd
edn (Louisville, Ky.: Westminster/John Knox Press, 1993), p. 33.

42. *Adv. Haer.* 1.28.1.

43. Frederik Wisse, 'The Nag Hammadi Library and the Heresiologists', *VC* 25 (1971),
pp. 205–23 (218–19).

tinian.' But that there was a Valentinus or a Ptolemy no one denies ...
The decision to abandon an overarching construct called 'gnosticism'
would not require abandoning research on specific categories of texts
that manifest some relationship by tradition.[44]

Certain fragments from Valentinus himself have been preserved in the
works of other writers,[45] and a comparison can be undertaken between them
and Nag Hammadi works commonly thought to be Valentinian, such as the
Gospel of Truth, the *Treatise on the Resurrection*, and the *Gospel of Philip*.
However, while significant similarities in vocabulary and ideas have indeed
been found, it is far from certain whether the category 'Valentinianism' is
the best way of accounting for them. Such similarities are not confined to
texts traditionally regarded as 'Valentinian'; as Simone Pétrement and Bentley Layton have argued, they also extend to other documents such as the
Apocryphon of John and the *Gospel of Thomas*.[46] A 'Valentinianism' as broad
as this would be a category devoid of meaning.

I was still left, however, with the practical need to limit the texts to be
included in the project to a manageable number. Might it be possible instead
to confine myself to a particular codex? This possibility suggested itself to
me after encountering Williams' suggestion that the Nag Hammadi codices
do not represent random collections of unrelated texts, but were instead
consciously compiled with particular aims in view.[47] Seeking a codex that
might be seen as representative of the library as a whole, I decided to focus
my attention on the contents of Codex 2, since it has been recognized to
offer an 'unusually varied' cross-section of 'gnostic' texts.[48] For my purposes
here, the most interesting tractates proved to be the *Gospel of Philip*, the
Exegesis on the Soul, the *Hypostasis of the Archons* and the *Gospel of
Thomas*. Tractates from other codices are introduced where relevant or
useful.

44. Williams, *Rethinking 'Gnosticism'*, p. 51.
45. Most notably in Clement of Alexandria, *Stromateis* 2.114.3–6; 2.36.2–4; 3.59.3;
4.89.1–3; 4.89.6–4.90.1; 6.52.3–4; also in Hippolytus, *Ref.* 6.42.2.
46. Pétrement, *A Separate God*, pp. 364, 376; Bentley Layton (ed.), *Nag Hammadi Codex
II, 2–7*, i (Leiden: E.J. Brill, 1989), p. 6: 'despite the presence of only one originally Valentinian
work in Codex II, we have strong circumstantial evidence that the manuscript as such was
compiled with a view to Valentinian needs and tastes.'
47. Michael A. Williams, 'Interpreting the Nag Hammadi Library as "Collection(s)" in
the History of "Gnosticism(s)" ', in Louis Painchaud and Anne Pasquier (eds), *Les textes de
Nag Hammadi et le problème de leur classification*, Bibliothèque Copte de Nag Hammadi
Etudes 3 (Quebec: Les Presses de l'Université Laval/Louvain: Editions Peeters, 1995), pp. 3–50.
48. Layton, *Nag Hammadi Codex II, 2–7*, i, p. xiii.

Part I

Paul

Chapter 1

Marriage in 1 Corinthians

> If only you . . . would listen to me I would make of you the crème de la crème.
>
> Muriel Spark, *The Prime of Miss Jean Brodie*

Muriel Spark's charismatic and unconventional schoolmistress Jean Brodie offers much that is enticing to the ten-year-old girls in her charge. Finding the curriculum followed by the rest of the school to be most useful as a cover for the kind of lesson she prefers to give ('Hold up your books . . . in case of intruders'), Miss Brodie fascinates her pupils with highly romanticized and partial accounts of Renaissance art, the emergence of fascism in Europe, and her own love life. Association with this woman in her prime confers privileged status: 'all my pupils are the crème de la crème'. Such privilege carries a price, however: an expectation of loyalty the demands of which escalate as the novel progresses. Observing Miss Brodie's disapproval of the Girl Guides, Sandy Stranger comes to understand that this organization is in Miss Brodie's eyes a 'rival fascisti' to her own set, which is 'all knit together for her need'. Struck by a momentary impulse to join the Brownies, Sandy soon thrusts the idea aside, 'because she loved Miss Brodie'. Towards the end of the novel, more serious events lead Sandy to see Miss Brodie's influence in a much less benign light, and she overcomes her 'group-fright' to 'betray' her former teacher to the school authorities, giving them the opportunity they have been waiting for to expel this troublesome member of staff from their establishment. In the years that follow, Sandy not only converts to Roman Catholicism (the one Christian denomination with which Miss Brodie would have nothing to do) but also becomes a nun. Yet when, following the publication of her book on psychology, she receives a visitor at the convent who asks her about her early influences, she can only reply, 'There was a Miss Jean Brodie in her prime.' Even in the case of Sandy, it seems, Miss Brodie's early assertion is borne out: 'Give me a girl at an impressionable age, and she is mine for life.'

At first glance, there may not appear to be a great deal in common between St Paul and a fictional Edinburgh schoolmistress. There is, however, at least one important similarity: both offer to their respective communities something highly desirable – and both do so at a price. While their connection with Miss Brodie confers on her 'set' of girls an elite status, in return for their loyalty, those who belong to the group established by Paul are promised nothing less than salvation and victory over death, providing they obey their leader's instructions. These commodities have proved to be desirable not only to the first recipients of Paul's letters but also to many readers from every generation since. Perhaps it is because they too have such an investment in his texts that, as Elizabeth Castelli points out, many of Paul's interpreters have failed to ask questions about the power relations that are developed in his discourse.[1] Such vested interests and bids for authority will figure prominently in my discussion of Paul's interpreters in later chapters, but it is also essential to consider these matters when discussing Paul himself. To set the scene for my examination of his teachings on marriage and on women, therefore, I shall begin by considering briefly the ways in which Paul establishes and exercises his authority over his readers.

'What would you prefer?' demands Paul in 1 Cor. 4.21. 'Am I to come to you with a stick, or with love in a spirit of gentleness?' This question is the culmination to the argument for unity that has dominated the first four chapters of the letter, and demonstrates to the reader that Paul is prepared to employ any means required to achieve his end. The contrast between his encouragements to loving concord and his warnings to those whom he perceives to be endangering that ideal state can appear stark. He is able in the same letter to address his readers as 'my beloved children' (4.14), and then threaten them with non-recognition if they do not do as he says (14.37–38). Similarly, he urges the handing over to destruction of the unfortunate individual living with his father's wife (5.1–5), while at the same time insisting that the members of his church are knitted together like a body, in which 'if one member suffers, all suffer together with it' (12.26). The harsh discipline of 'the stick' and the supposed gentleness of love are not for Paul mutually exclusive tactics, but are instead inextricably intertwined.

As Castelli has shown, one of the most important strategies used by Paul to establish his authority is that of imitation, or mimesis: 'Be imitators of me', he urges the Corinthians in 4.16 and 11.1. Castelli argues convincingly that the call to imitate Paul is neither a matter of social expediency nor simply a natural outcome of Paul's special status in the early church.[2] Mimetic relationships are inherently hierarchical: the model (in this case, Paul) is supposed already to possess the perfection the copy hopes to attain, and he exerts the authority to which the copy submits.[3] Imitation

---

1. Elizabeth A. Castelli, *Imitating Paul: A Discourse of Power* (Westminster/John Knox Press, 1991), pp. 14–15. She goes on to note that most interpreters tend to adopt one of two paths: either they skirt the issue of power altogether, or else they authorize and reinscribe the text's claim to power, muting any evidence there might be for dissent (pp. 23–24).

2. Castelli, *Imitating Paul*, p. 16.

3. Castelli, *Imitating Paul*, p. 86.

also valorizes the idea of sameness:[4] any individual traits which stand in the way of the copy's emulation of the model must be eschewed. Mimesis therefore reinforces Paul's privileged position in constructing the Corinthian community and its identity: 'the exhortation to imitation underwrites the apostle's demand for the erasure of difference, and links that erasure to the very possibility of salvation'.[5]

Of course, Paul appears to engage in a little imitation himself. According to 1 Cor. 9.22–23, for the sake of the gospel he has 'become all things to all people', while in Gal. 4.12 he begs his readers to 'become as I am, for I also have become as you are'. Yet W.P. de Boer argues persuasively that this parallelism is only apparent: Paul's giving up the Law may have had the *result* of making him like the Gentiles, but he was not motivated by any *intention* to achieve such a likeness. By contrast, his converts are called upon to free themselves from their former lives precisely by consciously endeavouring to become like Paul.[6] Paul also presents himself as taking the subordinate copy's role in relation to Christ: 'Be imitators of me, as I am of Christ' (1 Cor. 11.1). Brian Dodd suggests that the imitation of Paul serves only as a middle step in enabling readers to follow Christ directly for themselves.[7] But could Paul really have seen himself as dispensable in this way? Stephen Moore thinks not, arguing that the essential point of the verse is really to 'imitate my obedience by obeying me'. As he sharply observes, '[t]o appeal to one's own exemplary subjection to a conveniently absent authority in order to legitimate the subjection of others . . . is a strategy as ancient as it is suspect.'[8]

Yet the success of mimesis in establishing hierarchical relationships and a group identity based on sameness is dependent on the willingness of one's community to imitate. As Bengt Holmberg defines it, authority consists in 'social relations of asymmetric power distribution *considered legitimate by the participating actors*'.[9] Statements such as 'in Christ Jesus I became your father through the gospel' (1 Cor. 4.15) could have had effect only insofar as the Corinthians too assented to them and shared Paul's assumptions about the behaviour such a relationship entailed. Of course, the fact that he found it necessary to write to them as he did would suggest that they were not fully

4.   Castelli, *Imitating Paul*, p. 16.

5.   Castelli, *Imitating Paul*, p. 17.

6.   W.P. de Boer, *The Imitation of Paul: An Exegetical Study* (Kampen: Kok, 1962); cited in Castelli, *Imitating Paul*, p. 115.

7.   Brian Dodd, *Paul's Paradigmatic 'I': Personal Example as Literary Strategy*, JSNTSup 177 (Sheffield: Sheffield Academic Press, 1999), p. 21.

8.   Stephen D. Moore, *God's Gym: Divine Male Bodies of the Bible* (New York and London: Routledge, 1996), p. 30.

9.   Bengt Holmberg, *Paul and Power: The Structure of Authority in the Primitive Church as Reflected in the Pauline Epistles* (Lund: CKW Gleerup, 1978), p. 3; my emphasis.

living up to these requirements: his discussion of their factionalism (a direct threat to the unity that mimesis was intended to foster) and other supposed misconduct signals a divergence of opinion on a number of important issues. On the other hand, that he wrote to them at all is indicative of his expectation that such an approach would be useful and effective, at least to some degree, and the terms in which he makes his appeal suggest that there is substantial common ground between the apostle and his converts.

As Castelli and Moore have found, Michel Foucault's analysis of the workings of power is particularly helpful in discussing the nuances of this complicated state of affairs. 'Power', in Foucault's vocabulary, is not a thing to be possessed, but instead consists in unstable and ever-shifting relationships. 'Where there is power, there is resistance', of many and various kinds, which is not to be understood as 'only a reaction or a rebound, forming with respect to the basic domination an underside that is in the end always passive, doomed to perpetual defeat'.[10] Contrary to appearances, perhaps, the status quo is not inevitable, and power never lies solely or permanently in the hands of one individual. With this analysis in mind, Paul's first letter to the Corinthians can be seen as an attempt to restore the balance of power in his favour.

Was Paul successful in this attempt? Margaret Mitchell for one thinks not, delivering the verdict that 'Paul's rhetoric of reconciliation in 1 Corinthians was a failure'.[11] Drawing on the evidence of 2 Corinthians, Mitchell suggests that Paul succeeds only in incurring the enmity of all the factions, rather than their mutual reconciliation. Certainly 2 Cor. 12.20 suggests that the old problems were still very much present: Paul writes, 'I fear that when I come, I may find you not as I wish, and that you may find me not as you wish; I fear there may perhaps be quarrelling, jealousy, anger, selfishness, slander, gossip, conceit, and disorder.' Indeed, that factionalism still troubled Corinth at the end of the first century CE is confirmed by the author of *1 Clement*, who looks back with nostalgia to the divisions with which Paul had had to deal, 'since [then] you were partisans of notable apostles and of a man whom they endorsed. But think now who they are who have led you astray and degraded your honourable and celebrated love of the brethren' (*1 Clem.* 47.4–5).

Yet this apparent lack of practical success (as far as Paul's own intentions are concerned, at any rate) has done little to dim the enthusiasm of later readers for capitalizing on the authority attendant on his name and

10. Michel Foucault, *The Will to Knowledge*, tr. Robert Hurley (Harmondsworth: Penguin, 1998), pp. 95–96.
11. Margaret M. Mitchell, *Paul and the Rhetoric of Reconciliation: An Exegetical Investigation of the Language and Composition of 1 Corinthians* (Tübingen: J.C.B. Mohr [Paul Siebeck], 1991), p. 303.

embodied in his letters; as far as this characteristic at least is concerned, the diverse heirs to Paul's tradition have been extremely interested in imitating him. His communications with the Corinthians may not have brought about the end he had in view, but having been written down, they became available to be used by new and diverse groups of readers for purposes he could never have envisaged. As I have shown in the Introduction, the reading of documents such as these is never an innocent procedure, but is instead always bound up with questions of power and vested interests. Texts never simply 'speak for themselves', as Castelli correctly observes,[12] and any claim that they do can only be disingenuous, especially when the text in question is as ambiguous as 1 Corinthians 7. In this chapter, Paul is engaging in the difficult and delicate task of attempting to persuade different people to do different things at the same time, and a large part of the aim of the exegesis that follows will be to draw attention to those elements of the passage that make it such an ambivalent and malleable text.

The Context for Paul's Teaching on Marriage[13]

As I have argued in the Introduction, meaning is always context-bound. This is especially true in the case of 1 Corinthians 7, which appears to have been composed in response to both oral reports and written communication from one particular community. The opening verse of ch. 7 shows that Paul was responding to a letter from the Corinthians themselves. The περὶ δὲ formulation, used only rarely by Paul elsewhere,[14] flags the matters which they had raised: in this chapter, the question of whether a man ought to touch a woman (7.1), and the question of virgins (7.25).

The content of Paul's replies appears to be determined in large part by an overwhelming concern with sexual immorality, πορνεία, which figures prominently in the two preceding chapters. πορνεία or a related term is used in 5.1, 9, 10, 11 and 6.9, 13, 15, 16, 18. Several other kinds of sexual offenders are condemned in 6.9 – adulterers (μοιχοί), 'ladies' men'

---

12. Elizabeth A. Castelli, 'Paul on Women and Gender', in Ross Shepard Kraemer and Mary Rose D'Angelo (eds), *Women and Christian Origins* (New York and Oxford: Oxford University Press, 1999), pp. 221–35 (222).

13. I deal in this brief section only with the immediate literary context for 1 Corinthians 7. More general observations on the relationship of the text to its social and cultural context will be offered at relevant points in the exegesis.

14. James D.G. Dunn, *1 Corinthians*, New Testament Guides (Sheffield: Sheffield Academic Press, 1995), p. 19.

(μαλακοὶ),[15] and men who engage in homosexual relations (ἀρσενοκοῖται) – and these are apparently what some of the Corinthians used to be (6.11). Paul writes at length and with considerable agitation on this subject, repeatedly lamenting that the Corinthians ought to have known better; 'do you not know . . .?' he beseeches them several times over (5.6; 6.9, 15, 16). Yet even now one of them is living with his father's wife (5.1), something 'even' the pagans do not condone; and some of them may be using prostitutes (6.15–16). The Corinthians' πορνεία is deleterious to the group's unique identity, bringing the community into disrepute, and sullying the boundaries between it and the world. It is in Paul's eyes a problem of the utmost seriousness, and in 1 Corinthians 7 he uses the opportunity afforded by his correspondents' own letter to lay down a solution for this deeply worrying state of affairs.

7.1–5: Behaviour in Marriage

It would be somewhat unfortunate if the heated debate over the provenance of the maxim of 7.1 were permitted to detract attention from its contents. Even if it was the Corinthians who first suggested that 'it is good for a person [ἀνθρώπῳ] not to touch a woman', it remains true, as Loveday Alexander points out, 'that Paul is in no great hurry to distance himself from the proposal'.[16] Hans Conzelmann has noticed the apparent one-sidedness of the statement, and comments that 'this is the prevailing approach in the ancient world'.[17] It is necessary to say a little more than this, however, for in its one-sidedness the saying stands in sharp contrast to the laboured reciprocity of much of what follows. How does this rather ascetic-sounding statement relate to the pervasive πορνεία of chs 5 and 6, which Paul is explicitly trying to combat in the present passage?

If the idea that 'it is good for a person not to touch a woman' did originate with the Corinthians themselves, the statement would seem to testify to a striking divergence of opinion on sexual morality within the Corinthian

---

15.   Dale B. Martin (*The Corinthian Body* [New Haven and London: Yale University Press, 1995], p. 33) has argued convincingly that μαλακός does not refer to a man who engaged in homosexual practices. Instead, the term (which means 'soft') was used to describe a man whose physical characteristics fell closer to the 'feminine' end of the spectrum; that is to say moist, soft and cold, as opposed to dry, hard and warm. Such a man was thought to have an eye for those things similar to himself, and was therefore overly fond of sex with women.

16.   Loveday Alexander, ' "Better to Marry than to Burn": St. Paul and the Greek Novel', in Ronald F. Hock, J. Bradley Chance and Judith Perkins (eds), *Ancient Fiction and Early Christian Narrative*, SBL Symposium Series 6 (Atlanta: Scholars Press, 1998), pp. 235–56 (238).

17.   Hans Conzelmann, *1 Corinthians*, tr. J.W. Leitch, Hermeneia (Philadelphia: Fortress Press, 1975), p. 115 n. 10.

community, with some members apparently happy to indulge in the kind of activities Paul condemns in chs 5 and 6, while others endeavour to avoid sex altogether. A particularly interesting explanation for this difference of opinion is suggested by Antoinette Clark Wire: namely, that it was gendered.[18] She notes that all those who are accused of sexual immorality in chs 5 and 6 are male;[19] but the solution which Paul proposes, marriage, is one that depends above all on the cooperation of women.[20] Wire alerts her readers to the possibility that a slogan such as 'It is good for a person not to touch a woman' could actually have been promoted by women themselves, in particular those who felt led by their devotion to Christ to give up sexual relations.[21] In this scenario, both in the problem and in the remedy Paul sets out, the connection between the social body and the individual body is very much in evidence. Just as the sexual immorality of some men harms not only them but also the whole community,[22] so some women (if Wire's thesis is correct) are called upon to give up what is good for them for the sake of the well-being of the whole community. Paul gives the impression that he shares and affirms the women's principle,[23] but he still requires them to sacrifice any individual aspirations they may have for the benefit of the group which he is constructing.

Monogamous heterosexual marriage, within which the couple are to engage in sexual relations, is thus prescribed as the remedy for πορνεία (7.2–4). Dale Martin suggests that marriage thus acts 'as a mechanism for protecting the boundaries of the church's body from external contamination through sex with those outside'.[24] However, 5.1 makes it clear that πορνεία is already ἐν ὑμῖν, within the boundaries of the church; it is not only a pervasive characteristic of the world (5.10), but is also found within the

---

18.　Antoinette Clark Wire, *The Corinthian Women Prophets: A Reconstruction through Paul's Rhetoric* (Minneapolis: Fortress Press, 1990), p. 73. While Wire exhibits more confidence than I can share in the possibilities for definitively reconstructing the world behind the text, the scenario she suggests here does offer an interesting illustration of Castelli's idea of Paul's imposition of sameness on his community (insofar as women's individual aspirations and independence are required to be given up).

19.　Wire, *The Corinthian Women Prophets*, p. 74. Wire recognizes that the fact that no women are so accused of course only constitutes an argument from silence and therefore cannot be conclusive.

20.　Wire, *The Corinthian Women Prophets*, p. 78.

21.　Wire, *The Corinthian Women Prophets*, p. 94. Given the connection between celibacy and prophecy (of which more below, and further in Chapter 2), the slogan may have proved especially congenial to women who wished to prophesy.

22.　Cf. 1 Cor. 12.26: 'If one member [of the Body of Christ, the church] suffers, all suffer together with it; if one member is honoured, all rejoice together with it.' Similarly, if one member of the Body engages in sexual immorality, all are dishonoured by this act. Thus 6.15, 'Shall I therefore take the members of Christ and make them members of a prostitute? Never!'

23.　Wire, *The Corinthian Women Prophets*, p. 80.

24.　Martin, *The Corinthian Body*, p. 212.

community itself (5.11). Paul appears to be resigned to the state of the world, but he is not prepared to let the Corinthian community of believers remain in a state of imperfection (5.13). Marriage, and engagement in sexual relations within it, is proposed not simply as a preventative prophylactic but as a cure for an already existent disease.

As Martin points out, it is not only inaccurate but also anachronistic to describe Paul as having some kind of 'pathological aversion' to sex;[25] but it is just as much of a distortion to uphold him as the founder and champion of 'Christian family values'.[26] Conzelmann,[27] Martin[28] and Daniel Boyarin[29] all assert that Paul offers no positive grounds for getting married.[30] As David Horrell puts it, marriage 'is allowed primarily on the grounds of lack of self-control and passion, and [is] thus portrayed as a second-best option'.[31] Such an attitude sets Paul at odds with most of his contemporaries. As Sarah Pomeroy has observed, in Roman society marriage and childbearing were elevated to the level of a moral, religious and patriotic duty,[32] an outlook of which the Stoic writer Musonius Rufus (*c.* 30–100 CE) provides an eloquent example: '[I]t [is] each man's duty to take thought for his own city, and to make of his home a rampart for its protection. But the first step toward making his home such a rampart is marriage.'[33] Paul exhibits no interest in such ideals of civic duty, and (unsurprisingly) even less in the concern with family honour and advancement which characterized upper-class nuptials. His reluctant endorsement of the married state as a necessity for some reflects his ambivalence with regard to the world, the society of which marriage is a bulwark:[34] he does

---

25.   Martin, *The Corinthian Body*, pp. 211–12.

26.   I am of course aware that in using such loaded terms as 'inaccurate' and 'distortion' here, I am in effect claiming superiority for my own reading of Paul against those of scholars who adhere to one or other of these 'distortions'! What I am attempting to do here, however, is to determine as far as possible what Paul was trying to do with this text *in his situation*, and as answers to this specific question I would assert that such readings are indeed mistaken.

27.   Conzelmann, *1 Corinthians*, p. 116.

28.   Martin, *The Corinthian Body*, p. 209.

29.   Daniel Boyarin, *A Radical Jew: Paul and the Politics of Identity* (Berkeley: University of California Press, 1994), p. 177.

30.   Whether 7.14 and 16 constitute an exception to this assertion will be discussed below.

31.   David G. Horrell, *The Social Ethos of the Corinthian Correspondence: Interests and Ideology from 1 Corinthians to 1 Clement* (Edinburgh: T&T Clark, 1996), p. 158.

32.   Sarah B. Pomeroy, *Goddesses, Whores, Wives, and Slaves: Women in Classical Antiquity* (London: Robert Hale, 1975), p. 132.

33.   Musonius Rufus 14, in Cora E. Lutz, 'Musonius Rufus "The Roman Socrates" ', *Yale Classical Studies* 10 (1947), pp. 3–147 (93).

34.   As Ben Witherington remarks, 'In Roman Corinth, one who advocated singleness as a better state than marriage would hardly be seen as one who was baptizing the status quo' (*Conflict and Community in Corinth: A Socio-Rhetorical Commentary on 1 and 2 Corinthians* [Grand Rapids: Eerdmans/Carlisle: Paternoster, 1995], p. 174).

not want the Corinthians to cut themselves off from the world (5.10), but he also reminds them that they will judge it (6.2), and that its present form is passing away (7.31).[35]

Such is the danger of πορνεία that only prayer is an adequate reason for those who are married to abstain from sexual relations, and even this must be for a limited time and by mutual consent (7.5). It is not immediately clear why prayer should require abstinence from sexual activity. John Poirier and Joseph Frankovich make the intriguing suggestion that Paul prescribes such seasons of prayer in accordance with the demands of Jewish ritual purity. By way of comparison they cite *T. Naph.* 8.8: 'There is a time for having intercourse with one's wife and a time to abstain for the purpose of prayer.'[36] However, Paul does not *command* such periods of abstinence; he merely *permits* them. It is also by no means obvious that Paul sees it as necessary for people to abstain from sex in order to be pure; on the contrary, his assertion that 'you were washed, you were sanctified, you were justified in the name of the Lord Jesus Christ' (6.11) has the ring of the final word on the subject.

The instructions in 7.5 may perhaps best be explained as the apostle's limitation of a practice initiated by some of the Corinthians themselves, whereby he tries to make temporary what they had intended to be a permanent arrangement. Such prolonged abstinence, as Martin points out, would prevent the fulfilment of the mutual duty (ὀφειλή) of sexual accessibility husband and wife owe to one another, thus exposing them to the danger of temptation because of the lack of self-control that makes the duty necessary in the first place.[37] One can imagine such temptation being particularly strong where one partner is more committed to abstinence for the sake of prayer than is the other; the spouse who wishes to resume sexual activity may be lured to do so outside the marriage relationship. In such a situation, Paul appears once again to be urging that the more resolute partner sacrifice their ideals for the sake of the weaker spouse and the purity of the group as a whole.

---

35. This attitude to the world does not mean that Paul is not anxious about the Corinthians' reputation. On the contrary, for the sake of spreading the gospel, and for the sake of his own honour and ultimately that of Christ, he shows considerable concern with how their actions will look to outsiders, imagining with horror the likely reaction of any outsiders who witness one of the Corinthians' unruly gatherings for worship where all are speaking in tongues: 'will they not say that you are out of your mind?' (14.23).

36. John C. Poirier and Joseph Frankovich, 'Celibacy and Charism in 1 Corinthians 7.5–7', *HTR* 89 (1996), pp. 1–18 (4).

37. Martin, *The Corinthian Body*, p. 209.

7.6–9: Paul's Preference for Celibacy

'This [τοῦτο] I say by way of concession, not command' (7.6) – but what exactly is it that Paul concedes? Bruce Winter observes that this τοῦτο is 'important . . . in determining the overall interpretation of the passage';[38] I would suggest that the reverse is also true. If, like Anthony Thiselton, one finds in 1 Corinthians 7 a Paul who advocates marriage and celibacy both as gifts of God, then it makes sense to assume that it is abstinence for the sake of prayer that is conceded; such a reading also has the advantage of leaving 'no apparent linguistic or exegetical difficulty'.[39] However, if on the other hand one finds it impossible to escape the impression that Paul displays a marked preference for celibacy throughout the chapter,[40] then it seems more appropriate to read everything contained within the frame of the favourable remarks on celibacy in 7.1 and 7.7 as the concession, a large concession which is made necessary because of the threat of πορνεία.[41]

Paul makes his ideal quite clear: 'I wish that all were as I myself am' (7.7). This preference for celibacy again sets him decidedly at odds with his contemporaries, who were of the opinion that 'whoever destroys marriage destroys the whole human race';[42] but the likes of Musonius Rufus may have drawn some comfort from the words which immediately follow. Paul may wish that everyone could pursue the celibate life, but he recognizes that this is impossible, for 'each has a particular gift [χάρισμα] from God, one having one kind and another a different kind' (7.8). This provides an interesting illustration of the dynamics of the mimetic relationship, as Paul sets himself up as a model whom most of his readers (by his own decree) will find it impossible fully to emulate, thereby enabling him to retain his own unique

---

38.   Bruce W. Winter, *After Paul Left Corinth: The Influence of Secular Ethics and Social Change* (Grand Rapids and Cambridge: Eerdmans, 2001), p. 234.

39.   Anthony C. Thiselton, *The First Epistle to the Corinthians: A Commentary on the Greek Text*, NIGTC (Grand Rapids and Cambridge: Eerdmans/Carlisle: Paternoster, 2000), pp. 606 and 511. See also, for example, G.J. Laughery, 'Paul: Anti-Marriage? Anti-Sex? Ascetic? A Dialogue with 1 Corinthians 7.1–40', *EvQ* 69 (1997), pp. 109–28 (121), and Witherington, *Conflict and Community in Corinth*, p. 175.

40.   As, for example, does Horrell, *Social Ethos*, p. 158.

41.   Thiselton makes a distinction between those who apply τοῦτο to all of 7.2–5 and those who apply it only to 7.2, finding the latter option preferable, since the instructions concerning mutual sexual accessibility of husband and wife have the air of obligatory precepts (*First Epistle*, p. 510). I am not convinced that such a distinction can be easily drawn. Marriage may only be conceded as a necessity for some, but if it is undertaken, then the relationship must be conducted in the way that Paul sets out and no other. For those lacking self-control, what takes place within the marital relationship is just as important as the fact of its existence; v. 2 cannot be separated from the verses that follow. Of course, taking all of vv. 2–5 as the concession removes the difficulty of improbable distance between τοῦτο and that to which it refers (Thiselton, *First Epistle*, p. 510).

42.   Musonius Rufus 14, in Lutz, 'Musonius Rufus', p. 93.

position and his hold on power. All gifts may come from God, but some are more highly valued than others.

The relationship between celibacy and χάρισμα is worthy of further consideration. Is celibacy itself a gift, or is the connection less direct? Ben Witherington straightforwardly asserts that for Paul both singleness and marriage in the Lord are gifts.[43] C.K. Barrett, on the other hand, understands only celibacy to be a gift; those who lack it (and therefore ought to marry) have other charisms instead.[44] Poirier and Frankovich, however, observe that celibacy is not called a charism anywhere else in the Pauline corpus; but something else is, and that is prophecy.[45] Drawing upon a tradition of Moses' celibacy,[46] they suggest that Paul understood celibacy to be an obligation attendant on his prophetic gift, an obligation he apparently wishes all could share even as he acknowledges that he cannot impose it because all do not have the same gifts.[47] Paul's express wish in 7.7 that all could be like himself would therefore be echoed by 14.5, where he says he wants all the Corinthians to engage in prophecy, the most desirable of the spiritual gifts (14.1).[48]

This theory becomes even more intriguing when one recalls the significance attached to the sexual status of *women* prophets in the New

43. Witherington, *Conflict and Community in Corinth*, p. 176. Thiselton agrees (*First Epistle*, p. 606).

44. C.K. Barrett, *A Commentary on the First Epistle to the Corinthians* (London: A. & C. Black, 1968), pp. 158–59.

45. Poirier and Frankovich, 'Celibacy and Charism', p. 16. See for example 1 Cor. 12.10 and 14.1.

46. Poirier and Frankovich, 'Celibacy and Charism', p. 15. Cf. Philo, *Vit. Mos.* 2.68–69: 'But, in the first place, before assuming this office [the priesthood], it was necessary for him to purify not only his soul but also his body, so that it should be connected with and defiled by no passion, but should be pure from everything which is of a mortal nature, from all meat and drink, and from all connection with women. And this last thing, indeed, he had despised for a long time, and almost from the first moment that he began to prophesy and to feel a divine inspiration, thinking that it was proper that he should at all times be ready to give his whole attention to the commands of God.' See also the texts cited in Geza Vermes, *Jesus the Jew: A Historian's Reading of the Gospels* (London: Fontana/Collins, 1973), pp. 99–102.

47. Poirier and Frankovich, 'Celibacy and Charism', p. 16. It is true that Paul is nowhere explicitly called a prophet (as Poirier and Frankovich themselves admit, p. 11), and for this reason the theory must remain at the level of a hypothesis. However, the way in which prophecy is described in 1 Cor. 14.3–4 sounds not dissimilar to the way Paul may have understood his primary task: 'those who prophesy build up the church'.

48. Paul is writing to a church where speaking in tongues appears to be the predominant activity, a source of concern because of its negative impact on the community's relations with outsiders (14.23). Prophecy, delivered in comprehensible language, is therefore much to be preferred. As with celibacy, however, while prophecy may be the ideal, it is not granted to all (12.4–10); just because Paul expresses a desire that all should prophesy does not mean he expects that they will in fact do so.

Testament.[49] 1 Cor. 11.5 is a clear indication that there were women prophets in Corinth; and if Wire is correct in her theory of the provenance of the maxim in 7.1, then it is these women who represent the fulfilment of Paul's stated wish that his readers resemble him in having the gift of prophecy and accepting the obligation to celibacy that went along with that gift. It is possible, then, to read 7.7 as an endorsement of women prophets in Corinth; but this is to forget that many of these women may have been expected to forgo their own commitment to celibacy in order to comply with Paul's instructions on marriage as a defence against πορνεία. For example, any among them who were married but had forsaken sexual relations with their husbands are now apparently required to resume them (7.3–5). Such women may continue to exercise their prophetic gift, but only under the conditions laid down by Paul.[50]

Paul's instructions to the unmarried and widows in 7.8 strike a number of familiar notes. Once again a particular state is recommended as καλὸν, good (cf. 7.1, and later 7.26); and for the second time in as many verses Paul expresses the wish that his readers follow his own example. A literal reading of the Greek is 'it is good for them [those who once were married but now are not] if they remain as I also [κἀγώ] am', and this has led some scholars to speculate that Paul himself, like those whom he addresses, was a widower.[51] It would certainly be highly unusual for a person in Paul's position never to have married, since marriage was very much the norm in both Jewish and Graeco-Roman culture.[52] It has already been noted that Paul's preference for celibacy in this letter runs contrary to custom; when it leads him to encourage widows not to remarry, it also runs contrary to law. The Augustan laws made marriage mandatory for women between twenty and fifty years of age, and for men over twenty-five.[53] Under the Lex Julia, widows were required to remarry in ten months, and a divorced woman in six.[54] Lack of compliance was penalized; cooperation and the production of sufficient children were rewarded with control over one's own financial affairs.[55] How effective these regulations actually were in practice is hard to

49.   Wire, *The Corinthian Women Prophets*, p. 83. See for example the references to the widowed Anna in Luke 2.36–37, and the four unmarried daughters of Philip in Acts 21.9.

50.   Most notably in 11.2–16, to be discussed in detail in Chapter 2.

51.   So William Orr and James Arthur Walther, *1 Corinthians*, AB 32 (Garden City, NY: Doubleday, 1976), p. 209.

52.   Conzelmann, *1 Corinthians*, p. 114.

53.   Elaine Fantham *et al.*, *Women in the Classical World: Image and Text* (New York and Oxford: Oxford University Press, 1994), p. 302.

54.   Aline Rouselle, *Porneia: On Desire and the Body in Antiquity*, tr. Felicia Pheasant (Oxford: Basil Blackwell, 1988), p. 91. The Lex Papia extended this period to a year.

55.   Margaret Y. MacDonald, 'Reading Real Women through the Undisputed Letters of Paul', in Kraemer and D'Angelo (eds), *Women and Christian Origins*, pp. 199–220 (212).

gauge, but at the very least they reflect a level of unease about threats to the household[56] which a call to celibacy such as Paul's would have done little to assuage.

For the unmarried and widows too, being celibate (and being like Paul) is a path open only to those who possess the necessary self-control. To those who lack it, marriage is once again presented as the advised alternative, the lesser of two evils: 'it is better to marry than to burn with passion' (7.9), though the ideal is to do neither. Martin wrestles with the idea that Paul appears to be suggesting here that marriage 'functions not as a legitimate avenue for the expression of desire but as what will preclude it altogether', a notion that he reasonably assumes the modern reader will find 'completely counter-intuitive'.[57] It would indeed be difficult to comprehend why a married couple would engage in sexual relations (as Paul instructs them to do) without there being at least some glimmer of passion to incline them towards it; but it may not be necessary to try. Marriage, as Paul intends it to be conducted, can instead be seen as the safe site where the burning of desire can be quenched in a controlled way, with no risk of it erupting into an uncontainable conflagration. Still, Martin's engagement with such a 'counter-intuitive' idea is an important reminder of the vast cultural gap that lies between modern readers and *all* Paul's writings, not just the most obviously strange or shocking.

7.10–16: Divorce

Unhindered by any conception of marriage as an ideal state, Paul is willing to engage at length with the practical problems with which the institution is beset.[58] His prohibition of divorce is one of the few instances where he makes direct appeal to the teaching of Christ: 'not I but the Lord' (7.10). This rare (and therefore noteworthy) addition of Christ's authority to his own (of which he has rather a high opinion, as 7.25 and 40 make plain) serves to underscore the seriousness of the prohibition on divorce which he here lays down. While in the previous section Paul was concerned that anyone currently attempting to live a celibate life without being equipped for the task should get married, his utilization here of this 'command of the Lord' against divorce appears to make it impossible for anyone who is currently married to adopt a celibate life, even if they happen to have the gift for it.

Yet Paul subverts the absolute nature of the prohibition on divorce, and

---

56. MacDonald, 'Reading Real Women', p. 212.
57. Martin, *The Corinthian Body*, p. 214.
58. In contrast to the approach of the author of Ephesians, as I shall show in Chapter 3.

the authority of Christ which he has just invoked, by making an exception to the rule in the very next verse! It would seem that his relationship to dominical commands was a creative one, to say the least. Unlike the Synoptic versions of Jesus' prohibition on divorce, Paul addresses the woman first,[59] and makes a lengthy exception in her case with no corresponding flexibility extended to the man. The similarity to the lack of parallelism that was encountered in 7.1 may well prove to be instructive.

Some scholars have suggested that Paul's rash move in 7.11 must be a response to actual circumstances in Corinth: some women have already separated from their husbands, and this fact Paul takes into account by permitting them to remain separated if they will not be reconciled to their husbands.[60] However, a consideration of the grammar of the verse rather undermines this solution; the construction of ἐάν with the subjunctive does not allow this kind of certainty that the events in question have already occurred. On the contrary, as Stanley Porter explains, 'A third class conditional with ἐάν and the subjunctive . . . is more tentative and simply projects some action or event for hypothetical consideration.'[61] It is therefore possible that Paul recognizes that some women in Corinth were likely *in future* to disobey the command not to separate from their husbands, and he thus attempts to legislate accordingly. Does this modification of the Lord's command suggest sympathy on Paul's part with the principles of those married women who wish to adopt a celibate life? Perhaps; but as I have noted previously, such sympathy does not necessarily mean that permission will be granted to live those principles out, especially when the good of the community and Paul's own position in it are at stake. It should not be overlooked that Paul concludes his aside to the women by encouraging them to be reconciled to their husbands.

Paul's modification of Jesus' command continues in 7.12–16, where he takes into account the specific circumstance of mixed marriages between a believer and a non-believer. The believer herself seems to be permitted no power of decision over her marriage. Either she complies with Paul's instructions and continues with the marriage, or she submits to the desire of the unbelieving partner to dissolve it. It is not an option for her to separate from her husband, nor may she protest if he instigates a separation which she does not want. Although Paul addresses both men and women in this section, the use of feminine pronouns here is not inappropriate. Margaret MacDonald has shown that women were more likely than men to find

59. Cf. Mark 10.11–12; Matt. 5.32.

60. So Conzelmann, *1 Corinthians*, p. 120, and Laughery, 'Paul: Anti-Marriage?', p. 122.

61. Stanley Porter, *Idioms of the Greek New Testament*, 2nd edn (Sheffield: Sheffield Academic Press, 1994), p. 262. See also BDF, p. 188: 'Ἐάν with the subjunctive denotes that which under certain circumstances is expected from an existing general or concrete standpoint in the present'.

themselves in this situation, for it was expected that a woman should adhere to her husband's religious tradition.[62] Plutarch's *Coniugalia Praecepta* (140D) states this requirement clearly:

> A wife ought not to make friends of her own, but to enjoy her husband's friends in common with him. The gods are the first and most important friends. Wherefore it is becoming for a wife to worship and to know only the gods that her husband believes in, and to shut the front door tight upon all queer rituals and outlandish superstitions. For with no god do stealthy and secret rites performed by a woman find any favour.

Therefore, if a man became a Christian, his wife might be expected to follow his example, but the reverse was not the case for a woman who converted. Indeed, by encouraging Christian women to remain with their non-Christian husbands without giving up their Christian belief, Paul is in effect 'sanctioning what might be understood as a kind of marital infidelity'.[63] Here is further evidence that Paul does not feel himself bound by social convention.

In 7.14 Paul declares that the unbelieving spouse is made holy through the believing spouse. Is it possible that here (at last) is the attribution of a positive function to marriage? Probably not; it seems more likely that Paul affirms the transferral of holiness from the believer to the non-believer primarily in order to deny the reverse process: that the non-believing spouse makes the believing spouse unclean.[64] Thus the perfect tense ἡγίασται (7.14) foregrounds the idea of sanctification, to emphasize that it is indeed this process and not any other which takes place in a mixed marriage. If any believer were considering severing their marriage ties for fear of contamination, they need not do so. This amounts at best, however, to a reassurance for those already in mixed marriages: it is presented as justification for the instruction of 7.13. It is not presented as a motivation to contract new marriages of this type, nor is it a sufficient reason for the believing partner to prevent their spouse from breaking off the relationship if that is what they wish (7.15). Furthermore, this sanctification is not the same as

---

62. Margaret Y. MacDonald, *Early Christian Women and Pagan Opinion: The Power of the Hysterical Woman* (Cambridge: Cambridge University Press, 1996), p. 189.

63. MacDonald, *Early Christian Women and Pagan Opinion*, p. 189.

64. So Martin, *The Corinthian Body*, p. 218. Given Paul's dire warnings on the effects of sex with a prostitute in 1 Cor. 6.16–18, it is perhaps not surprising that this kind of misunderstanding should have arisen. Some of the Corinthians may have come to think that any kind of sexual relations with a non-believer, even within the bonds of marriage, would similarly threaten one's spiritual connection with Christ and the integrity of the whole body. Paul in 7.13–14 attempts to make clear that this is not the case: though the unbelieving partner may indeed belong to 'the world', the prophylactic effects of marriage are such that the contamination the believing spouse fears is not in fact a danger, and nor therefore is it grounds for separation.

salvation; the contrast between the certainty of the one in 7.14 and the doubtfulness of the other in 7.16 does not allow this equivalence to be made. The salvation of the unbelieving spouse is not impossible; but it is not so certain as to justify the preservation of the marriage at all costs.

7.17–24: 'Remain as you are'

The new vocabulary in 7.17–24 would at first glance appear to indicate a new topic. Paul begins to speak of circumcision and uncircumcision, of slavery and freedom, matters seemingly unrelated to marriage and celibacy. Some commentators, therefore, view this passage as a mere digression[65] – glad, perhaps, to be able to relegate to secondary status verses that can be read (by modern eyes) as a morally dubious endorsement of the status quo as far as slavery is concerned. Others, however, correctly recognize it as a central link in Paul's argument.[66] How, then, does this link function? Horrell suggests that '[Paul's] comments on the position of circumcised and uncircumcised, slave and free are primarily illustrative':[67] in other words, these states can be seen to function here as metaphors for marriage and celibacy, metaphors which (for the most part) Paul employs to encourage people to remain in their present state. This explanation has the advantage of accounting for what might otherwise appear to be an unwarranted intrusion of unrelated material in the midst of Paul's discussion of a vitally important subject.

Any reader familiar with Paul's other letters will soon recognize that circumcision and slavery are not random examples. They immediately call to mind the radical formula of Gal. 3.28: 'There is no longer Jew or Greek, there is no longer slave or free; there is no longer male and female; for all of you are one in Christ Jesus'. Almost as quickly, one realizes that in 1 Corinthians there is something missing. Not only is there no explicit reference to 'male and female' in 7.17–24, but this third pair is also missing from the more exact parallel with Gal. 3.28 that is found in 1 Cor. 12.13: 'For in the one Spirit we were all baptized into one body – Jews or Greeks, slaves or free – and we were all made to drink of one Spirit'. However, it can be argued that insofar as he advocates marriage, Paul is in effect endorsing specific male and female gender roles.[68] Those whom he encourages to be celibate,

---

65. Orr and Walther, *1 Corinthians*, p. 216.

66. See for example Laughery, 'Paul: Anti-Marriage?', p. 122.

67. Horrell, *Social Ethos*, p. 161.

68. Bruce J. Malina (*The New Testament World: Insights from Cultural Anthropology* [Louisville, Ky.: Westminster/John Knox Press, 1993], p. 49) shows that honourable male and female behaviour was construed almost entirely in relation to their respective roles in the household. Boyarin (*A Radical Jew*, p. 190), meanwhile, offers the observation that in Paul's

on the other hand, are those who possess the self-control to abstain from sexual relationships and who may therefore live beyond the confines of traditional gender roles. Given his insistence on the necessity of marriage for most, however, it appears that the scope of his declaration that 'there is no male and female' is, in the Corinthian community at least, significantly restricted.

Paul deploys both metaphors, that of circumcision and that of slavery, to the same end, namely to encourage his readers to remain in the same situation as when they were called; however, the two examples are not put to use in exactly the same way. Differences in ethnicity are more easily swept aside as irrelevant. The circumcised man and the uncircumcised man are addressed in turn (7.18), before Paul asserts that 'circumcision is nothing, and uncircumcision is nothing, but obeying the commandments of God' (7.19). If this is applied to marriage and celibacy, then it can be said that Paul is presenting the two states as different but equal, and relativizing both of them to the fundamental task of keeping God's commandments.

The slavery metaphor is a little more complicated. Paul does not here address both sides of the opposition in turn, but only the slave. The etymological connection between δοῦλος (7.21) and the perfect passive of δουλόω in 7.15 would suggest that it is the married person (the one who is 'bound') whom the slave represents.[69] Any who find themselves in this situation are encouraged not to worry about it; but if they find themselves 'freed' (by divorce or widowhood), then they ought to make the best of this new situation. Again, Paul is anxious that existing marriages be preserved as far as possible, and he is therefore at pains to show that all earthly positions – slave, free, married, unmarried – are insignificant compared to one's standing in Christ (7.22); one is reminded of his insistence in 7.7 that 'each has a particular gift from God'. However, Paul does not find it necessary to extend any words of consolation to those who are free (celibate); equal though all may be in Christ, one still finds it hard to escape the impression that celibacy is the preferable state, even though for many it is an impossibility.

---

cultural context '[i]t is (hetero)sexuality . . . that produces gender' and the hierarchical relationship between men and women, since male and female bodies in sexual relationship with one another could hardly be imagined to be in any other condition than dominant and dominated respectively.

69. A passage from Epictetus may also be called upon to lend weight to this reading. In *Diss.* 1.29.59 he writes: 'it is disgraceful to consider these things [philosophical enquiries] like runaway slaves; nay, sit rather free from distractions [ἀπερισπάστως] and listen . . . not as these runaways do' (cited in Alexander, ' "Better to Marry than to Burn" ', p. 242). Here too slavery is associated with 'distractions', that is to say with all the practical concerns, particularly those attaching to marriage, that hinder the sage in his devotion to God's service. Paul himself goes on to address the problem of distractions in 7.32–35.

7.25–35: Marriage as a Source of Anxiety

Paul now turns his attention primarily to those who have not been previously married. 1 Cor. 7.25–35 not only has a new set of principal addressees; it also displays a rather different attitude to marriage from that of the preceding verses. The dominant concern in this part of the chapter is no longer sexual immorality, but the 'imminent crisis' (7.26), in the light of which marriage is presented not as a remedy for a troublesome complaint, but rather as a source of trouble in itself (7.28). As before, it is not wrong to marry, but the reader is left in no doubt that to refrain is the better option (7.38).

Paul begins the section by acknowledging that on this subject 'I have no commandment from the Lord, but I give my opinion as one who has received mercy from the Lord and is faithful' (7.25). Given what Paul has already done with a commandment of the Lord in 7.10–11, it would be mistaken to read this disavowal as an expression of humility on the apostle's part. Indeed, the opposite is true: unshackled by dominical tradition, Paul can legislate for this particular situation entirely as he sees fit. Even if any of his readers has so far failed to recognize the authority the apostle has claimed for himself, one who is trustworthy 'by the Lord's mercy' is hardly to be disobeyed lightly.

For the third time Paul offers his opinion on what is καλὸν, good, for a person. Continuing the theme of the previous section (7.17–24), he proposes that what is good is that a person – married or single – should remain as they are. Having suggested in 7.25 that he is here going to deal with the question of virgins (παρθένοι), Paul almost immediately (7.27) switches his attention back to men: 'Are you bound to a wife?' This is not simply a case of apostolic absent-mindedness; 7.36–38 make it quite clear that Paul assumes the man has the prerogative as far as marriage arrangements are concerned.[70] 'If you are married to a wife, do not seek separation [λύσιν]; if you have been separated [λέλυσαι] from a wife, do not seek a wife' (7.27). Orr and Walther wish to read λέλυσαι as a reference to the wife's death,[71] but the parallel relationship between the two halves of the verse makes a broader interpretation preferable. It is unlikely that the situation in Corinth was quite so dire that Paul had to warn his congregation not to actively seek the state of widowerhood! 7.27b may refer to the death of a spouse, but that cannot be the only situation Paul envisages. He may also have in mind here those whose marriages have been dissolved at the instigation of a non-believing partner (7.15). Such people are free to remarry, but it is better for them if they do not. Still bearing in mind that marriage is a necessity for

---

70. MacDonald, *Early Christian Women*, p. 148; Martin, *The Corinthian Body*, p. 227.
71. Orr and Walther, *1 Corinthians*, p. 219.

some because of a lack of self-control (7.9), Paul reminds his readers that marriage is not a sin (7.28); this is hardly a glowing commendation of the institution. Barrett paraphrases him in inimitable style: 'If you seek to lose your freedom in marriage, you may be foolish, but you are not sinful.'[72] Pointing out the distress contingent on the married state, Paul underlines again the superiority of his own celibate position, while at the same time trying not to deter those who need marriage to ward off πορνεία. It is such attempts simultaneously to promote two opposing courses of action (as his particular circumstances and aims required him to do) that help to make Paul's teachings such a fertile resource for a diverse body of later readers.

In a manner somewhat similar to that of 7.17–24, in 7.29–31 Paul encourages the Corinthians to adopt an attitude to their lives consistent with their experience of a radically transformative event. There, that event was their entry into a relationship with Christ; here, it is the prospect of the imminent end that is expected to engender a life-altering effect. Sandwiched between warnings that 'the appointed time [καιρὸς] has grown short' (7.29) and that 'the present form of the world is passing away' (7.31) is advice on how believers ought to live in such a situation. It is revealing to view this advice as a single unit: Paul urges the Corinthians to live from now on as though they had no wives, as though mourning and rejoicing were both as naught, and as though they had no possessions or dealings with the world. This cannot be explained as simple anti-cosmism; Paul has already acknowledged that complete separation from the world is impossible, and he does not advocate such a stance (5.10). Yet given that the world is passing away, the only wise course of action is not to invest much in it.[73] These verses serve to remind readers that Paul's advocacy of marriage in this chapter is by no means an endorsement of worldly values: it is recommended only as a necessity, a solution to a particular problem – a problem from which Paul himself happens not to suffer. Insofar as the celibate person transcends the traditional roles enshrined in marriage, celibacy is not part of the present form of this world; presumably such a way of life better equips those who adhere to it to weather the impending storm.

The development of these ideas continues in 7.32, where Paul expresses the desire that the Corinthians be 'free from anxieties [ἀμερίμνους]'. To be anxious, then, appears to be a bad thing. Yet Paul immediately proceeds to observe that 'the unmarried man is anxious about the things of the Lord, how he might please the Lord'; is it then wrong to be anxious about pleasing the Lord? If so, then women also are making the same mistake: 'the

---

72. Barrett, *A Commentary on the First Epistle to the Corinthians*, p. 175.

73. Witherington (*Conflict and Community in Corinth*, p. 180) is thinking along similar lines when he writes that what is important here is not the *degree* of interaction with the world, but rather the *quality* of such interaction.

unmarried woman and the virgin are anxious about the things of the Lord, that she might be holy both in body and spirit' (7.34). MacDonald opines that 'while married life can be subject to anxiety, anxiety [of the bad kind] can also result from an attempt to be holy that is motivated primarily out of a rigid preference for celibacy'.[74] She and Barrett therefore argue that 7.32 does not constitute a commendation of the unmarried man, nor 7.34 of the unmarried woman.[75] According to this view, Paul is at pains here to portray marriage and celibacy as equally valid (or, in this case, equally anxiety-ridden) states; he presents himself as enabling people to live in 'unhindered devotion to the Lord' in the way that is appropriate for them.

However, such a reading does not sit easily with the clear preference for celibacy that has been seen to run throughout this chapter. The unmarried man may be anxious about the 'affairs of the Lord', but in Paul's eyes these surely are a much more worthy cause for concern than the 'affairs of the world' that trouble the married man. And the latter has a problem that the former does not share: 'his interests are divided' (7.34 NRSV); or, to give a more literal rendering of the Greek, 'he has been divided [μεμέρισται].' The attention drawn to this verb by rendering it in the perfect tense would suggest that, as far as Paul was concerned, this was the real issue: the married man has other concerns that hamper devotion to the Lord 'without distraction [ἀπερισπάτους]' (7.35). Epictetus takes a similar position when considering the Cynic's position:

> in such an order of things like the present, it is a question, perhaps, if the Cynic ought not to be free from distraction [ἀπερίσπαστον], wholly devoted to the service of God . . . not tied down by the private duties of men, nor involved in relationships which he cannot violate and still maintain his role as a good and excellent man, whereas on the other hand, if he observes them, he will destroy the messenger, the scout, the herald of the gods that he is. For see, he must show certain services to his father-in-law, to the rest of his wife's relatives, to his wife herself; finally, he is driven from his profession, to act as a nurse in his own family and to provide for them.[76]

This quotation sheds light on why celibacy is so important to Paul's own position: it sets him apart from other people, not only practically but also in terms of status (it frees him to be a 'messenger of God'). Martin suggests that 7.32–35 were included in the letter because there were some in Corinth who (like modern readers) needed some explanation for Paul's negative

---

74. MacDonald, *Early Christian Women and Pagan Opinion*, p. 136.
75. MacDonald, *Early Christian Women and Pagan Opinion*, p. 136, and Barrett, *A Commentary on the First Epistle to the Corinthians*, p. 175.
76. Epictetus, *Diss.* 3.22.69ff.; cited in David L. Balch, '1 Cor. 7.32–35 and Stoic Debates about Marriage, Anxiety, and Distraction', *JBL* 102 (1983), pp. 429–39 (431).

attitude to marriage and sex.[77] One is left to wonder just how this explanation would have been received by those readers who were married, and who had been told by Paul earlier in this chapter to remain so, even though their situation is a source of such trouble.

7.36–40: The Betrothed and the Widowed

In these concluding verses of the chapter, Paul dispenses advice to people in two particular situations: the engaged couple (7.36–38) and the widow (7.40). The interpretation of the first of these has been notoriously difficult. 1 Cor. 7.36–38 has been read as referring not to a man and his fiancée, but to a father and his unmarried daughter.[78] This latter reading has primarily been based on the use of the causative γαμίζω, usually meaning 'to give in marriage', in 7.38. However, Blass and Debrunner suggest that in this context the verb serves merely as an equivalent of γαμέω.[79] From the woman's point of view, the distinction may well be only academic. Wire correctly observes that it is the man's right to cause his virgin to marry that is at stake in these verses;[80] the woman herself is offered no opportunity to decide her own fate. The male prerogative in marriage is once again in evidence.

The exegete's problems with these verses do not end with determining the identity of the protagonists. Both the subject and the meaning of ὑπέρακμος in 7.36 are ambiguous. The subject may be either the man or the virgin [παρθένος], while the word itself may refer either to one who is past the age for marriage, or to one who is experiencing strong passions. These alternative meanings have often been gendered, the former applied to women, the latter to men.[81] Thus it would seem that if the interpreter can decide upon a meaning, then she has also found her subject, and vice versa. However, Martin has questioned not only the way in which interpreters have gendered the alternative meanings of ὑπέρακμος, but also the very dichotomy between age and desire. He suggests that 7.36 refers to the young *woman's* passions, for which marriage is the remedy.[82] Martin's work is important because it takes into account the views of the medical writers and philosophers which prevailed in Paul's day. Nevertheless, in the context of these verses, and of 1 Corinthians as a whole, it does seem more appropriate

---

77. Martin, *The Corinthian Body*, p. 210.

78. Orr and Walther (*1 Corinthians*, p. 224) are two modern scholars who adopt this interpretation.

79. BDF, p. 51.

80. Wire, *The Corinthian Women Prophets*, p. 88.

81. See for example UBS Greek New Testament, 4th revd edn, Greek–English Dictionary, p. 187.

82. Martin, *The Corinthian Body*, pp. 219–20.

to read ὑπέρακμος as referring to the passions of the man. If he is unable to control himself, then he is to marry; in this situation, any desire on the part of his fiancée to remain celibate is to be sacrificed. As at the beginning of the chapter, some women are to give up their aspirations because of some men's (potential or actual) πορνεία. Paul does not wish to discourage marriage when it must take place, but it is better when it is not necessary (7.38). He appears to hope that the virgin who wishes to remain in that state will be allowed to do so, but at the same time he has removed from her hands the power to make that decision.

Finally Paul turns to widows (7.39–40). Ignoring the apparent exception he made in 7.11, he asserts that 'a wife is bound for as long as her husband lives' (7.39). When her spouse dies, however, she is free to be married to whom she wishes; 'but in my judgement she is more blessed if she remains as she is' (7.40). Only after she has already been married and become a widow does a woman have the chance to make her own decisions.[83] Once again, Paul's parting disclaimer only serves to reinforce his authority. The 'opinion' of one who has the Spirit of God is not to be dismissed lightly.

Concluding Remarks

Many of Jean Brodie's attempts to mould her pupils in her own image went severely awry; the outcome of her educational enterprises was certainly not what she would have expected (or desired). Yet throughout her novel Spark shows her readers that this singular schoolmistress made a deep and lasting impact on all her girls. Similarly, it is hard to imagine that Paul's instructions in 1 Corinthians 7 had quite the effect on their original readers that he desired. His influence too, however, reached into the future in ways he could not have anticipated, and it is not difficult to see how Paul's later interpreters have been able to mine so many different gems from this difficult but potential-laden passage. If, when the hope of an imminent parousia has faded and the church's sojourn in the world is starting to feel more permanent, one wishes to promote traditional marriage, this portion of Paul's writings can help. If others for different reasons wish to promote celibacy as the ideal way of life, with marriage as the resort of the weak who lack self-control, then Paul has already made the case for such a position. In new contexts, 1 Corinthians 7 can take on many different complexions. Some of these new contexts will be the topics of later chapters; but before leaving Paul himself, and 1 Corinthians, behind, I turn in the following chapter to consider his similarly complex, intriguing, and at times frustrating discussion of women.

83. Wire, *The Corinthian Women Prophets*, p. 89.

Chapter 2

WOMEN IN 1 CORINTHIANS

> So also our beloved brother Paul wrote to you according to the wisdom given to him . . . There are some things in [his letters] hard to understand, which the ignorant and unstable twist to their own destruction, as they do the other scriptures.
>
> 2 Pet. 3.15–16 NRSV

Few passages in the Pauline correspondence seem to be more deserving of this assessment of 2 Peter than Paul's instructions concerning women in 1 Cor. 11.2–16 and 14.33b–40. These are passages over which many scholars have laboured long and hard, and the particular interpreters one chooses to regard as 'ignorant and unstable' very much depends on one's point of view. As was the case with Paul's teaching on marriage addressed in the previous chapter, no reader can honestly claim to approach these texts without some kind of vested interest. While not wishing to ignore the oppression of women which they have been used to justify over the centuries, it is my primary objective here to discern, as far as it is possible to do so, what Paul was aiming to achieve with these sections of his letter in the context of first-century Corinth, and the ways in which he uses discourse to further those aims.[1]

I shall begin with an examination of 1 Cor. 11.2–16 in which I shall argue that Paul, motivated by both theological concerns and a desire for conformity with society at large, commands that women cover their heads when actively participating in worship. Such instruction runs contrary to the practice that the women themselves have been following, and the rhetorical tactics to which Paul resorts indicate that this was for him a matter of considerable importance. Following this, I shall consider the rather more heated 14.33b–40, arguing that the disputed vv. 34–35 are authentic. This then requires me to assess the various attempts that have been made to reconcile the apparent contradiction between this passage and 11.2–16.

---

1. I use the term 'discourse' in the sense elaborated by Elizabeth Castelli, to mean not just simple representation, but language used to persuade, to coerce, and to construct power relations (*Imitating Paul: A Discourse of Power* [Louisville, Ky.: Westminster/John Knox, 1991], p. 53).

While a tentative verdict may be offered as to which of these attempts is the least unsatisfactory, it is my primary intention here to highlight the ambivalence which characterizes Paul's teaching on women as a whole, rather than try to resolve it once and for all.

A Note on the Authenticity of 11.2–16

Before beginning to 'disambiguate'[2] 1 Cor. 11.2–16, it is necessary to note briefly the argument made by a few scholars that this passage is a non-Pauline interpolation.[3] As William Walker himself acknowledges, there is no direct manuscript evidence to support such a position,[4] and his main reason for adopting it appears to be that this passage does not concur with the treatment of women in what he refers to as Paul's 'authentic writings'.[5] While one might sympathize with Walker's reluctance to attribute what he sees as blatant sexism to such a revered authority figure as Paul, such worthy concerns in this instance only give rise to dubious conclusions. The authorship of controversial passages like the one under discussion here simply cannot be decided on the basis of scholars' own presuppositions concerning what Paul 'ought' to have said about women, discomforting though the implications might be of having to accept seemingly misogynistic statements as authentically Pauline. With this in mind, and lacking any conclusive evidence to the contrary,[6] I proceed to the exegesis of 1 Cor. 11.2–16 assuming that it is indeed an authentic Pauline text.

---

2. I borrow this term from Dennis Ronald MacDonald, 'Corinthian Veils and Gnostic Androgynes', in Karen L. King (ed.), *Images of the Feminine in Gnosticism* (Philadelphia: Fortress Press, 1988), pp. 276–92 (276). It seems singularly appropriate.

3. See especially William O. Walker, '1 Corinthians 11.2–16 and Paul's Views Regarding Women', *JBL* 94 (1975), pp. 94–110. See also Lamar Cope, '1 Corinthians 11.2–16: One Step Further', *JBL* 97 (1978), pp. 435–36, and G.W. Trompf, 'On Attitudes toward Women in Paul and Paulinist Literature: 1 Corinthians 11.3–16 and its Context', *CBQ* 42 (1980), pp. 196–215.

4. Walker, '1 Corinthians 11.2–16', p. 97.

5. Walker, '1 Corinthians 11.2–16', p. 104. Walker accepts Gal. 3.28 and the various statements about Paul's female co-workers as authentic, but provides no justification for giving these excerpts priority over the relevant passages from 1 Corinthians.

6. Jerome Murphy-O'Connor has shown that much of the data to which Walker appeals is 'evidence which fits' rather than 'evidence which proves' ('The Non-Pauline Character of 1 Corinthians 11.2–16?', *JBL* 95 [1976], pp. 615–21 [619]). For example, similarities to deutero-Pauline epistles such as Ephesians may just as easily be explained by their borrowing from 1 Corinthians, rather than the other way round.

11.2: Evoking a Favourable Response

That this passage is also a difficult text becomes apparent in the very first verse, in which Paul addresses the Corinthians thus: 'Now I commend you because you continue to remember me in all things and, just as I handed on to you, you are keeping the traditions' (11.2; my translation). How is Paul able to praise them in this way when already in this letter he has had to contend with their factionalism (1.10–13), their toleration of sexual immorality (5.1–5), their boasting (5.6), and their taking one another to court (6.1–8)? As if all that were not enough, in ch. 11 he proceeds to correct a practice that has put them out of kilter with both Paul's theology and church custom (11.2–16), and he takes them to task for abuses at the Lord's Supper (11.17–34). Finally, in ch. 15, he must even deal with some who fail to believe in the resurrection. In short, there seems to be very little for Paul to commend, and the Corinthians themselves can hardly now be unaware of the apostle's displeasure at certain aspects of their behaviour. So what is 11.2 supposed to achieve?

John P. Meier proposes one solution, reading the verse as a *captatio benevolentiae* designed to flatter the Corinthians and dispose them more favourably to the argument which follows.[7] This recognition that the commendation is intended to evoke a certain response from the readers is a useful starting point. If the language of the verse is examined more closely, it is possible to be more specific about the nature of the desired response, and how the verse is designed to achieve it.

First, adherence to the traditions the Corinthians have received from Paul is evaluated positively as an activity that begets praise. They are thus encouraged to apply themselves to a pattern of behaviour in which they have not as yet enjoyed unequivocal success. Secondly, the use of the present tense (κατέχετε) shows obedience to Paul's teaching to be a task that continues through time. By thus presenting as good a *continuing* openness and obedience to his teaching, Paul appears to be preparing the ground for a modification of this teaching that will not damage his authority.

What might have provoked such a move? By way of a preliminary response to this question, I would suggest that Paul was troubled by certain practices in the Corinthian church which he believed to have arisen from their misappropriation of his previous teaching. He therefore feels it necessary to clarify his position in such a way as to remove any theological basis the Corinthians might claim for their undesirable activities. The question of the nature of the modification, and why it was necessary, will be addressed more fully as the exegesis proceeds.

---

7. John P. Meier, 'On the Veiling of Hermeneutics (1 Corinthians 11.2–16)', *CBQ* 40 (1978), pp. 212–26 (215).

11.3: Headship: the Source of Authority

Having thus wooed the Corinthians, Paul begins his reformulation in the following verse. The threefold series of relationships in 11.3 is presented as a given, for which Paul feels no need to provide either justification or proof; the emphasis is on making his readers understand (εἰδέναι) its implications. If the Corinthians were already familiar with this material, it must be assumed that they had understood it rather differently, for the instructions which follow from it in the ensuing verses of Paul's letter seem clearly designed to counteract an existing practice.

The metaphorical polyvalence of κεφαλή makes it quite plausible that Paul and the Corinthians could have had rather different understandings of its meaning. Indeed, there is still little scholarly consensus on what the nuances of κεφαλή might be in this context. The question is often posed as an either/or choice between 'ruler'[8] and 'source'.[9] Paul's usage here must be determined in the light of the rest of the passage, and his extended use of the Genesis creation narratives lends considerable weight to the 'source' interpretation. This concurs with the evidence from both the LXX and secular Greek.[10] But this does not rule out any notion of hierarchy or authority. Dale Martin, in drawing attention to the importance of priority of origin in ancient ideology of status,[11] has shown that the dichotomy between these two options is, to a considerable extent, a false one.[12] Even if

---

8.   This option is preferred by J.A. Fitzmyer, 'Another Look at ΚΕΦΑΛΗ in 1 Corinthians 11.3', *NTS* 35 (1989), pp. 503–11; Antoinette Clark Wire, *The Corinthian Women Prophets: A Reconstruction through Paul's Rhetoric* (Minneapolis: Fortress Press, 1990), p. 117; and Ben Witherington, *Conflict and Community in Corinth: A Socio-Rhetorical Commentary on 1 and 2 Corinthians* (Grand Rapids: Eerdmans/Carlisle: Paternoster, 1995), p. 237.

9.   Scholars adopting this interpretation include F.F. Bruce, *1 and 2 Corinthians*, NCB (London: Oliphants, 1971), p. 103; Gordon D. Fee, *The First Epistle to the Corinthians*, NICNT (Grand Rapids: Eerdmans, 1987), p. 502; L. Ann Jervis, ' "But I Want You to Know . . .": Paul's Midrashic Intertextual Response to the Corinthian Worshipers (1 Corinthians 11.2–16)', *JBL* 112 (1993), pp. 231–46 (240); and Meier, 'On the Veiling of Hermeneutics', p. 217.

10.   Fitzmyer, although presenting the case for the 'ruler' interpretation, also discusses the evidence for the alternative. He notes, for example, that when ראש in the Hebrew Bible bears the sense of 'ruler', it is more usually rendered in the LXX by ἄρχων or ἀρχηγός ('Another Look', p. 505).

11.   Dale B. Martin, *The Corinthian Body* (New Haven and London: Yale University Press, 1995), p. 232. As an example, he offers the Greek claim to higher status, which was based upon acknowledged Roman borrowing of older Greek things (p. 295 n. 14).

12.   Another text where 'head' appears to be used with this double connotation is Philo, *Praem. Poen.* 125: 'the virtuous one, whether single man or people, will be the head of the human race and all the others like the limbs of a body which draw their life from the forces in the head and at the top'. One may also note Hippolytus, *Ref.* 8.11, in which he describes Basilides' Great Archon as 'Head of the World', and goes on to say of this figure that 'imagining himself to be Lord, and Governor . . . He turns Himself to (the work of) the creation of every object in the cosmical system'.

'source' is taken to be the basic meaning of the word, 'authority' is not just a possible but a necessary connotation. This observation will also be important later in my treatment of 11.7–9.

Having established the value of its key term, it is now possible to consider briefly the meaning of 11.3 in its entirety. The first pairing, Christ and man (ἀνήρ), is perhaps the most puzzling: in what sense can Christ be the 'source' of the male human being but not the female? Christ's role as agent in creation[13] (if read in the light of Genesis 2) provides a less unsatisfactory answer to this question than does his redemptive role as head of every believer.[14] However, neither the severity of the problem nor the distinction between these two solutions ought to be pressed too hard. Paul is setting out his theological position in such a way as to promote the difference between male and female that he wants to see manifested in community practice. The use of the more inclusive ἄνθρωπος at this point would only have served to blur the desired gender distinction. A more elaborate reflection on Christ as source may be found in 1 Cor. 8.6: 'for us there is one God, the Father, from whom are all things and for whom we exist, and one Lord, Jesus Christ, through whom are all things and through whom we exist'. In light of the discussion in the previous paragraph, it is pertinent to note that Christ is referred to here (and repeatedly throughout 1 Corinthians) as 'Lord'. He is thus presented as both source and authority figure.

The third pairing, God and Christ, may be understood in a similar way, once again drawing on evidence from elsewhere in 1 Corinthians. 15.24–28 portrays Christ as ruling over all things – except God: 'When all things are subjected to him, then the Son himself will also be subjected to the one who put all things in subjection under him, so that God may be all in all' (15.28). As in 11.3, it is God who is the undisputed head of the whole structure. Martin correctly surmises that if these first and third pairs are hierarchical, then the second, man and woman, which they frame, must be also.[15] Moreover, this relationship between man and woman, originating in creation, has not been abrogated with the coming of Christ.

11.4–6: (Un)covering the Head and Shaming the 'Head'

Having laid out the theological basis, Paul now proceeds to the practical instructions which are his real concern. Of course, in the strictest sense, Alan Padgett is correct in his assertion that the statements found in 11.4–6

13. C.K. Barrett, *A Commentary on the First Epistle to the Corinthians* (London: A. & C. Black, 1968), p. 249.

14. Fee, *The First Epistle to the Corinthians*, p. 505.

15. Martin, *The Corinthian Body*, p. 232.

merely describe a certain state of affairs, rather than prescribe a course of action.[16] There is no imperative verb in these verses, nor any occurrence of δεῖ or ἔχεστιν. Nonetheless, only the most naïve reader could deny that these verses in fact make Paul's preferred mode of conduct manifestly clear.[17] His use of the language of shame serves as a powerful disincentive to those attracted to or already engaged in the practices described; and such an appeal to his readers' values may be far more effective in achieving his aims than simply laying down the Law. Cultural anthropologists have shown that honour and shame were fundamental values in ancient Mediterranean culture. However, Bruce Malina adds this important observation: 'honor and shame patterns do not determine what is honorable or shameful. The determination of what specific behaviors or objects are of worth depends upon factors other than these values.'[18] So, precisely what behaviours does Paul present as shameful in these verses, and what factors motivate him to do so?

The first part of this question is not as straightforward as it may initially appear. Scholars have long debated whether the issue at stake was that of veiling or hairstyle, and whether it was women alone or members of both sexes who were acting in ways that Paul found troubling. With regard to the practice itself, it is the somewhat enigmatic phrase κατὰ κεφαλῆς ἔχων in 11.4 that has caused most difficulties. The expression allows for two interpretations: hair hanging down from the head, or a covering resting upon the head. Jerome Murphy-O'Connor adopts the first alternative,[19] arguing that because Jewish priests prayed with turbans on, Paul was unlikely to be upset by men praying with covered heads.[20] In addition, Paul himself demonstrates further, more explicit, concern with hair in 11.14–15. However, Richard Oster, taking the second option, cites evidence from Plutarch to show that κατὰ κεφαλῆς ἔχων may indeed refer to a covering resting upon the head.[21] Oster goes on to show that in a Roman colony like Corinth, it would have been the usual custom for the head to be covered during

16.   Alan Padgett, 'Paul on Women in the Church: The Contradiction of Coiffure in 1 Corinthians 11.2–16', *JSNT* 20 (1984), pp. 69–86 (70).

17.   This is only one of the numerous examples in this passage of indirect illocutionary acts which, as Geoffrey Leech explains, are a useful means of reconciling conflicting goals, for example being polite (or in this case, keeping the Corinthians on side) and imposing one's will (*Principles of Pragmatics* [London and New York: Longman, 1983], p. 40). Other notable instances of this technique occur in 1 Cor. 11.13–15, when Paul appears to be asking the Corinthians' opinion, but clearly expects them to reiterate his own.

18.   Bruce J. Malina, *The New Testament World: Insights from Cultural Anthropology*, revd edn (Louisville, Ky.: Westminster/John Knox Press, 1993), p. 54.

19.   Murphy-O'Connor, 'Sex and Logic in 1 Corinthians 11.2–16', *CBQ* 42 (1980), pp. 482–500 (484).

20.   Murphy-O'Connor, 'Sex and Logic', p. 485.

21.   Richard Oster, 'When Men Wore Veils to Worship: The Historical Content of 1 Corinthians 11.4', *NTS* 34 (1988), pp. 481–505 (486).

religious activity, and that this practice set its adherents apart: 'it was clear to [Greeks] and Romans that the habitual propensity of Romans to wear head apparel in liturgical settings stood in sharp contrast to the practice of others'.[22] Thus there is a plausible historical background for Paul's less ambiguous reference to a man covering his head in 11.7.[23]

11.4 shows that while Paul speaks the same cultural language as his contemporaries, his theological stance as set out in 11.3 leads him to label as shameful practices which were for them a perfectly acceptable norm. For Paul, any man who prays or prophesies with his head covered shames his 'head', Christ – an unequivocally bad thing to do. Paul's position is all the more remarkable if Molly Levine is correct in her observation that such an act, especially on the part of a free man, was a dramatic gesture of submission to divine authority.[24] As Daniel Boyarin remarks, one clearly cannot attribute everything Paul says either to his Jewish background or to pagan culture![25] But does this mean that there actually *were* men in the Corinthian church who were covering their heads to pray and prophesy? It would not be entirely surprising and cannot be ruled out; but Paul does seem to be much more concerned with women's behaviour in this passage. It is to them that he devotes an extended aside in 11.5b–6, and it is they who are the subject of the passage's focal declaration in 11.10 and of the appeal to the Corinthians' own judgement in 11.14. Margaret MacDonald has shown that women's conduct was of paramount importance to the reputation of the entire group: 'Behaviour that might be judged by the outside world as shameful for women could dishonour men and bring disgrace to the whole community.'[26]

This might explain why, when it comes to women, Paul's theology appears to be much more in tune with cultural norms. 11.5 is an almost perfect parallel to the preceding verse, except that the instructions on head

22. Oster, 'When Men Wore Veils to Worship', p. 494.

23. Particularly in the case of women, however, one ought not to differentiate too starkly between hairstyle and head covering. Murphy-O'Connor notes that the head covering served also to keep the hair in order ('Sex and Logic', p. 488). Furthermore, Molly Levine observes that uncontrolled hair and an uncovered head on a woman had similar connotations of sexual impropriety ('The Gendered Grammar of Ancient Mediterranean Hair', in Howard Eilberg-Schwartz and Wendy Doniger [eds], *Off With Her Head! The Denial of Women's Identity in Myth, Religion, and Culture* [Berkeley: University of California Press, 1995], pp. 76–130 [92, 103]).

24. Levine, 'The Gendered Grammar of Ancient Mediterranean Hair', p. 103.

25. Daniel Boyarin, *A Radical Jew: Paul and the Politics of Identity* (Berkeley: University of California Press, 1994), p. 183.

26. Margaret Y. MacDonald, *Early Christian Women and Pagan Opinion: The Power of the Hysterical Woman* (Cambridge: Cambridge University Press, 1996), p. 146. As Malina explains, it was generally expected that a woman would be under the tutelage of some male (usually a father, husband or other male relative); and if she was seen to act in an unconventional or immoral way, she brought dishonour not only on herself, but also on the man who was supposed to control her (*The New Testament World*, p. 50).

covering are the opposite: what is honourable for men is shameful for women. The use of δὲ, a relatively weak adversative, may do no more than signal this fact. However, it might also hint that this difference between men and women in the context of worship was not what the Corinthians would have expected. Oster offers the following passage from Juvenal which suggests that Roman women, like their male counterparts, covered their heads for worship: 'There she stood before the altar, thinking it no shame to veil her head on behalf of a harper; she repeated, in due form, all the words prescribed to her; her cheek blanched when the lamb was opened.'[27] If Paul reversed the cultural norm for men in this regard, the Corinthians might ask, would he not also do the same for women?

Oster goes on to suggest that most Corinthian women conformed to this practice of worshipping with covered head.[28] But this is not the only form of religious practice for which there is evidence. Elisabeth Schüssler Fiorenza draws attention to the oriental cults in which women worshipped in an ecstatic frenzy with hair uncovered and unbound.[29] It is quite plausible that Corinthian women Christians with a background in these cults should wish to continue this kind of practice, especially when such frenzy was perceived as a mark of true prophecy.[30] However, it is also possible that some first experienced the setting aside of everyday constraints in the midst of ecstatic worship in a specifically Christian context. Wayne Meeks argues that the ritual that employed the baptismal formula preserved in Gal. 3.28, 'there is no longer Jew or Greek, there is no longer slave or free, there is no longer male and female . . .', induced in the initiate a liminal state in which they 'participat[ed] in divine power and therefore momentarily transcend[ed] the division between male and female'.[31] It would not be surprising if a desire to recapture such an ecstatic experience motivated the Corinthian women to remove during worship one of the prime markers of gender division: the veil.

That the veil did function in this differentiatory way is attested by both Jewish and pagan sources. In the Talmud, *Nedarim* 30b, one reads: 'men sometimes cover, sometimes uncover their heads, but women always cover their heads, and minors never cover their heads'.[32] The heroine of the story

27. Juvenal, *Satires* 6.390–92; cited in Oster, 'When Men Wore Veils to Worship', p. 503. It is not the woman's veiling her head that is the unusual circumstance in this scenario, but rather the fact that she does so for the sake of a humble musician.

28. Oster, 'When Men Wore Veils to Worship', p. 503.

29. Elisabeth Schüssler Fiorenza, *In Memory of Her: A Feminist Theological Reconstruction of Christian Origins* (London: SCM Press, 1983), p. 227.

30. Schüssler Fiorenza, *In Memory of Her*, p. 227.

31. Wayne A. Meeks, 'The Image of the Androgyne: Some Uses of a Symbol in Earliest Christianity', *HR* 13 (1973/74), pp. 165–208 (184).

32. Cited in Levine, 'The Gendered Grammar of Ancient Mediterranean Hair', p. 106.

of Joseph and Aseneth may be commanded by an angelic visitor to remove her veil, but both the content and the singular circumstances of the instruction lead the reader to infer that women being veiled was the normal custom.[33] Similarly, Plutarch writes: 'it is more common for women to go into the public place covered up, and for men to go uncovered'.[34] The difference thus displayed was a fundamental building block of the ancient Mediterranean world, which 'was, and still is, a world divided according to gender: every person, place, object, action is known either as male or female'.[35]

But this was not a difference of equals, either in theory or in practice. Philo of Alexandria, whose idea of the primal androgyne exerted much influence in Corinth according to at least one scholarly account,[36] has this to say: 'Progress is nothing else than the giving up of the female gender by changing into the male, since the female gender is material, passive, corporeal, and sense perceptible, while the male is active, rational, incorporeal and more akin to mind and thought.'[37] In this sort of ideological context, it is not surprising that, as Martin points out, it is usually women who 'become male' rather than the other way round.[38] As D.R. MacDonald succinctly puts it, 'the androgyne myth is not antiquity's answer to androcentrism; it is but one manifestation of it'.[39]

In practical terms, the veil functioned as a means of social control.[40] Words taken from Talmud *Berachot* 24a might be used to sum up its connotations concisely: 'The chaste wife covers her hair, hides her flesh, and silences her voice.'[41] The act of unveiling a woman was one created by and for men:[42] only the husband was entitled to unveil his wife; thus the veil symbolized his control over her sexuality.[43] As such it has a double meaning,

---

33. 'Remove the veil from your head, and for what purpose did you do this? For you are a chaste virgin today, and your head is like that of a young man' (*Jos. Asen.* 15.1). This is the inference taken up by George J. Brooke, 'Between Qumran and Corinth: Embroidered Allusions to Women's Authority', in James R. Davila (ed.), *The Dead Sea Scrolls as Background to Postbiblical Judaism and Early Christianity*, Studies on the Texts of the Desert of Judah 46 (Leiden and Boston: Brill, 2003), pp. 157–176 (71 n. 54).

34. Plutarch, *Moralia* 267, *Quaestiones Romanae* 14, cited in Levine, 'The Gendered Grammar of Ancient Mediterranean Hair', p. 106.

35. Jerome Neyrey, 'Maid and Mother in Art and Literature', *BTB* 20 (1990), pp. 65–75 (65), cited in MacDonald, *Early Christian Women*, p. 19.

36. Dennis Ronald MacDonald, *There Is No Male and Female: The Fate of a Dominical Saying in Paul and Gnosticism*, HDR 20 (Philadelphia: Fortress Press, 1987), p. 93.

37. Philo, *Quaest. in Gen.* 1.8; cited in MacDonald, *There Is No Male and Female*, p. 99.

38. Martin, *The Corinthian Body*, p. 230.

39. MacDonald, *There Is No Male and Female*, p. 101.

40. MacDonald, *There Is No Male and Female*, p. 89.

41. Cited in Levine, 'The Gendered Grammar of Ancient Mediterranean Hair', p. 105.

42. Levine, 'The Gendered Grammar of Ancient Mediterranean Hair', p. 99.

43. This comes across quite clearly in Tertullian's *De virginibus velandis* 16, in which he urges virgins to veil their heads: 'For wedded you are to Christ: to Him you have surrendered your flesh . . . Walk in accordance with the will of your Espoused.'

protecting the woman but also confining her. Martin puts it succinctly: 'To veil a woman . . . meant not only to protect her but also to civilize her; to guard her from invasion and penetration but also to protect society from the dangers and chaos represented by her femaleness. It meant to keep her intact, but also to keep her in place.'[44]

So the Corinthian women who choose to unveil themselves in worship take over a male prerogative, perhaps in order to re-experience the ecstatic liminal state they temporarily entered at baptism. This is no insignificant matter. It must not be forgotten that the church was in the public eye, domestic setting and fictive kin-language notwithstanding.[45] The use of the term ἐκκλησία, meaning a formal assembly of citizens, indicates that the early Christians also saw themselves as in some sense a political entity.[46] Christian women were visible, and both their actions and the communities to which they belonged were new and therefore subject to suspicion. Mary Rose D'Angelo observes that religious innovation often led to charges of sexual immorality.[47] Such charges needed no factual basis; they are a good example of the evaluative use of language for the purpose of discrediting a group regarded as suspect, for whatever reason. However, Paul is still anxious that the Corinthian women should not act in any way that will provide fuel for potential accusers' fire, even if this means that their religious activities must be curtailed. It is not surprising that when the baptismal formula appears in 1 Cor. 12.13, 'no male and female' is missing.

To drive home his point, Paul resorts to extreme measures and equates unveiling the head with shaving it. He takes something the Corinthians could unequivocally understand as shameful and juxtaposes it with their own practice, which they found perfectly acceptable. One can imagine the Corinthian women protesting at the idea that they should cut off their hair. Straight away Paul provides the solution: then they ought to cover their heads. He thus establishes a spurious pair of polar opposites between which the women must choose: being veiled, or being shorn. There is no middle way, and the option of being unveiled is effectively ruled completely out of play; the 'choice' offered in 11.6 really is no choice at all. As Wire puts it, 'Paul uses what he considers to be an unthinkable alternative to appear flexible without giving anything away.'[48]

---

44. Martin, *The Corinthian Body*, p. 235.
45. MacDonald, *Early Christian Women*, p. 37.
46. Wendy Cotter, 'Women's Authority Roles in Paul's Churches: Countercultural or Conventional?', *NovT* 36 (1994), pp. 350–72 (370).
47. Mary Rose D'Angelo, 'Veils, Virgins, and the Tongues of Men and Angels: Women's Heads in Early Christianity', in Eilberg-Schwartz and Doniger (eds), *Off With Her Head!*, pp. 131–64 (138).
48. Wire, *The Corinthian Women Prophets*, p. 119.

11.7–9: The Argument from Creation

From theological proposition through practical implications, Paul now turns to scriptural justifications, namely the accounts of the creation of human beings which are to be found in the first two chapters of Genesis. He assumes a position of power in relation to the text, not citing it directly so that his readers may draw their own conclusions, but providing only his own interpretation. Of course, it is quite possible that Paul adopts this approach because he feels it necessary to correct the Corinthians' prior (mis)understanding of a text which they already knew.[49] But the result is the same: this is still a Paul who is placing himself and his interpretation in a superior position to that of his readers.

As Elizabeth Castelli observes, Paul appeals to the creation narratives to demonstrate that gender difference is divinely created.[50] It did not originate only with the Fall, to which Paul does not refer in this passage.[51] In 11.7 Paul offers direction only to the man; the question of what the woman ought to do is deferred until 11.10. 'For a man ought not to cover his head, being the image and glory of God; but the woman is the glory of man' (11.7; my translation). The term 'image' has been imported from Genesis 1 into the two-stage account of the creation of human beings in Genesis 2, and the inference concerning woman's status is clear. The image of God ought not to be covered; woman has been told to be covered; therefore, woman is not the image of God.[52]

Morna Hooker's argument that the idea of woman sharing the divine image is not unacceptable to Paul, but only 'irrelevant' in the present context, points in the right direction[53] – although it is perhaps more accurate to say that the notion was *unhelpful* to Paul here, rather than irrelevant. Paul is not addressing ontological questions for their own sake, and to have acknowledged here that woman too is the image of God may have irreparably undermined his insistence that she cover her head in worship. Yet to call woman the 'image of man' when he is trying to differentiate between the

49.   Jervis, ' "But I Want You to Know . . ." ', pp. 234–35.

50.   Elizabeth A. Castelli, 'Paul on Women and Gender', in Ross Shepard Kraemer and Mary Rose D'Angelo (eds), *Women and Christian Origins* (New York and Oxford: Oxford University Press, 1999), pp. 221–35 (229).

51.   This difference is of course expressed in culture, as I have shown above, and such expression is very important to Paul. But it cannot be assumed that he held anything like the modern conception that gender is socially constructed. One may well wish to contend that this conception is accurate with regard to ancient Mediterranean society as much as to the modern West, but this would not have been Paul's own perception.

52.   Contra Barrett, *A Commentary on the First Epistle to the Corinthians*, p. 249, and Bruce, *1 and 2 Corinthians*, p. 105.

53.   Morna D. Hooker, 'Authority on her Head: An Examination of 1 Cor. XI. 10', *NTS* 10 (1963/64), pp. 410–16 (411).

two would not be particularly helpful either. It is in fact the term δόξα, which is absent from the Genesis accounts, that enables Paul to get around the problem.[54] As Ann Jervis perceives, this word allows Paul to avoid the problematic statement that woman is the image of man, while pointing out the contrast between male and female in Genesis 2.[55]

The interpretation of δόξα is therefore a matter of some importance. André Feuillet helpfully debunks the common translation of 'reflection', which has little or no basis in the LXX or secular Greek.[56] Feuillet and several others correctly prefer the sense of 'honour'.[57] Wire draws out the full cultural implications of this, reading δόξα as honour in contrast to the shame which Paul has just evoked.[58] That Paul thus describes woman as the 'honour of man' (and therefore also, by implication, as a potential source of shame for him) is consistent with the cultural anthropology discussed above.

Any well-meaning attempt to read this verse as supportive of gender equality[59] must fall away in the face of the statements which follow. 11.8–9 fills out the hierarchical concept of headship to which readers were introduced in 11.3. Man is the source of woman, and woman was created for his sake, not vice versa. The importance of priority of origin for status has already been noted above. Martin goes on to observe that persons of lower status exist for those of higher status (slaves and masters being an obvious example),[60] assumptions which are evident both in the deutero-Pauline epistles and in the so-called 'gnostic' literature. 1 Tim. 2.13–15 is a good example from the first group, directly juxtaposing man's priority in creation with woman's culpability in the Fall in an argument designed to limit women's religious activity and to promote their traditional domestic role.[61] As for the second group, perhaps the best example is the biblical demiurgical myth fundamental to many of the texts found at Nag Hammadi, in which the creator figure Yaltabaoth is a divine being of lower rank than the true God from whom he ultimately derives; furthermore, according to

---

54. Fee, *The First Epistle to the Corinthians*, p. 515.

55. Jervis, ' "But I Want You to Know . . ." ', p. 242.

56. André Feuillet, 'L'homme "gloire de Dieu" et la femme "gloire de l'homme" (1 Cor. 11.7b)', *RB* 81 (1974), pp. 161–82 (164).

57. Feuillet, 'L'homme "gloire de Dieu" ', pp. 175–76; see also Fee, *The First Epistle to the Corinthians*, p. 516.

58. Wire, *The Corinthian Women Prophets*, p. 120.

59. E.g. Feuillet, 'L'homme "gloire de Dieu" ', p. 178.

60. Martin, *The Corinthian Body*, p. 232.

61. Of course, while similar arguments are employed, the 1 Timothy passage is clearly intended to achieve rather different ends from 1 Cor. 11.2–16, which assumes throughout that women will pray and prophesy in church.

several of the accounts he makes matters worse by failing to recognize his secondary status.[62]

11.10: The Woman's Authority and the Angels

These verses lead up to the (slightly surprising) focal point of the argument in 11.10: 'Because of this a woman ought to have authority on her head [ἐξουσίαν ἔχειν ἐπὶ τῆς κεφαλῆς], because of the angels.' The verse is highlighted by means of a chiastic structure:

A. Man is the source of woman (11.8)
    B. Woman's existence depends on man's (11.9)
        C. Declaration (11.10)
    B′. Interdependence of woman and man 'in the Lord' (11.11)
A′. Woman is the source of man (11.12)

Given its obvious importance, it is rather unfortunate that 11.10 is so obscure for the modern reader. Women are not simply told to cover their heads, as a comparison with 11.7 might lead one to expect. After apparently subordinating her, Paul now speaks of woman's authority; and in addition angels suddenly appear, as if out of the blue.

To deal with the last problem first, it is easier to understand the angels' function here if it is assumed that they are actually connected in some way to the preceding argument. There are in fact material demonstrations that this is the case: first, the use of ὀφείλει in 11.10 (which echoes that in 11.7); and secondly, the repetition of διά in 11.9–10, which serves to connect the two parts of 11.10 with each other and with what precedes.[63] With this in mind, it is clear that the angels' role as guardians of the order of creation just described is prominent in Paul's mind.[64] More specifically, of course, Paul is concerned with orderly conduct at worship. Fitzmyer has argued that Paul was familiar with and influenced by the belief of the Qumran community that angels were present in the worship assembly.[65] For example, in 1QSa 2.5–9 one reads that 'everyone who is defiled in his flesh . . . with a blemish visible to the eyes . . . these shall not enter to take their place among the congregation of famous men, for the angels of holiness are among their

---

62. See for example the retelling of the early chapters of Genesis found in the *Hypostasis of the Archons* (which will be examined at greater length in Chapter 6); see also the *Apocryphon of John* (Codex II) 13.5–13.

63. Jason David BeDuhn, ' "Because of the Angels": Unveiling Paul's Anthropology in 1 Corinthians 11', *JBL* 118 (1999), pp. 295–320 (304).

64. Barrett, *A Commentary on the First Epistle to the Corinthians*, p. 254.

65. J.A. Fitzmyer, 'A Feature of Qumran Angelology and the Angels of 1 Cor. XI. 10', *NTS* 4 (1957/58), pp. 48–58.

congregation'.[66] As Martin points out, in a culture in which women were generally expected to be veiled, a woman's uncovered head in public constituted a bodily defect,[67] a deviation from the norm. Paul therefore seeks to promote measures that will allow for women's inclusion in the worshipping community without giving offence to the angels.

But this does not – indeed, cannot – eliminate the alternative interpretation, based upon Gen. 6.1–4, of the angels as sexual predators on women.[68] Orr and Walther's assertion that 'the angels would never have been thought of in contemporary Judaism as being subject to lust for a human female'[69] is really quite incomprehensible in the light of texts such as the Book of the Watchers in *1 Enoch*.[70] Indeed, Martin goes so far as to assert that the idea was so prevalent that it is present in 1 Cor. 11.10 whether Paul intended it to be or not.[71] As previously noted, the removal of the veil has connotations of both sexual seduction *and* disorder. It perhaps ought to be expected, then, that Paul's invocation of the angels in the course of his promotion of head-covering for women is addressed to both these concerns.

The interpreter is then left with the problem of ἐξουσία. What, if anything, does women's 'authority' have to do with their being veiled? Fitzmyer takes refuge in the subtle complexities of Semitic language to argue, on the basis of the similarities between the Aramaic term for 'veil' (*sltwnyh*) and the root of the Aramaic verb 'to have power over' (*slt*), that ἐξουσία in this instance is an equivalent of *sltwnyh*.[72] I cannot help but agree with Morna Hooker that this suggestion is a little too ingenious.[73] The idea that ἐξουσία refers to a husband's authority over his wife does not work either, for as Jason BeDuhn demonstrates, the expression must refer to the authority the

---

66. The translation used is that of Florentino García Martínez, *The Dead Sea Scrolls Translated: The Qumran Texts in English*, 2nd edn, tr. Wilfred G.E. Watson (Leiden: Brill/ Grand Rapids: Eerdmans, 1996), p. 127.

67. Martin, *The Corinthian Body*, p. 245.

68. Martin, *The Corinthian Body*, p. 243.

69. William F. Orr and James Arthur Walther, *1 Corinthians*, AB 32 (Garden City, NY: Doubleday, 1976), p. 261.

70. This text recounts the story of the two hundred angels who fell from heaven because of their desire for earthly women: 'And it came to pass when the children of men had multiplied that in those days were born unto them beautiful and comely daughters. And the angels, the children of the heaven, saw and lusted after them, and said to one another: "Come, let us choose us wives from among the children of men and beget us children" ' (*1 En.* 6.1–3).

71. Martin, *The Corinthian Body*, p. 245. Martin also points out that historically this has been the most common interpretation of 1 Cor. 11.10.

72. Fitzmyer, 'A Feature of Qumran Angelology', p. 52.

73. Hooker, 'Authority on her Head', p. 413. Fitzmyer also appears to undermine his own plea that at least some of the Corinthians would have understood these Semitic word games, given his lack of confidence concerning their knowledge of Jewish beliefs about fallen angels ('A Feature of Qumran Angelology', p. 54). It seems to me rather more likely that the Corinthians would have been familiar with these traditions than with the intricacies of Aramaic.

woman has over her own head: 'Paul *always* employs the term to mean authority held by the subject'.[74] That Paul attributes authority to women is initially surprising in the light of the preceding argument from creation, but this tactic is part and parcel of his rhetorical strategy.[75] Now, as in 11.5–6, Paul gives women a 'choice' as to what to do with their heads – a radical step indeed if the choice offered were genuinely free, but in the context of the argument as a whole, it is clear that there is really only one viable option. The veil itself is not a sign of true authority as a modern reader might understand that concept;[76] it is instead a sign of submission with which women choose to cover themselves.[77] In one verse Paul both attributes authority to women and tells them how they must use it.

11.11–12: A Cautionary Note

πλὴν at the beginning of 11.11 indicates a shift in Paul's argument. These verses correspond closely to, and appear to revise, 11.8–9. Paul now draws attention to the interdependence of man and woman (11.11), and notes that, unlike the first two human beings, it is now the case that man comes into being through woman (11.12). Should one then hear in these verses, as does Hans Conzelmann, a note of retreat?[78] This is unlikely. It would be surprising for Paul to make a move that would undermine all his labours thus far. Wire is correct in observing that these verses do not in fact concede much.[79] The demand that women cover their heads is not abrogated;[80] indeed, in the verse immediately following, Paul clearly expects the Corinthians to assent to the propriety of this practice (11.13). In fact, if 11.11–12 amend anything, it is the declaration just made in 11.10: they provide a further indication of just how Paul expects women to exercise their authority. For the first time in this passage Paul refers now to the woman first, and reminds her that she is still in a relationship of interdependence with man. The rhetorical strategy of according to the woman the choice to veil herself is not to be misconstrued as undoing the basic pattern of male–female

74. BeDuhn, ' "Because of the Angels" ', pp. 302–303; emphasis in original.
75. BeDuhn, ' "Because of the Angels" ', p. 303.
76. Contra Bruce, *1 and 2 Corinthians*, p. 106. George Brooke ('Between Qumran and Corinth', p. 171) also argues that 'for Paul women's authority is to be marked by customary decorum, either with a veil or with braided hair tied up'. However, as I have attempted to show previously, it is part of the very purpose of this 'customary decorum' to mark women's subordinate status.
77. Martin, *The Corinthian Body*, p. 246.
78. Hans Conzelmann, *1 Corinthians*, tr. James W. Leitch, Hermeneia (Philadelphia: Fortress Press, 1975), p. 190.
79. Wire, *The Corinthian Woman Prophets*, p. 128.
80. D'Angelo, 'Veils, Virgins and the Tongues of Men and Angels', p. 135.

relationships which Paul has elaborated thus far. χωρὶς, then, must be read in this instance as 'apart from', not 'different from'.[81] It is difference that Paul wants to uphold. Even and especially ἐν κυρίῳ, woman and man are not independent of one another.

It is perhaps a little less clear how 11.12 might serve to constrain women's authority. The verse does begin by reasserting the first woman's secondary status, but this appears to be somewhat mitigated by the ensuing statement the 'the man [comes] through the woman'. This phrase has generally been understood to refer to normal sexual reproduction, in which women give birth to (male) children, in contrast to Eve, who was brought forth from the man's body. If this interpretation is correct, then this verse may be a rare Pauline endorsement of the bearing and raising of children. The main point, however, is made clear by the concluding phrase: 'but all things [are] from God'. That it is now women who bring men into the world does not alter the fact of the first woman's secondary status, nor that of the generations of women who follow her. The divine order of creation is neither overturned nor contradicted. As in 11.3, God's place at the top of the hierarchy serves to preserve the status quo.

11.13–16: 'Judge for yourselves'?

'All things from God' being a suitably resounding note on which to conclude this part of the argument, Paul now turns to the Corinthians and challenges them in a direct address to 'judge for yourselves'. It is testimony to Paul's communicative skills that in a passage where he is working so hard to enforce his own will upon the Corinthians, the first imperative verb they encounter is one telling them to make up their own minds on the matter. This is hardly the act of a man who is unsure that his argument so far has been successful.[82] It may indeed have been the case that the Corinthians were accustomed to seeing women praying with their heads covered,[83] but Paul does not rely on that. His challenge is best paraphrased thus: '*In the light of all I have said*, does it seem proper to you that a woman should pray to God with her head uncovered?' Paul is confident that he has made his case effectively. Fee is thus correct in his assessment: 'once they have thus "judged for themselves", of course, Paul expects them to see things his way'.[84] Paul flatters the Corinthians by appealing to their judgement.

---

81. Contra Schüssler Fiorenza, *In Memory of Her*, p. 229.
82. Contra Conzelmann, *1 Corinthians*, p. 190.
83. Wire, *The Corinthian Women Prophets*, p. 128. See also the quotation from Juvenal on p. 44 above.
84. Fee, *The First Epistle to the Corinthians*, p. 525.

Having reduced the legitimate choices to one, he can afford to let them think that they are deciding their own conduct.

The rhetorical questions continue in 11.14.[85] Here, just in case there is still any doubt, Paul does make a more general appeal beyond the scope of his own argument, to 'nature' (φύσις). A modern understanding of nature renders the verse obscure, or even laughable. However, in its first-century CE context, φύσις has the sense of 'how things are',[86] or 'everything which by its origin or by observation of its constitution appears to be a given'.[87] Thus, as D'Angelo observes, there is a very close correlation between nature and propriety.[88] 'Nature' is what people expect to see, and what, therefore, they regard as proper and right. Helmut Koester has observed that hair and beard styles were particularly important indicators of nature.[89] For a male human being, short hair is 'natural', while long hair, which is contrary to cultural expectations, is a source of shame. On the contrary, for a female human being, long hair is the norm, and is therefore her δόξα; that is to say, it is honourable for her. This is what one would expect in light of the shaven female head being regarded as a source of shame (11.5–6). Paul's point is this: nature, by giving woman long hair, indicates that she ought to be covered; that is her natural state. Meier sums up the matter succinctly: 'Woman must follow in prayer the lead nature gives her in daily life.'[90] At least as far as women are concerned, sensitivity to cultural expectations is not suspended in the worship assembly.

Yet the women who were praying and prophesying with uncovered heads could not have been unaware of these cultural expectations. For them at least, the benefits of transgressing the norms outweighed the disadvantages. 11.16 appears to indicate that Paul expects that there may yet be some who are disinclined to accept his argument. His final tactic, superficially the most benign and perhaps even indicative of desperation, in fact lays down an ultimatum to those who wish to be contentious. The use of 'we' should not be underestimated in a strongly group-orientated society like the ancient Mediterranean. When Paul says of women praying and prophesying with uncovered heads that '*we* have no such custom', those who continue to

85. Fee, *The First Epistle to the Corinthians*, p. 525. Padgett's suggestion ('Paul on Women in the Church', p. 82) that 11.13–15 be read as a series of simple statements (e.g. 'it is proper for a woman to pray to God with her head uncovered') is an inventive way of reconciling Paul with modern sensibilities; but it is not a correct reading of the passage in its original context.

86. Fee, *The First Epistle to the Corinthians*, p. 527.

87. Helmut Koester, in *TDNT*, ix, p. 253.

88. D'Angelo, 'Veils, Virgins and the Tongues of Men and Angels', p. 135.

89. Koester, *TDNT*, ix, p. 263. It is thus unsurprising that Paul should talk about hair when he begins to argue from nature. There is no need to assume that he was in fact concerned with hairstyle rather than head covering. In any case, these two concerns are not unrelated (see n. 23 above).

90. Meier, 'On the Veiling of Hermeneutics', p. 223.

engage in the practice are effectively excluded from the community: by embracing this custom, they place themselves by definition outside the 'we'. These women (and their supporters) are thus forced to choose between a practice which they find liberating, and their membership of the community which made the practice possible in the first place. Paul allows for no debate.

11.2–16: Overall Assessment

It is too simplistic to write this passage off as a prime example of Pauline misogyny. Paul assumes throughout that women will pray and prophesy in the worship assembly, and that it is legitimate for them to do so; such an assumption is lamentably absent from later texts such as the Pastoral Epistles. However, he is not prepared to permit women to engage in these activities in the manner which they themselves see fit (that is, with unveiled heads). Paul is determined that his own concern for the community's honour take precedence over the women's willingness to transgress cultural norms for the sake of spiritual experience. The text thus represents his attempt to assume a position of considerable power over them.

14.34–35: The Question of Authenticity

Paul exercises this power much more transparently in 14.33b–40. Here Paul once again seeks to control women's behaviour; but whereas in 11.2–16 he was concerned only that they should be properly attired while praying and prophesying, in 14.33b–40 he attempts to prohibit these activities altogether. It is fitting to treat 14.33b–40 together as a unit because, as Wire recognizes, 'the sharp tone and severe demands [of 14.37–38] are rhetorically most appropriate to the categorical silencing of the women' which the earlier verses in the passage demand.[91] Once again Paul is attempting to change current practice in an area that is of considerable importance both to him and to his interlocutors.

To approach the passage in this way assumes the authenticity of the controversial verses 14.34–35. Due at least as much to the rather unappealing content of these verses (to modern eyes) as to their apparent contradiction with 11.2–16, several scholars have attempted to argue that they are a non-Pauline interpolation.[92] Fee argues that the verses' location after 14.40

---

91. Wire, *The Corinthian Women Prophets*, p. 155.

92. For example, Carolyn Osiek and David L. Balch see 14.34–35 as the projection of deutero-Pauline ideas back onto Paul himself; they insist that to read Paul through such a lens is 'disastrous', because 'it obscures the freedom women experienced in those early

in some manuscripts can best be explained if they were an early marginal gloss subsequently inserted at two different places.[93] However, Antoinette Wire and Curt Niccum have both demonstrated convincingly that the displacement in the manuscripts of the Western tradition can in fact be traced back to one archetype.[94] In sum, distasteful though the passage might be, 'the external evidence argues for the authenticity of 1 Cor. 14.34–35 in its traditional location'.[95] The internal difficulties of the text must be resolved by other means.

14.33b–35: The Veil of Silence

As in 11.16, in 14.33b Paul once again invokes the practice of other Christian assemblies as an authority to which the Corinthians must defer. The result is that the Corinthians' own Christian identity is at stake: if they wish to retain their place among the churches of the saints (which Paul has ascribed to them in the greeting in 1.2), then they must conform their conduct to that which Paul sets down. 14.33b–34 exhibits a chiastic structure in which the central prohibition on women's speech is flanked by two sources of authority, and proper submission is equated with silence:

    A. As in all the churches of the saints,
           B. let women be silent in the churches;
                  C. for it is not permitted to them to speak,
           B'. but let them be in submission,
    A'. as the Law also says.

As Jervis points out, it is not unknown for Paul to invoke the Law in this

---

communities' (*Families in the New Testament World: Households and House Churches* [Louisville, Ky.: Westminster/John Knox, 1997], p. 117). The use of such a strong term indicates how much is at stake for those readers of the Bible who have embraced the modern ideal of sexual equality, but who still wish to ascribe some kind of meaningful authority to texts like 1 Corinthians. Osiek and Balch's argument as a whole also raises the spectre of circularity that tends to haunt such debates: one's image of Paul influences which parts of his letters one will regard as authentic; but it is only from these letters that one can derive an image of Paul in the first place.

For other examples of arguments for the inauthenticity of 14.34–35, see Conzelmann, *1 Corinthians*, p. 246; D'Angelo, 'Veils, Virgins and the Tongues of Men and Angels', p. 138; Fee, *First Epistle to the Corinthians*, pp. 697–702; Martin, *The Corinthian Body*, p. 289 n. 2; Philip B. Payne, 'Fuldensis, Sigla for Variants in Vaticanus, and 1 Corinthians 14:34–35', *NTS* 41 (1995), pp. 240–62.

93. Fee, *First Epistle to the Corinthians*, p. 699.

94. Wire, *The Corinthian Women Prophets*, pp. 149–52; Curt Niccum, 'The Voice of the Manuscripts on the Silence of Women: The External Evidence for 1 Corinthians 14.34–35', *NTS* 43 (1997), pp. 242–55 (251–52).

95. Niccum, 'The Voice of the Manuscripts', p. 254.

manner.[96] It does not much matter which specific part of the Law, if any, he has in mind here. The pertinent point is that two major sources of authority are shown to lead to the same conclusion: it is not permitted for women to speak in the churches. Anyone minded to contravene Paul's command will find little encouragement here.

The point is reinforced in the following verse: 'but if they wish to learn anything, let them ask their own husbands at home; for it is shameful for a woman to speak in church'. Wire correctly perceives that this is no real concession to the women's wishes: all it does is confirm their confinement to the household.[97] Even the author of 1 Tim. 2.11 at least allows women to learn in the assembly. Once again Paul draws upon the values of honour and shame to drive his argument home. The term αἰσχρόν (shameful) was used in 11.6 of a woman praying or prophesying with her head unveiled; now it is employed to stop them speaking at all, whatever their attire. It would appear now that only silence is an adequate covering for women's modesty. As in 11.6, it is Paul who by his assertion declares shameful an activity which its practitioners would have experienced rather differently, and he appears to expect his readers to accept his judgement without question.

14.33b–40 and 11.2–16: Making Sense of the Contradiction

This uncompromising silencing of women, reinforced on either side by church custom and by the Law, does not sit easily with Paul's earlier assumption that women can and will pray and prophesy if properly covered. It is therefore necessary at this point to attempt to make sense (if sense can indeed be made) of the seeming contradiction between 14.33b–40 and 11.2–16. But how far can one go in trying to impose consistency on a highly complex text? I have suggested previously that even within one chapter (1 Corinthians 7), Paul appears to be capable of advocating two contrasting positions at once.[98] Yet in this case a plausible explanation for his apparent indecisiveness could be found in the distinct groups of people in the Corinthian community to whom Paul was addressing himself. It is possible that something similar may be the case here; I shall in due course test out the

---

96. L. Ann Jervis, '1 Corinthians 14.34–35: A Reconsideration of Paul's Limitation of the Free Speech of some Corinthian Women', *JSNT* 58 (1995), pp. 51–74 (58). Other positive appeals to the Law may be found in 1 Cor. 7.19 and 9.8.

97. Wire, *The Corinthian Women Prophets*, p. 154.

98. That is to say, Paul makes clear his own preference for celibacy (1 Cor. 7.7a) and expresses the wish that he could spare his readers the distress in this life that those who marry will experience (7.28b); yet at the same time he advocates marriage for those who apparently lack the self-control to follow the superior celibate way of life. He simultaneously sets up an ideal and forbids some of his readers from attempting to attain it.

idea that 14.33b–40 is intended to silence not all women, but only those who are married (the instructions in 11.2–16 would then be understood as concerned only with celibate women prophets).

Before proceeding to try out this hypothesis, however, it is necessary to consider another means of reconciling the two passages, in which it is not the speakers with whom Paul is primarily concerned, but rather the type of speech in which they engage.[99] This theory requires λαλεῖν in 14.34–35 to be read as referring not to inspired speech (which is the sense in which the verb has been used throughout the preceding chapter) but to disruptive chatter or questions which interrupt the worship service. This argument is highly unconvincing, for a number of reasons. Paul does indeed unambiguously call for order and peace in the worship service (14.32); but disorder arises not from mere questions or chatter, but rather from the fact that 'whenever [the Corinthians] assemble, each one has a hymn, a teaching, a revelation, a tongue, or an interpretation' (14.26). It is an over-abundance of *inspired* speech that is the problem.

Furthermore, if Paul really were dealing with disruptive chatter here, then the remedy he proposes seems an alarmingly severe one for such a relatively mild disease. That he must invoke the combined forces of church custom, the Law and shame suggests that the speech taking place was something in which the speakers had a great deal invested and which they would not relinquish easily. And why, in any case, should it only be women's questioning that is singled out as shameful? Is it not implausible that only women would have had things that they wished to know? Indeed, Paul has just encouraged prophecy 'so that *all* may learn' (14.31, my emphasis). In sum, it is difficult to avoid the conclusion that it is not the type of speech that troubles Paul, but rather the identity of the speakers.

But precisely who might comprise this group of speakers whom Paul is so determined to silence? This brings me to the hypothesis mentioned above. If at least some consistency with 11.2–16 is to be assumed – that is to say, if Paul does permit at least some women to pray and prophesy in the assembly – then 14.33b–35 cannot be addressed to all women. The recommendation of 14.35 that those women who wish to learn anything should ask their husbands at home suggests the possibility that it may be *married* women whom Paul has in view here. If so, the instructions of 11.2–16 must be directed to unmarried celibate women, for (according to Paul) it is only they who may legitimately prophesy. But here lies this solution's stumbling block: looking at 11.2–16 in isolation, it contains no obvious signs that it refers only to a certain group of women; while Paul can elsewhere refer

99. Commentators adopting this thesis include Jervis, '1 Corinthians 14.34–35', p. 52, and Orr and Walther, *1 Corinthians*, p. 313.

specifically to unmarried women, virgins and widows,[100] he does not do so here. Are there any grounds, then, on which the suggestion that Paul's attitude to women prophets depended on their marital status becomes plausible?

It may be noted first of all that at least one other author contemporaneous with Paul finds women's submission enshrined in the Law; and when he does, it is expressly *wifely* submission. Thus Josephus writes: 'The woman, says the Law, is in all things inferior to the man. Let her accordingly be submissive, not that she be sexually violated by the man, but that she be ruled; for God gave the power to her husband.'[101] Secondly and more important, however, there does appear to be a tradition of celibate female prophecy in the New Testament and related literature. Luke 2.36–38 informs the reader that the elderly prophet Anna has been a widow for much of her adult life, while the four prophesying daughters of Philip are described in Acts 21.9 as unmarried. Philo, in his discussion of the Therapeutae, refers to women, 'most of them aged virgins, who have kept their chastity not under compulsion, like some of the Greek priestesses, but of their own free will in their ardent yearning for wisdom'.[102]

In addition, there is John Poirier and Joseph Frankovich's intriguing suggestion that Paul understood celibacy to be incumbent on him because of his prophetic status.[103] As I discussed in Chapter 1, they draw attention to the Jewish tradition of Moses' celibacy, necessary because of the inviolability and unpredictability of the word of God.[104] Is it possible that Paul extends this requirement to women prophets as well? If he does, his instructions in 1 Corinthians 7, which (if my analysis in the previous chapter is correct) appear to require many women to get or remain married, would narrow the field of potential candidates considerably, and I am unable to convince even myself that 11.2–16 would be addressed to such a small group as this without some indication in the passage itself that this is in fact the case.

Ultimately irreconcilable though they may be, the two passages are not utterly foreign to one another. 11.2–16 makes clear that even if women are permitted to exercise their prophetic gift, Paul still seeks to maintain strict control over the manner in which they do so; they are not permitted to forget the secondary status that is theirs on account of creation (hence the veil must still be worn). 14.33b–35 simply takes this assessment of women's position to its logical conclusion. The vehemence of 14.33b–40 can leave the reader in little doubt that women were prophesying in Corinth, whether

---

100.   See for example 1 Cor. 7.8, 25, 34.

101.   Josephus, *Apion* 2.200–201.

102.   Philo, *Vit. Cont.* 68.

103.   John C. Poirier and Joseph Frankovich, 'Celibacy and Charism in 1 Corinthians 7.5–7', *HTR* 89 (1996), pp. 1–18 (17).

104.   Poirier and Frankovich, 'Celibacy and Charism', p. 15.

Paul liked it or not; he is not dealing here with a mere hypothetical problem. How immediately successful his conflicting attempts to deal with it might have been must be left to the reader's imagination.

14.36–40: The Concluding Challenge

The final verses of ch. 14 drive Paul's argument home with biting rhetorical force. After speaking about women in the third person, 14.36 reverts to the second person in a sudden direct challenge to the Corinthians: 'Or did the word of God originate with you? Or are you the only ones it has reached?' Wire argues that these questions are addressed to the women themselves, in an attempt by Paul to ridicule their claim to any speaking role.[105] However, it is perhaps more likely that he challenges the whole community here, chastising them for their toleration of such shameful activities, just as he does in 5.1–2. The questions function to make any acceptance of women speaking in the assembly a preposterous thing, on a par with claims that the word of God originated with the Corinthians, and that it has reached them only. Both such claims are patently untrue and there is no reason to suppose the Corinthians would make them. Paul thus attempts to re-evaluate women's prophecy and render it equally unacceptable. His two questions also serve to remind the Corinthians once again that their very Christian identity is at stake in this matter: the word of God did not originate with them but with Paul, who brought it to them and to others as well, and who is writing to them now. How can they dare to dismiss the commands of the one from whom they received the message of salvation?

Paul appears to recognize that the Corinthians will not capitulate easily, however, and wields a further rhetorical weapon in 14.37–38. Should his own authority not be enough to convince them by itself, he boldly equates his instructions with a command of the Lord, and makes acknowledgement of this equation the criterion by which a person can be recognized as a prophet. There is no need to find in 14.38 the threat of eschatological judgement[106] to understand the seriousness of this move. In equating his restrictive instructions with the 'command of the Lord', Paul is effectively setting up himself and his understanding of the Lord's requirements against the women's experience of the Lord as the one who has bestowed upon them the gift of prophecy. Having reminded them in 14.36 of his role in proclaiming Christ to them, he appears to stake everything on the assumption that, as broker between the Corinthians and Christ, they cannot afford to sever their relationship with him, whatever it may cost them.

---

105. Wire, *The Corinthian Women Prophets*, p. 154.
106. As Fee does, *First Epistle to the Corinthians*, p. 712.

Women prophets are effectively given two choices. Either they may continue to utter inspired speech in defiance of Paul's command and in so doing renounce their prophetic status (a choice Paul clearly does not expect them to take); or they may confirm their prophetic status by ceasing to prophesy! As Wire puts it, 'he seems to misgauge the women prophets by thinking they will demonstrate their status as prophets by agreeing they can never speak as prophets'.[107] Yet other prophets in the Corinthian community are also placed in a difficult position, for if they affirm the married women's prophetic status contrary to Paul's instructions, they thereby forfeit their own. To help them make the 'right' choice, Paul concludes by urging the brothers (ἀδελφοί) to engage in prophecy (14.39), an activity which they know brings many benefits: it calls unbelievers to account and discloses the secrets of their hearts (14.24–25); it enables all to learn and to be encouraged (14.31) – but only if it is carried out by the proper persons. Paul's egotistical tirade concludes on a demure note as he asks that all things be done decently and in order (14.40); the troublesome women have been dealt with and dismissed. One can only hope that they did not go as quietly as Paul might have liked.

Concluding Remarks

The means which Paul uses to achieve his ends in 1 Cor. 11.2–16 and 14.33b–40 are quite similar. In both passages he prioritizes his sensibilities and concerns over those of the women whom he seeks to control; in both he demonstrates his power over all the Corinthians by assuming the right to determine their identity as Christians on the basis of their reaction to his commands. His attitude to female prophecy appears to be one of extremely reluctant acceptance of a phenomenon which he cannot fully control, but which he nonetheless seeks to limit as far as possible.

The importance of the theological and societal concerns by which Paul was motivated should not be underestimated, and on account of this alone modern readers ought not to rush to demonize him. However, his efforts to secure his own authority over his community would appear to have had a considerable cost for some of its members. It is also possible to see how Paul's contradictory teachings on women in 1 Corinthians laid the basis for a wedge to be driven between prophetic speech and the traditional female roles of marriage and child-bearing. Later texts reveal this wedge firmly in place; thus on the one hand we find the total confinement of women to the household in the Pastoral Epistles, and on the other hand the motif of women fleeing such roles and 'becoming male' in texts such as the *Acts of*

107. Wire, *The Corinthian Women Prophets*, p. 155.

Paul and Thecla and 'gnostic' writings like the *Gospel of Thomas*. In 1 Cor. 14.33b–40, the ground has been laid for 'true' prophecy to be gendered male, and for the presence of women in leadership roles to be presented as a distinguishing mark of 'heretical' groups. That both 'orthodox' and non-'orthodox' groups, however, were able to find inspiration and ammunition for their respective causes in Paul's first letter to the Corinthians will be amply demonstrated in the chapters that follow.

Part II

DEUTERO-PAULINE LETTERS

Chapter 3

MARRIAGE IN THE DEUTERO-PAULINE LITERATURE: COLOSSIANS AND EPHESIANS

> The author is . . . the ideological figure by which one marks the manner in
> which we fear the proliferation of meaning.
>   Michel Foucault, 'What is an Author?'

I move on in this second part of the book to examine the interpretations of
Paul found in some other New Testament texts that also bear his name: the
letters to the Colossians and Ephesians (the focus of the present chapter)
and the Pastoral Epistles (the subject of Chapter 4). That these documents
are written in Paul's name presents, for the purposes of the argument
developed in the current work, both an advantage and a potential problem.
The advantage consists in the openness of these authors' interest in the
apostle's teachings: by appropriating his name, they consciously and plainly
position themselves in relation to the Pauline tradition. The problem, however, lies in the even more obvious initial implication of the letters' stated
source: might not Colossians, Ephesians and the Pastorals actually be, as
they say, written by Paul himself? This problem requires me not only to
assert but also to justify my belief in these documents' pseudonymity; this I
propose to do for each text individually before examining those sections of
their contents pertinent to my particular topical concerns of women and
marriage.

A few general remarks are in order before embarking on this task. As this
and the following chapter will show, the positions on marriage and women
adopted by the deutero-Pauline letters differ in many important respects
from those set out in 1 Corinthians. Clearly, then, the authors of these later
texts are not interested in Paul simply because they find his teaching on
these topics congenial; if this were the case, why would they take it upon
themselves to change it to the degree that they do? The source of Paul's
attraction for these writers must be sought elsewhere. Margaret MacDonald
is on the right track when she suggests that the motivation for the pseud-
epigraphical enterprise can be found in 'a desire on the part of [Paul's]
associates to communicate his authoritative word when he was no longer

able to do so'.[1] It is primarily the desire to exercise Paul's authority that leads these authors to appropriate his name; and in order to exercise it effectively in situations different from those encountered by the apostle in his lifetime, the practical teachings found in the authentic letters need to be adapted in certain ways. One might say that – in their own eyes, at least – the deutero-Paulinists were maintaining the spirit, if not the letter, of the output of their literary namesake.

Evidence from the epistles themselves would suggest, however, that the problem of adapting to a new context was not the only one they were composed to address. They also appear to be designed to combat other interpretations of Paul, of which their authors for various reasons disapprove.[2] The deutero-Pauline letters may therefore be understood as attempts to halt what Foucault calls 'the proliferation of meaning',[3] to pin down the significance of Paul and establish their own interpretation of him as the correct one by appropriating his name. To reject these letters' own testimony as to their authorship (as I do), and furthermore to give serious consideration to the works of other readers of Paul who have previously been dismissed as 'heretics' (as I shall do in Chapters 5 and 6), effectively removes the constraints which the deutero-Pauline authors sought to impose on the interpretation of the apostle, and thus enables the 'proliferation of meaning' to proceed freely once again. But for now it is necessary to consider in a little more depth why the deutero-Paulinists wished to stop it in the first place.

'Absent in the flesh but present in spirit': Colossians as Pseudepigraphy

Who, then, wrote Colossians? Was it Paul, as the letter itself asserts in its opening verse, or did some other, unknown author compose the epistle under the cloak of the apostle's name? J.D.G. Dunn professes the opinion that, since Colossians appears to form a bridge between Pauline and post-Pauline thought, the side of the bridge on which one chooses to place its author does not matter as much as some might suppose.[4] The cynical observer might suspect that Dunn's reluctance to come out more strongly in

---

1. Margaret Y. MacDonald, *The Pauline Churches: A Socio-Historical Study of Institutionalization in the Pauline and Deutero-Pauline Writings*, SNTSMS 60 (Cambridge: Cambridge University Press, 1988), p. 124.

2. This assertion will be subject to more detailed discussion when I come to examine the individual texts in turn.

3. Michel Foucault, 'What is an Author?', in David Lodge (ed.), *Modern Criticism and Theory: A Reader* (London and New York: Longman, 1988), pp. 197–210 (209).

4. J.D.G. Dunn, *The Epistles to the Colossians and to Philemon: A Commentary on the Greek Text*, NIGTC (Grand Rapids: Eerdmans/Carlisle: Paternoster, 1996), p. 19.

favour of Colossians' pseudonymity[5] could be governed by factors other than the evidence in the text. Such a cynic may well believe she has a point when she turns to the work of Markus Barth. Having noted with regret that 'cumulative experience has shown that the verdict "inauthentic" leads to a depreciation and devaluation of some elements, at times even of the essential substance and character of this letter', Barth himself goes on to declare for Pauline authorship.[6] One can only assume that he has been guided to some extent in reaching this verdict by his own appreciation and evaluation of the text's worth.

It is, however, unfair to single out Dunn and Barth for criticism in this regard, for it is invariably and unavoidably the case that commentators' assessments of biblical texts are influenced by vested interests. I have already attempted to come clean about my own: for the purposes of my argument here, it is undeniably convenient for me to read Colossians as pseudepigraphy, or as A.J.M. Wedderburn puts it, as 'an experiment in the interpretation of the Pauline heritage'.[7] However, I hope to demonstrate in the remainder of this section that the letter itself does contain ample evidence to support this position. Previous discussions of authorship have tended to devote a good deal of attention to matters of vocabulary and literary style; while not wishing to deny the relevance of these phenomena in connection with other factors, I intend to focus here instead on less technical matters pertaining to Colossians' implied situation.

Col. 2.1 confirms that the letter's implied author and implied recipients have not met in person: 'For I want you to know how much I am struggling for you, and for those in Laodicea, and for all who have not seen me face to face.' The reader may already have discerned this to be the case from various clues in the preceding chapter: the author has heard of (but not seen for himself) the Colossians' faith (1.4), and it was not he but Epaphras who first brought the gospel to them (1.7). The author identifies himself closely with Epaphras, calling him 'our beloved fellow-slave' and commending him warmly (1.7), and at the same time he reminds his readers of the positive outcome of their listening to Epaphras and learning from him: 'the gospel has been bearing fruit among yourselves from the day you heard it and truly comprehended the grace of God' (1.6). In this way he prepares the ground for the Colossians to receive his instructions in a similarly enthusiastic fashion.

If a person wishes to send a pseudonymous letter, it is obviously convenient if his intended readers have no first-hand knowledge of the individual

---

5. This is the position to which he eventually commits himself (Dunn, *Epistles*, p. 36).

6. Markus Barth, *Colossians*, tr. Astrid B. Beck, AB 34B (New York: Doubleday, 1994), pp. 114, 125.

7. Andrew T. Lincoln and A.J.M. Wedderburn, *The Theology of the Later Pauline Letters* (Cambridge: Cambridge University Press, 1993), p. 62.

whose name he adopts. This circumstance should therefore alert the commentator to the possibility of pseudonymity; on its own, however, it does not constitute sufficient evidence to prove the fact conclusively. Romans, for example, was also written to a congregation not personally acquainted with Paul, yet its authenticity is rarely disputed. One important feature which distinguishes Romans from Colossians is the former's reiteration of the author's wish or intention to visit his readers in person (Rom. 1.10, 11, 13, 15; 15.22–24); no such desire is expressed in the latter. That such emphasis is laid on the potential visit in Romans would suggest that there is at least a possibility that it may come about; conversely in Colossians, where there is no such possibility, the subject is not even raised. The closest the author comes is to mention visits by some of Paul's associates (Col. 4.7–10). Colossians also lacks the characteristic Pauline address to his readers as 'brothers' (ἀδελφοί), which may be found in abundance in Romans.[8]

The issues of the Colossian church's relation to the world and of the opponents whom the author is seeking to confound will be addressed in more detail in the following sections. However, since Colossians differs from undisputed Pauline letters such as 1 Corinthians in these respects, and differs from them in such a way as to suggest a later and significantly altered situation, it is relevant to mention them briefly in this discussion of pseudepigraphy. Paul in 1 Corinthians may see the world as morally bankrupt and subject to the judgement of the saints, but he does not order his readers to withdraw from it (1 Cor. 5.10; 6.2). While these instructions to his congregation are clearly formulated with public opinion in mind, his main concern seems to be directed toward healing internal divisions and fostering church members' relationships to one another. In Colossians, however, a shift has occurred, so that a harmonious and unified church is now defined against a threat coming from outside. Margaret MacDonald has observed that Colossians was written at a time when hostility to the church was beginning to grow, while the church on its part was developing an increasing interest in social respectability.[9] With this in mind, I would therefore suggest that Colossians is an interpretation of the Pauline tradition composed with social respectability as its driving concern. This motivation manifests itself in the author's description of the opponents (in particular his rejection of their ascetic practices)[10] and in his socially conformist ethical instruction set out in the form of the household code. Such apparent conservatism does not derive from any great love for the world, but rather from the need to survive in uncongenial surroundings until Christ is revealed: 'Set your

---

8.   See for example Rom. 1.13; 7.1, 4; 8.12; 10.1; 11.25; 12.1; 15.14, 30; 16.17.

9.   Margaret Y. MacDonald, 'Citizens of Heaven and Earth: Asceticism and Social Integration in Colossians and Ephesians', in Leif E. Vaage and Vincent L. Wimbush (eds), *Asceticism and the New Testament* (New York and London: Routledge, 1999), pp. 269–98 (271).

10.   MacDonald, 'Citizens of Heaven and Earth', pp. 277, 286.

minds on things that are above, not things that are on earth, for you have died, and your life is hidden with Christ in God' (Col. 3.2–3).

'Philosophy and empty deceit': The Opponents in Colossians

The inclusion in this section of at least a brief discussion of the identity of the Colossian opponents seems unavoidable, confusing and consensus-free though the topic might be. I shall even venture to proffer my own solution to the problem, speculative though it will inevitably be. Mark Kiley neatly summarizes the difficulty facing scholars who wish to identify the opponents with a reasonable degree of specificity:[11] 'the heresy as presented in Colossians bears some connections with aspects of a whole host of sects and ideologies of various periods, but fits no one of them precisely'.[12] Predictably, however, this state of affairs has not prevented many from attempting such an identification. Dunn decides that the opponents subscribe to 'an apocalyptic or mystical Judaism transposed into the diaspora that has been able to make itself attractive to those sympathetic to Judaism by playing on familiar fears and making more impressive claims'.[13] Eduard Lohse, on the other hand, resorts to the well-worn tactic of labelling the opponents 'gnostic', describing their typically 'gnostic' traits with a predictably negative spin. Not only does their system emphasize knowledge and display a world-negating character, a 'gnostic understanding of the world is also exhibited in the desire to be filled with divine power as well as in the boastful arrogance of those who think they have experienced such fullness and possess wisdom and knowledge'.[14] A more thorough survey of the scholarly literature than is possible here would yield a variety of permutations on various points on the spectrum between these two options, including at least one denial that the author of Colossians was responding to alternative teaching at all.[15]

11. Such a wish would in any case appear to be in marked contrast to the author of Colossians himself, who portrays his antagonists in rather vague terms, never ascribing to them any more precise epithet than τις (Mark Kiley, *Colossians as Pseudepigraphy* [Sheffield: JSOT Press, 1986], p. 63).

12. Kiley, *Colossians as Pseudepigraphy*, p. 61.

13. Dunn, *Epistles*, p. 34. See also his discussion of Col. 2.23 in 'The "Body" in Colossians', in Thomas S. Schmidt and Moisés Silva (eds), *To Tell the Mystery: Essays on New Testament Eschatology in Honor of Robert H. Gundry* (Sheffield: JSOT Press, 1994), pp. 163–81 (172–73).

14. Eduard Lohse, *Colossians and Philemon*, tr. W.R. Poehlmann and R.J. Karris, Hermeneia (Philadelphia: Fortress Press, 1971), p. 129. I take issue not so much with the characteristics Lohse adduces as with his labelling them 'gnostic'.

15. Thus Morna D. Hooker, 'Were There False Teachers in Colossae?', in Barnabas Lindars and Stephen Smalley (eds), *Christ and Spirit in the New Testament: Studies in Honour of C.F.D. Moule* (Cambridge: Cambridge University Press, 1973), pp. 315–31.

All these scholars are working with more or less the same body of evidence. As with the question of authenticity, criteria other than 'hard facts' help to determine what conclusions are drawn here. Just as the author of Colossians was keen to show how these opponents were both different from and inferior to his own group, so modern scholars in their turn can be tempted to find in these 'outsiders' (since that is what they are from the viewpoint of the canonical text) a foil for what they want early Christianity to be.[16] The work of the social psychologist Henri Tajfel helps to explain this phenomenon. He observes that 'the value connotations . . . of group membership can only be derived through comparisons with other relevant groups'.[17] In a situation like that pertaining in Colossians and the other deutero-Paulines, where it is a viable option for individuals to shift their allegiance from one group to another, any group leader wishing to retain the loyalty of his adherents must emphasize the differences between his own group and its rivals, and furthermore present those differences in terms favourable to himself. The portrayal of the opponents, whether by the author of Colossians himself or by many later commentators, is not a disinterested one, but is designed with particular aims in view.

The need for a group to distinguish itself in this way is of paramount importance when those against whom it is defining itself are in actual fact quite similar to it. It is circumstances like this, I would suggest, with which the author of Colossians is attempting to deal. Once again, some openness about presuppositions may be in order; and it is one of mine that early Christianity was a good deal less irenic and more conflict-ridden than may once have been supposed. Although the author of Colossians may disagree, it seems to me likely that the opponents to whom he alludes, and other similar groups, thought of themselves as insiders to the Christian movement; it may therefore prove interesting, and maybe even fruitful, for modern commentators to do likewise. Indeed, in the case of Colossians I should like to be even more specific and suggest that the opponents in view are fellow-Paulinists, who are promoting a different interpretation of the Pauline tradition which this author finds both unpalatable and ill advised.

Writing as 'Paul', the author of Colossians leads into his extended treatment of the opponents in the following way: 'I am saying this so that none may deceive you with attractive arguments. For though I am absent in the flesh, I am with you in spirit, rejoicing to see the orderliness and firmness of your faith in Christ' (Col. 2.4–5). Paul's 'absence in the flesh' takes on a whole new significance after the apostle's death, but through the

16. To give him his due, Dunn recognizes this problem and points out that there was no clearly delineated 'orthodoxy' and 'heresy' at the time Colossians was written, and that the opponents should not simply be dismissed out of hand (*Epistles*, p. 24).

17. Henri Tajfel, *Differentiation between Social Groups* (London: Academic Press, 1978), p. 9.

pseudonymous author's assumption of his name, the Colossians may feel his presence just as powerfully as did the Corinthians when he pronounced judgement of the man who had his father's wife (1 Cor. 5.3). That the author produced this letter at all testifies to his anxiety that it should be *his* Paul whom the Colossians welcomed among them, rather than one of the other appropriations and interpretations of the apostle that must have been on offer in the period of uncertainty following his death. Hence he commends them again for their faith in Christ, the faith which they learned from Epaphras, to whom this author is so close, and from which they are emphatically not to turn aside: 'As you therefore have received Christ Jesus the Lord, continue to live your lives in him, rooted and built up in him and established in the faith, just as you were taught' (2.6–7). The full efficacy of the faith they have been taught is stressed in 2.10 and 2.14, with the perfect forms πεπληρωμένοι and ἦρκεν foregrounding the coming to fullness and the removal of debt which have already taken place.

The potential threat to this faith is described in the following terms as 'philosophy and empty deceit, according to human tradition, according to the elements of the world and not according to Christ' (2.8). This is largely evaluative language which does not actually tell the reader a great deal. 'Empty deceit' clearly contrasts with the fullness of the true faith, while the repeated use of κατὰ (according to) serves to directly oppose human tradition and the 'elements of the world' to Christ, who is lord not only of the Colossians (2.6) but of the whole world (1.15–20). Wedderburn notes that this reference to the elements (στοιχεῖα) may also be used to denigrate the opponents' religion, rather than give an accurate description of what it entails.[18] The belief that human life was directed by heavenly bodies was widely held at this time, but Philo for one regards it with some disdain:

> We must, therefore, look on all those bodies in the heaven, which the outward sense regards as gods, not as independent rulers, since they are assigned the work of lieutenants, being by their intrinsic nature responsible to a higher power. . . . And if anyone gives up the service due to the everlasting and uncreated God, transferring it to any more modern and created being, let him be set down as mad and as liable to the charge of the greatest impiety.[19]

Just as Philo sets belief in the powers of the heavenly bodies in opposition to correct worship of God, so the author of Colossians establishes an absolute contrast between the στοιχεῖα and Christ.[20] There can be no compromise

18.   Lincoln and Wedderburn, *The Theology of the Later Pauline Letters*, p. 13. MacDonald similarly suggests that this mention of the elements is designed to associate the opponents with worldly, unstable and base phenomena ('Citizens of Heaven and Earth', p. 274).

19.   Philo, *Spec. Leg.* 1.19–20.

20.   A similar contrast may be found in Gal. 4.3.

between the two; as Lohse points out, the choice the readers ought to make is obvious.[21]

But is not this treatment of the opponents rather harsh if, as I have suggested, they are (or were) fellow-members of the Pauline school? Is it not more likely that Dunn is correct when he opines that 'the Colossian "philosophy" seems to have been quite separate from the Colossian Christian group'?[22] With regard to this aspect of my theory at least, a ready defence can be offered. Testimony to a comparable acrimonious split in a previously unified group can be found in 1 John. Here there is explicit evidence that those whom the author now vilifies he once counted as brothers (2.19), yet this erstwhile closeness does not prevent him branding them as liars, people who walk in the darkness, and even (indirectly) the antichrist.[23] Both 1 John and Colossians illustrate the phenomenon described by MacDonald: 'from the perspective of those labelling their opponents, deviance is most often perceived as moving people from inside to outside. . . . Adherence to false teaching is depicted as regression into the world.'[24] Furthermore, it is precisely when those whom one now faces as opponents once belonged to the same group that there is the sharpest need to distinguish between 'them' and 'us', and to do it in terms unfavourable to 'them'; when rivals used to be brothers, the risk of further defections is all the greater.

Some scholars have suggested that Colossians is primarily concerned with future rather than present danger; Kiley, for example, reads 2.6–23 as 'a warning against a possible heresy perhaps, but only perhaps, having some roots in the actual situation of the addressees'.[25] I find this argument unconvincing. The traditional understanding that commands expressed in the form found in Col. 2.6 and 2.18 – μή plus present imperative – have the sense of 'do not continue an action' may have long since been called into question;[26] but this need not mean that the Colossians were not already being confronted with the opponents' attempts to condemn them (2.16). On the contrary, if in fact 'the same aspectual distinctions maintained in all of the other moods are maintained in the imperative as well',[27] then the use of the present tense here foregrounds the command, and might be said to

21.   Lohse, *Colossians and Philemon*, p. 121.

22.   Dunn, *Epistles*, p. 25.

23.   In drawing this comparison I do not mean to suggest that the Pauline and Johannine schools are in every way identical to one another (though of course both are scholarly hypotheses), nor that their divisions resulted from the same issues.

24.   MacDonald, 'Citizens of Heaven and Earth', p. 273.

25.   Kiley, *Colossians as Pseudepigraphy*, p. 64.

26.   See, for example, C.F.D. Moule, *An Idiom Book of New Testament Greek*, 2nd edn (Cambridge: Cambridge University Press, 1959), pp. 20–21.

27.   Stanley E. Porter, *Idioms of the Greek New Testament* (Sheffield: Sheffield Academic Press, 1994), p. 225.

bestow upon it a certain sense of urgency[28] which would suggest that the author is dealing with something more immediately pressing than some hypothetical future concern. In addition to this, 2.20 seems to suggest that some of the Colossians are already 'submitting to regulations as if they lived in the world'.

In what do these undesirable regulations consist? Barth argues that '[i]t is presumed that all these [things] are characteristic of a piety that is not sanctioned by Paul'.[29] I wish to suggest, however, that – in the opponents' eyes, at least – their practices do indeed represent the true outworking of the apostle's teaching. A few phrases by way of example must suffice. First, one might mention 'taking their stand on visions' (ἃ ἑόρακεν ἐμβατεύων) in 2.18. Paul himself was no stranger to visions and was prepared to invoke them in his own defence: 'It is necessary to boast; nothing is to be gained by it, but I will go on to visions and revelations of the Lord' (2 Cor. 12.1). It is almost tempting to speculate that the textual variant on this phrase in Colossians (some manuscripts read ἃ μή ἑόρακεν ἐμβατεύων) reflects some degree of controversy over this aspect of the Pauline heritage. One may be on slightly firmer ground with the three regulations in 2.21: 'Do not touch, do not taste, do not handle'. Lohse and Barth both insist that these refer to food only and have nothing to do with sexual practice,[30] but MacDonald argues convincingly that sexual renunciation is involved as well.[31] The verb for 'touch' (ἅπτω) is also found in 1 Cor. 7.1: 'It is good for a man not to touch a woman'; as I argued in Chapter 1, this slogan represents Paul's own opinion at least as much as that of any Corinthian ascetic. Might it be, then, that the opponents take up, with what the author of Colossians sees as undue enthusiasm, Paul's preference for sexual renunciation as well as his restrictions on the eating of idol meat, which are now upheld for their own sake rather than that of the weak?[32]

---

28. As Porter suggests is the case in 2 Cor. 13.11–12 (*Idioms of the Greek New Testament*, p. 225).

29. Barth, *Colossians*, p. 385.

30. Lohse, *Colossians*, p. 123; Barth, *Colossians*, p. 356.

31. MacDonald, 'Citizens of Heaven and Earth', p. 276.

32. The presence of a Jewish element in the author's depiction of his opponents (the festivals, new moons and sabbaths referred to in Col. 2.16) may be thought to throw an obstacle in the path of the hypothesis I am trying to advance. It is possible to resolve this difficulty: one could call on Daniel Boyarin's observation that '[t]he Palestinian Judaism of Paul's time was strongly dualist in mood and at best powerfully ambivalent about sexuality' (*A Radical Jew: Paul and the Politics of Identity* [Berkeley: University of California Press, 1994], p. 159) and on this basis suggest that the Colossian opponents were a group of Jewish converts to Pauline Christianity who found sexual renunciation attractive and who were also inclined to preserve distinctive dietary practices. It is perhaps more helpful, however, to continue to be mindful of Kiley's observation (quoted at the beginning of this section) that the portrayal of the opponents includes a disparate range of characteristics that are hard to reconcile; since the

Unsurprisingly, the rebukes issued by the author of Colossians are also strongly Pauline in character. He accuses the opponents of being 'puffed up [φυσιούμενος]' (2.18; cf. 1 Cor. 4.18; 5.2; 8.1), and most importantly of 'not holding fast to the head, from which the whole body, nourished and held together by its ligaments and sinews, grows with a growth that is from God' (Col. 2.19). Like the strong in 1 Corinthians, the opponents at Colossae are elevating their own concerns over the good of the community as a whole.[33] The opponents' apparent ascetic bent threatens the church in another way, however: not only do their regulations create divisions,[34] they also have the potential to draw unfavourable attention from outsiders, which the author is anxious to avoid at all costs. His discussion of Christ in 2.9–15 has already shown that such practices are unnecessary; his readers' salvation has already been accomplished. He returns to the theme of these verses in 3.1–4, in which he makes his climactic point: 'for you have died, and your life has been hidden with Christ in God' (3.3). Believing in Christ, the Colossians have broken from their old life so decisively it is as if they have died; the new life they now enjoy does not need the kind of conspicuous outward display that the opponents' ascetic habits represent. The perfect κέκρυπται stresses this hiddenness, and it is this which the ethical instructions set out in the household code are designed to foster, even as believers live 'physically integrated within the dominant social environment'.[35]

'As is fitting in the Lord': Marriage in Colossians

After the long and complex treatment of marriage found in 1 Corinthians 7, the reader may well be (pleasantly) surprised to discover that the author of Colossians sets out his views on the matter in just two short verses: 'Wives, be subject to your husbands, as is fitting in the Lord. Husbands, love [ἀγαπᾶτε] your wives and never treat them harshly' (Col. 3.18–19). There is no mention here of divorce or widowhood, let alone a preference for celibacy, nor any sense that marriage serves only a negative function as a protection against πορνεία. Instead, marriage is assumed to be the normal state of existence, in which most if not all members of the community will

author's aim is to discredit, not to represent accurately, and to make as wide as possible the gulf between him and his opponents, not everything he says about them can or should be regarded as a 'fact' to be accounted for.

33.   In fact, Barth (*Colossians*, p. 385) sees the unity and well-being of the church as the main emphasis of 2.19.

34.   Eduard Schweizer (*The Letter to the Colossians: A Commentary*, tr. Andrew Chester [London: SPCK, 1982], p. 153) notes that legal demands are 'the very means humans use to establish their superiority'.

35.   MacDonald, 'Citizens of Heaven and Earth', p. 279.

find themselves. Indeed, whereas Paul hesitates to commend marriage because of the investment in worldly structures that it represents, the author of Colossians might almost be said to promote it for precisely the same reason. As Dunn observes, the whole point here is (in this respect at least) not to be different from the world,[36] so as to maintain an honourable reputation in the eyes of the surrounding society.

As Wayne Meeks observes, it is the context in which these admonitions are set, rather than their content, that gives them the Christian stamp;[37] Lohse concurs, noting that while the instructions in Colossians conform to Hellenistic moral teaching, they have now been given a new motivation, as duties to be fulfilled 'in the Lord'.[38] L. Hartman offers a comprehensive survey of theories on where exactly the sources of Colossians' ethical teaching are to be located in Graeco-Roman society,[39] before offering his own suggestion that this oldest of the New Testament household codes derives from general social thought patterns and not from any specific literary forms.[40]

Hartman suggests that the reciprocity of the Colossian household code, where not only wife and husband but child and parent and slave and master are all addressed in turn, cannot be put down to convention, but should instead be seen as apt for this particular situation 'in the Lord'.[41] However, while it is true that both members of each pairing are spoken to directly, the hierarchical relationships between them are left largely undisturbed. Lohse observes that wives, called upon to be subordinate, are required to go along with the prevalent social order; but with this behaviour being described as 'fitting in the Lord', their submission to their husbands becomes obedience to Christ as well.[42] This divine endorsement of the moral status quo is developed and expanded in a striking way in the letter to the Ephesians, as I shall now show.

---

36. Dunn, *Epistles*, p. 245.

37. Wayne A. Meeks, ' "To Walk Worthily of the Lord": Moral Formation in the Pauline School Exemplified by the Letter to Colossians', in Eleanore Stump and Thomas P. Flint (eds), *Hermes and Athena: Biblical Exegesis and Philosophical Theology* (Notre Dame, Ind.: University of Notre Dame Press, 1993), pp. 37–58 (49).

38. Lohse, *Colossians and Philemon*, p. 156.

39. See L. Hartman, 'Some Unorthodox Thoughts on the "Household Code Form" ', in Jacob Neusner *et al.* (eds), *The Social World of Formative Christianity and Judaism* (Philadelphia: Fortress Press, 1988), pp. 219–32.

40. Hartman, 'Some Unorthodox Thoughts', p. 229. He notes that no literary household code before Colossians has yet been found (p. 226). Some examples of prevalent social thought patterns will be offered in the discussion of Eph. 5.21–33 below.

41. Hartman, 'Some Unorthodox Thoughts', p. 227.

42. Lohse, *Colossians and Philemon*, pp. 157–58.

The Context of Ephesians

The tenor of the letter to the Ephesians has much in common with Colossians. Once again 'Paul' is presented as not particularly well acquainted with his readers: 1.15 and 3.2 suggest that the implied author and implied audience have heard certain things of one another, but have not actually met. Again the fictive kin-language of brotherhood, which was so prominent in 1 Corinthians and which both described and reinforced a strong affective relationship between author and audience, is absent. Not only is the literary style of Ephesians markedly different from the undisputed Pauline letters, displaying longer sentences and fewer questions,[43] the point of view of its implied author is later than that of Paul.[44] The tensions which dominated the Pauline communities in the apostle's own lifetime appear to have been resolved, most notably that between Gentile and Jewish Christians, so that 'in [Christ's] flesh he has made both groups into one and has broken down the dividing wall, that is, the hostility between us' (Eph. 2.15).

Dunn suggests that Colossians provides a model for Ephesians as an expression of late Paulinism by someone other than the apostle.[45] In comparison with the former, the latter appears if anything to be even more general in outlook and in the situation it is intended to address. Opponents are not so prominent here, and are painted with the broadest of brushstrokes, as the author assures his readers that 'no fornicator or impure person, or one who is greedy . . . has any inheritance in the kingdom of Christ and of God' (5.5) and warns them to 'let no one deceive you with empty words' (5.6). Overall, David Meade's assessment of this document is persuasive: 'Ephesians can be seen as a creative attempt to secure the Pauline heritage of [particular] communities and to relate it to the church at large . . . [L]iterary attribution in Ephesians is primarily an assertion of authoritative Pauline tradition, not of literary origins'.[46] What happens, then, to Paul's teaching on marriage and celibacy in this particular creative appropriation?

Marriage as an Image of Salvation in Ephesians 5.21–33

Rudolf Schnackenburg observes that the author of Ephesians knows the Colossian household code, and takes it as the basis for his own ethical

---

43.   Ernest Best, *Ephesians*, New Testament Guides (Sheffield: JSOT Press, 1993), p. 18.
44.   Andrew T. Lincoln, *Ephesians*, WBC 42 (Dallas: Word, 1990), p. lxii.
45.   Dunn, *Epistles*, p. 37.
46.   David G. Meade, *Pseudonymity and Canon* (Tübingen: Mohr, 1986), pp. 153, 157.

instructions,[47] although he expands his treatment of marriage considerably from the concise two verses offered in Colossians. As one might expect, the instructions on marriage to be found in Eph. 5.21–33 are, like those in Col. 3.18–19, of a much more general cast than those in 1 Corinthians 7, with little if any attention being directed toward the particular practical problems with which Paul was so concerned. Of Paul's careful attempts to address a variety of practical issues – widowhood, divorce, mixed marriages between a believer and non-believer, the status of virgins – no sign remains; the author of Ephesians addresses himself only to wives and husbands (and then to children and parents and slaves and masters in the following sections of the household code).

This excision of the disadvantages which can afflict the married state coincides with the transformation of Paul's ambivalent attitude into an uncomplicated and highly traditional support for and assumption of marriage. As in Colossians, celibacy is no longer mentioned, let alone preferred. The main concern of this passage, then, is not whether one ought to marry, but rather how one ought to conduct oneself having entered the married state. Instructions to this end are interwoven by way of analogy with reflections on the relationship between Christ and the church. In this way, the author's idealized vision of marriage comes to function as an image of the bond between Christ and his people, in what Andrew Lincoln describes as this author's 'unique addition to the early Christian household code tradition'.[48] At the same time, the analogy bestows divine sanction upon a socially conservative, hierarchical version of the marriage partnership, and gives the teaching an air of permanence which Paul's provisional instructions lack.

The call for mutual submission in 5.21 is the last echo to be heard of the laboured reciprocity of Paul's teaching in 1 Corinthians 7. While the author of Ephesians does go on to address wives and husbands in turn, the directions he gives to each are different in kind. Wives are urged to submit 'to your husbands as to the Lord' (5.22). (The verb ὑποτάσσομαι is supplied from the preceding phrase.) ὡς may bear a number of connotations here: taken in a comparative sense, wives are to defer to their husbands in the same manner as they defer to Christ; in the temporal sense, they should submit to husbands for as long as they submit to Christ, that is to say, submission to her husband is the particular form a woman's service to Christ ought to take. Probably both ideas are present here. Nowhere in 1 Corinthians 7 does Paul call upon women to submit to their husbands; however (assuming the passage is authentic), he does use ὑποτάσσομαι in its

---

47. Rudolf Schnackenburg, *Ephesians: A Commentary*, tr. Helen Heron (Edinburgh: T&T Clark, 1991), p. 241.

48. Lincoln, *Ephesians*, p. 363.

imperative form in 1 Cor. 14.34. In this instance the subject of concern is not marital relations but rather orderly conduct in the worship service, and women's submission is largely equivalent to their silence. There is no indication the author of Ephesians has this particular context in mind; indeed, his insistence in 5.24 that wives submit to their husbands ἐν παντί rather suggests the opposite.

The wife's submission finds its counterpart in the husband's headship (5.23). Markus Barth asserts, rather puzzlingly, that 'the proposition, "The husband is the head of his wife" must be understood as original with the author of Ephesians'.[49] On the contrary, the statement ἀνήρ ἐστιν κεφαλὴ τῆς γυναικὸς sounds to this interpreter like a clear echo of κεφαλὴ δὲ γυναικὸς ὁ ἀνήρ in 1 Cor. 11.3. The author of Ephesians, however, has appropriated Paul's reflection on the relationship between man and woman in the light of the Genesis creation account, and applied it to the relationship between husband and wife in the light of Christ's relationship to the church. Little trace remains of κεφαλή's double nuance of 'source' and 'authority'; only the latter is now in view. While in 1 Corinthians 11 Christ was said to be the head of man just as man was of woman, in Ephesians 5 Christ and man are effectively presented as analogous equals. While presumably men are counted as part of the church which submits to Christ, this subordinate aspect of their role receives little explicit attention.

5.23c offers a short elaboration on the way in which Christ's headship of the church is realized: 'he is the saviour of the body'. The metaphor of the church as body is of course not original to this author, but in Paul's presentation of this image in 1 Corinthians 12, the head appears to be just one part of the body like any other; thus we read in 1 Cor. 12.25, 'The eye cannot say to the hand, "I have no need of you," nor again the head to the feet, "I have no need of you" '. However, the author of Ephesians develops it so that now Christ is the head of the body, into whom believers must grow, and 'from whom the whole body, joined and knit together in every ligament with which it is equipped, as each part is working properly, promotes the body's growth in building itself up in love' (Eph. 4.14–15). One may note also that in this presentation of the body metaphor, Paul's radical emphasis on the particular honour due to the weaker members of the body is absent; instead, the prerequisite for growth is simply that each part of the body work 'properly' (ἐν μέτρῳ), with the result that the author of Ephesians is rather closer than Paul to the socially conservative uses to which the body imagery was conventionally put.[50]

49.   Markus Barth, *Ephesians*, AB 34A (Garden City, NY: Doubleday, 1974), p. 618.

50.   Dale Martin notes that *homonia* ('concord') speeches 'always assume that the body is hierarchically constituted and that illness or social disruption occurs when that hierarchy is disrupted. . . . The ideological purpose of [such] speeches was to mitigate conflict by reaffirming and solidifying the hierarchy of society' (*The Corinthian Body* [New Haven and London: Yale University Press, 1995], p. 40).

'Nonetheless, as the church submits to Christ, so also wives to husbands in all things' (5.24). The submission required of wives is complete and absolute, although it is interesting to observe that no imperative is used to enforce it. Of course, in promoting wifely subordination, this author is not attempting to introduce a radically new mode of behaviour. Instead, he appears to be seeking to set out a specifically Christian rationale for what was already a fundamental expectation for female conduct. Plutarch's *Coniugalia Praecepta* at several points urges wifely submission, of which 139D may serve as a representative example: 'Whenever two notes are sounded in accord, the tune is carried by the bass; and in like manner every activity in a virtuous household [ἐν οἰκίᾳ σωφρονούσῃ] is carried on by both parties in agreement, but discloses the husband's leadership and preferences'. Juvenal's sixth satire rather gives the lie to Plutarch's rosy picture of marital concord, as he rails against the tyranny of women, suggesting to his friend who is contemplating marriage that other options might be preferable:

> Boys don't quarrel all night, or nag you for little presents
> while they're on the job, or complain that you don't come
> up to their expectations, or demand more gasping passion . . .
> But if your mind is set, with uxorious obsession,
> on one woman and one only, then bow your neck to the yoke
> in voluntary servitude.[51]

Juvenal's disgust with the situation he describes is abundantly clear, however, and he looks fondly back to the 'old days' of honest poverty before 'the ills of long peace' and 'loose foreign morals' brought about the current sorry state of affairs (286–300). The author of Ephesians, far from overturning these norms for female behaviour, reinforces them with specifically Christian warrant.

The instructions to husbands, however, diverge a little from the norm, as married men are told not to rule or control their wives, but rather to 'love [ἀγαπᾶτε] your wives, just as Christ also loved the church and gave himself for her' (5.25). In the same way as the wife must model her behaviour on the church, so the husband is to emulate Christ in this self-giving love. 5.26–27 elaborates on the role of Christ in presenting the church to himself in splendour, 'without a spot or wrinkle or anything of the kind, so that she may be holy and without blemish'. There are clear echoes here of Ezekiel's narration of God's preparation of his bride, Israel: 'Then I bathed you with water and washed off the blood from you, and anointed you with oil . . . Your fame spread among the nations on account of your beauty, for it was perfect because of my splendour that I had bestowed on you, says the Lord God' (Ezek. 16.9, 14).

Luce Irigaray remarks of this extended metaphor: 'Defining her [i.e. Christ's "wife"] as the Church, as Israel is defined as the bride of Yahweh, is tantamount to saying that Christ is wed to his work alone, which is not the fulfillment of humanity but a model of the patriarchal and the phallocratic.'[52] This caustic observation calls the reader's attention to the implications of the metaphor for the conduct of actual married couples, and particularly that of women. In 2 Cor. 11.2, Paul also expressed a desire to present (παραστῆσαι) the Corinthian church to Christ as a pure virgin bride; his concern that the Corinthians should be led astray by false teaching into unfaithfulness to Christ was manifested in a comparison with Eve, who was seduced by the serpent and thus committed infidelity against her husband Adam. Similarly in Ephesians, the splendour of the church consists in holiness and (moral) purity, concern with which was focused particularly on the sexual exclusivity of women, since '[t]he activity of women in Paul's communities may have been understood as a visible sign of the nature of the Pauline sect'.[53] Therefore, just as the church should not let herself be led astray by empty words (whose proponents are presented in 5.3–14 as more likely than not to be engaging in shady sexual practice as well), so also sexual faithfulness should be part of the submission which wives offer their husbands.

It is interesting that both the bride's betrayal of her husband, described by Ezekiel in such gratuitous detail, and the anxiety felt by Paul on the Corinthians' account, are absent from Eph. 5.21–33. The reader is reminded once again that this is a highly idealized portrayal of marriage. In light of this it is not surprising that no mention is made of the problem of mixed marriages, with which Paul dealt at length in 1 Corinthians 7. Yet it is likely that at least some readers of Ephesians would have found themselves in this situation, and the implications of the author's teaching for them are not clear. Turid Karlsen Seim maintains that such persons are required to abide by the instructions relevant to them without expecting their partners to reciprocate.[54] In other words (since women were over-represented in early Christian communities and thus more likely to find themselves in this position), the author of Ephesians wants Christian wives to submit to

---

52.   Luce Irigaray, 'Equal to Whom?', in Naomi Schor and Elizabeth Weed (eds), *The Essential Difference* (Bloomington and Indianapolis: Indiana University Press, 1994), pp. 63–81 (66).

53.   MacDonald, *The Pauline Churches*, p. 116.

54.   Turid Karlsen Seim, 'A Superior Minority? The Problem of Men's Headship in Ephesians 5', in David Hellholm, Halvor Moxnes and Turid Karlsen Seim (eds), *Mighty Minorities? Minorities in Early Christianity – Positions and Strategies* (Oslo: Scandinavian University Press, 1995), pp. 167–81 (171).

non-Christian husbands, who presumably do not feel themselves to be under any kind of obligation to love their wives as Christ loved the church. On the other hand, one might argue that the comparison of husband and wife with Christ and the church militates against such a one-sided reading of the instructions. Christ's love seeks out and compels the church's whole-hearted and reverent subordination; the church's submission is a response to Christ's self-giving love. The action of one without the other is unthinkable. If one accepts this reading, then believers in mixed marriages are simply ignored. Either way, the author of Ephesians offers little practical assistance to those whose marriages are, for whatever reason, less than splendid.

'In the same way husbands ought to love their wives as their own bodies. He who loves his wife loves himself. For no one ever hated his own flesh, but nourishes and tends it, just as Christ does the church, because we are members of his body' (5.28–30). These verses lay the ground for the climactic quotation of Gen. 2.24, which in turn is the basis upon which the author's analogy between Christ and the church and husband and wife must rest. Christ has already been described as 'the saviour of the body'; vv. 26–27 describe how that salvation was accomplished; and v. 28 identifies the wife with the husband's body. While the identification is used to urge the husband to love his wife,[55] the accompanying connotations of authority are not far beneath the surface. Philo provides an illustration of how the head was understood in relation to the body:

> as nature has assigned the chief position in the body to the head, having bestowed upon it a situation the most suitable to that pre-eminence, as it might give a citadel to a king (for having sent it forth to govern the body it has established it on a height, putting the whole composition of the body from the neck to the feet under it, as a pedestal might be placed under a statue) . . .[56]

Connotations of authority may also accompany the use of the first person plural in v. 30: 'we are members of his body'. The pronoun 'we' establishes a connection between author and readers and implicitly assumes that they will see things from his point of view, and it forcefully reminds the readers that in doing what he has done for the church, Christ has done it for them – 'for us' – and that the teaching on marriage which follows on from Christ's actions applies to them with equal force.

'For this reason a man shall leave his father and his mother and be united with his wife, and the two shall become one flesh' (5.31). In its original

---

55. 'Christ nourishing and cherishing his body, the Church . . . functions as more than an analogy, it is also the model for the husband–wife relationship' (Andrew T. Lincoln, 'The Use of the OT in Ephesians', *JSNT* 14 [1982], pp. 16–57 [31]).

56. Philo, *Spec. Leg.* 3.184.

context in Genesis, 'for this reason' referred to the woman's having been created out of Adam's rib: as the primeval man and woman once shared the same flesh, so the fundamental relationship between the genders expresses itself in the melding of the flesh of the partners. Paul in 1 Cor. 6.16 takes the shocking step of applying the verse to the union of a man with a prostitute, and as Lincoln points out, the relationship between Christ and believers is expressly contrasted with this purely physical connection.[57] Here in Ephesians, the quotation serves to confirm the nature of the union of husband and wife as the author has just described it: the wife is identified with the husband's body; the two are indeed 'one flesh'. Yet the citation of Gen. 2.24 also allows the author to draw together the two facets of the analogy that have been interwoven throughout Eph. 5.21–33: 'This is a great mystery; but I am talking about Christ and the church. Nonetheless, let each of you also love his wife as himself, and let wives fear their husbands' (5.32–33). The description of human marriage in Genesis finds its true fulfilment in the relationship between Christ and the church; yet its significance for human marriage is not thereby set aside, but on the contrary, deepened and transformed. Marriage, which provides a means for talking about Christ and the church, is now to be modelled on the relationship which it is used to describe.

Concluding Remarks

As Lincoln observes, the exalted view of marriage expressed in Ephesians contrasts strongly with that found in 1 Corinthians, and suggests the belief (shared by Colossians, but not by the authentic Pauline text) that the church has a future in the world with which it needs to come to terms.[58] All traces of Paul's decidedly ambivalent attitude to marriage have been driven out by the needs of a new situation; however, as I shall attempt to show in Chapter 5, some of these traces may resurface in certain Nag Hammadi documents' treatment of the subject. Before turning my attention in this direction, however, it is necessary first to examine the appropriation of Paul's teaching on women by another group of deutero-Pauline texts: the Pastoral Epistles.

---

57. Lincoln, 'The Use of the OT in Ephesians', p. 36.
58. Lincoln, *Ephesians*, p. lxxxvi.

Chapter 4

WOMEN IN THE DEUTERO-PAULINE LITERATURE: THE
PASTORAL EPISTLES

Every spinster should be assumed guilty before she is proved innocent . . .
Muriel Spark, *The Mandelbaum Gate*

Such is the exasperated wish of Barbara Vaughan, the central character of
The Mandelbaum Gate, frustrated as she is by the inability of the people she
encounters to perceive in her anything other than a typical mid-twentieth-
century English spinster. To her relatives, she is 'by definition a woman, but
sexually differentiated only by a narrow margin . . . a definite spinster, one
who had embraced the Catholic church instead of a husband, one who had
taken up religion instead of cats.' True, when Barbara herself looks in the
mirror she sees someone whose appearance is 'neat, prim, and unnotice-
able'; but she knows that there is a lot more to her than meets the eye, and
Spark makes sure that the reader knows it too. Under the very noses of her
unseeing relatives, Barbara embarks on a love affair with Harry Clegg, a
divorced Qumran archaeologist. On a visit to Jerusalem, she transgresses a
much more dangerous boundary, passing through the Mandelbaum Gate
from Israel to Jordan, despite the great dangers of such an enterprise
because of her Jewish blood. Assumed by those around her to be safe,
unadventurous and predictable, Barbara Vaughan proves herself to be
anything but.

'Every spinster should be assumed guilty before she is proved innocent . . .' Transposed into the world of the Pastoral Epistles, this axiom
takes on a very different tone. In the context of Spark's novel, the words can
be read as one woman's plea that her individuality be recognized, not
smothered by cultural norms. Imagining the words on the Pastor's lips,
however, they become not a request but a command; they reinforce cultural
norms rather than protest against them. 'Guilty' is no longer an amusing
synonym for 'interesting', but takes on its most prosaic, and deadly serious,
sense. The Pastor appears to have little difficulty in assuming not only spin-
sters but all women 'guilty', and it seems to be up to them to prove themselves 'innocent' by acting in the way he prescribes. What I aim to do in this
chapter is to explore how the Pastor's perception of women and his instructions regarding them fit into his general cultural context, and particularly

into the interpretative struggle over Paul in which he is engaged. Confronted by opponents whose teaching he sees as detrimental to his community's stability and reputation, he seeks to implement measures that will restore order and ensure respectability, and on both these counts women are an especial cause for concern.

The Question of Authorship

For the purposes of this book, as set out in the Introduction, I am assuming that the Pastoral Epistles are pseudonymous. This assumption puts me in the company of the majority of modern scholars, for which reason it is tempting simply to state it without comment. However, Luke Timothy Johnson's warning that 'the majority view needs to become something more than what it too often is today, an assumed and unexamined verity'[1] presents a challenge that is worth taking up. A brief review not just of the evidence that is usually brought to bear on the authorship question, but also of the various ways in which it is used by different commentators, yields some interesting results. '[F]ashions in scholarship by no means guarantee the truth,' says Johnson.[2] The question is: what, if anything, does?

P.N. Harrison, writing in 1921, evinces a touching, if naïve, optimism that the time will come when one side of the authorship debate 'is compelled by sheer weight of evidence to quit the field'.[3] To this end, he urges the reader to approach the question with 'an absolutely open mind and a single eye to truth' and 'complete impartiality'.[4] Therein lies the difficulty. How can it be that two different scholars, such as J.N.D. Kelly and Burton Scott Easton, are able to examine the same body of evidence and come to opposite conclusions about its cumulative effect?[5] The answer is that 'complete impartiality', even if it were desirable, is impossible; as Ceslas Spicq has observed, 'the assessment of these varied elements is subjective'.[6] Any decision on the authorship of the Pastorals is a matter of interpretation.

---

1.   Luke Timothy Johnson, *Letters to Paul's Delegates: 1 Timothy, 2 Timothy, Titus* (Valley Forge, Pa.: Trinity Press International, 1996), p. 3.

2.   Johnson, *Letters to Paul's Delegates*, p. 4.

3.   P.N. Harrison, *The Problem of the Pastoral Epistles* (London: Oxford University Press, 1921), p. 19. Over forty years later in 1964, he is still confident that there is a flaw on one side or the other that will come out sooner or later (*Paulines and Pastorals* [London: Villiers, 1964], p. 38).

4.   Harrison, *The Problem of the Pastoral Epistles*, p. 3.

5.   J.N.D. Kelly, *A Commentary on the Pastoral Epistles* (London: Adam & Charles Black, 1963), p. 34; Burton Scott Easton, *The Pastoral Epistles: Introduction, Translation, Commentary and Word Studies* (London: SCM Press, 1948), p. 15.

6.   C. Spicq, *Les Epitres pastorales*, 4th edn, 2 vols (Paris: Gabalda, 1969), p. 212. Translations of this work are my own.

For aid in developing the discussion of the issue at stake here, I turn to the work of Stanley Fish.[7] Fish observes that evidence 'is always a function of what it is to be evidence for':[8] in other words, it is the questions and the presuppositions that the reader brings to the material she is dealing with that determine what will count, and how. Unfortunately for Harrison, '[d]is-agreements are not settled by the facts, but are the means by which the facts are settled'.[9] What counts as a 'fact' is not objectively determined, but depends on the reader's point of view. When agreement or consensus is achieved (and this is never final), it is due not to the stability of facts, but to the power of what Fish calls 'interpretive communities',[10] that is to say groups of readers who share interpretative strategies. Johnson's 'fashions in scholarship' are perhaps better described as 'canons of acceptability',[11] by means of which the community decides which readings are legitimate and worthy of attention ('true'?), but which themselves always change.

So scholars, writing as members of different 'interpretive communities', come to divergent conclusions on such matters as style and vocabulary,[12] how the Pastorals fit into what is known of the chronology of Paul's life (or not), and the nature of the opposition faced by the author and its implications for the dating of the letters. I shall return to this issue in the following section, but for now, to illustrate the problem, I shall focus briefly on two factors, on which the proponents of Pauline authorship have seemed particularly reliant: the personal elements in the letters themselves, and the

---

7. I do not believe it inappropriate to draw here on the theories of a scholar whose primary concern is textual interpretation. While it may be argued that this activity presents a different kind of problem from that of determining who wrote a given document (the latter, at least in theory, does have a correct answer), in the case of the Pastorals that difference is greatly reduced, since almost all the evidence brought to bear on the authorship question is textual: the Pastoral Epistles themselves, other early Christian works that refer to them or quote from them, and of course the undisputed Paulines as well.

8. Stanley Fish, *Is There a Text in This Class? The Authority of Interpretive Communities* (Cambridge, Mass. and London: Harvard University Press, 1980), p. 272.

9. Fish, *Is There a Text in This Class?*, p. 338.

10. Fish, *Is There a Text in This Class?*, p. 338.

11. Fish, *Is There a Text in This Class?*, p. 349.

12. Johnson makes some important observations in relation to this topic (which has been treated most notably and exhaustively by Harrison in the two books cited above in n. 3), arguing that '[s]tyle, in Paul's time, was less an expression of the inner self than of a social presence' (*Letters to Paul's Delegates*, p. 6). Such a hypothesis seems just as applicable to the current time, even if modern readers have been more inclined to think in terms of an unchanging inner self than Paul and his contemporaries. Johnson correctly notes that the style and vocabulary of the Pauline corpus vary considerably with the context, subject matter and recipients of each individual letter (*Letters to Paul's Delegates*, p. 18). The question of how far such variation can go before it must be attributed to the presence of a new author is one which can be answered in a number of ways, depending on the criteria applied by different commentators.

apparent testimony to their authenticity found in other early Christian works.

If the Pastor composed such passages as 2 Tim. 4.6–9 with a view to moving his readers, then in some quarters at least he has achieved a great deal of success. Harrison is so affected by passages like this – 'They have the genuine Pauline stamp. They ring true'[13] – that he convinces himself they are authentic fragments from Paul himself in the midst of an otherwise pseud-onymous letter. Other interpreters who endorse the Pastorals' authenticity in a more wholehearted manner also devour these verses with relish. Spicq, who admits that there are difficulties with both positions,[14] finds that 'the personal, exhortative character of the Pastorals is a serious mark against the hypothesis that they are an artificial "fabrication" '.[15] Kelly likewise asserts that '[i]t is obvious that features like these provide a powerful argument for authenticity',[16] while Donald Guthrie goes so far as to insist that the idea that the personalia are fictional 'may at once be discounted because it fails to account for the obvious realism of the personal allusions'.[17] Obvious? Obvious to whom, and on what grounds? It seems just as 'obvious' to this interpreter that an author trying to write a letter in another's name will do his best to give his text an air of verisimilitude by means of just the kind of personal details as those found in the Pastorals. The idea that a pseud-onymous author should be incapable of wielding language in such a power-ful way rightly provokes an impatient response from Lewis Donelson: why 'must' such passages be Pauline, 'as if a forger could not be bright and clever with words, or as if Paul were the only intelligent person in early Christianity'?[18]

The appeal to external evidence appears to be most often made in the light of the assumption that the early church could never have appealed to or found useful any document that was pretending to be something it was not. So when such a towering figure as Irenaeus opens his magnum opus *Adversus Haereses* by quoting from 1 Timothy as the words of 'the Apostle', what further evidence can be required? Donelson writes that '[n]o one ever seems to have accepted a document as religiously and philosophically prescriptive which was known to be forged'.[19] This relationship between

---

13.   Harrison, *The Problem of the Pastorals*, p. 96.

14.   Spicq, *Les Epitres pastorales*, p. 213: 'That is to say, if there are real difficulties in attributing these letters to St Paul, there are even more in rejecting his authorship'.

15.   Spicq, *Les Epitres pastorales*, p. 211.

16.   Kelly, *A Commentary on the Pastoral Epistles*, p. 32.

17.   Guthrie, *The Pastoral Epistles: An Introduction and Commentary* (Leicester: Inter-Varsity Press, 1957), p. 19.

18.   Lewis Donelson, *Pseudepigraphy and Ethical Argument in the Pastoral Epistles* (Tübingen: J.C.B. Mohr [Paul Siebeck], 1986), p. 57.

19.   Donelson, *Pseudepigraphy and Ethical Argument*, p. 11.

accepting a document and 'knowing' it to be forged needs to be unpacked, however. Consider Tertullian's judgment of the *Acts of Paul and Thecla* in *De Bap.* 17:

> But if the writings which wrongly go under Paul's name, claim Thecla's example as a licence for women teaching and baptising, let them know that . . . the presbyter who composed that writing, as if he were augmenting Paul's fame from his own store, after being convicted, and confessing that he had done it from love of Paul, was removed from his office. For how incredible would it seem, that he who has not permitted a woman even to learn with over-boldness, should give a female the power of teaching and baptizing!

When the passage is quoted in full like this, it gives the strong impression that Tertullian's main problem with the *Acts of Paul and Thecla* was not the identity of its (actual) author, but the practices it endorsed. This is not a document that was happily embraced until its exposure as a piece of pseudepigraphy required it to be rejected, however reluctantly; it is rather a work that, to Tertullian at any rate, was never acceptable, and its denunciation as a forgery simply helped to seal its fate. Guthrie notes that Marcion likewise rejected the Pastoral Epistles because of 'dogmatic concerns'. Unfortunately he then goes on to insist that 'Marcion's lone voice, biased as it undoubtedly was, must not be allowed to outweigh the strong attestation from orthodox early Christian writers',[20] apparently ignoring the fact (amply demonstrated by Tertullian in the passage just quoted) that 'orthodox' writers had plenty of dogmatic concerns of their own. As Donelson puts it, 'Apparently early Christians were quite eager to admit the genuineness of a document if it suited their sense of orthodoxy'.[21]

Other scholars, however, appear to find value in the Pastorals despite, or even because of, their pseudonymity. A.T. Hanson concludes that '[i]f they are Pauline, they represent a dismal conclusion to Paul's writings; if they are post-Pauline, they are an admirable and indispensable illustration of the state of the church at the end of the first century'.[22] Yet Frances Young is still concerned that a negative verdict on Pauline authorship has destroyed the possibility of readers 'welcoming the Pastorals with courtesy, of beginning without distrust'.[23] Her plea for an ethical reading of the letters, one in which the audience is open to being persuaded as well as prepared to cast critical judgement, raises some interesting points. Is pseudonymity really the most pressing and serious obstacle to such a reading? Even Wayne Booth,

20.   Guthrie, *The Pastoral Epistles*, p. 14.
21.   Donelson, *Pseudepigraphy and Ethical Argument*, p. 45.
22.   A.T. Hanson, *Studies in the Pastoral Epistles* (London: SPCK, 1968), p. 120.
23.   Frances Young, 'The Pastoral Epistles and the Ethics of Reading', *JSNT* 45 (1992), pp. 105–20 (106).

whose development of friendship as a metaphor of reading Young relies upon heavily in her article, admits that some texts are inherently unfriendly, 'the author tyrannical, bossy, preachy; the reader placed as an underling or passive receptacle'.[24] Perhaps others will, like me, find themselves reminded of these words when I turn to examine the passages in 1 Timothy dealing with women and widows. Young's concerns notwithstanding, I for one should feel no more kindly disposed to a text containing such material even were I to have every assurance that it came from the pen of Paul himself.[25]

(False) Teaching and the Purpose of the Pastorals

1 Tim. 3.14–15 may be read as a summary of the purpose of the Pastorals:[26] 'I am writing these things to you, hoping to come to you soon; but if I am delayed, so that you may know how one ought to behave in the household of God, which is the church of the living God, the pillar and foundation of the truth.' A desire on Paul's part to be present in person rather than by means of a mere letter is a familiar motif in his undisputed writings,[27] and as Jouette Bassler points out, it is a particularly useful device for the pseudonymous author on this occasion, when the delay in Paul's coming is likely to be rather protracted.[28] In the absence of the apostle himself, a text written in his name allows his authority to be addressed to a new situation.[29]

The most important feature of this new situation is the presence of those who, for want of a better word, may be designated 'the opponents'.[30] They

---

24.   Wayne C. Booth, *The Company We Keep: An Ethics of Fiction* (Berkeley and London: University of California Press, 1988), p. 185.

25.   I am of course aware that a comparison may be drawn here between my attitude to the Pastorals and that of Tertullian to the *Acts of Paul and Thecla*: I dislike the contents of the text, therefore I declare it inauthentic. Suspecting that Tertullian and I might make rather uncomfortable bedfellows, I submit the following observation in my defence. In Tertullian's eyes, Pauline authorship confers on a text a privileged, authoritative status; in my eyes, it does not. Therefore a declaration on my part that a supposedly Pauline text is in fact pseudonymous has rather different implications from a similar declaration by the author of *De Baptismo*. (For the record, I happen rather to like some aspects of the *Acts of Paul and Thecla*, but I don't think it is authentic either.)

26.   As noted by Donelson, *Pseudepigraphy and Ethical Argument*, p. 171.

27.   See for example Rom. 1.13; Phil. 2.24; 1 Thess. 2.18.

28.   Jouette M. Bassler, *1 Timothy, 2 Timothy, Titus* (Nashville: Abingdon, 1996), p. 72.

29.   Margaret Y. MacDonald, *The Pauline Churches: A Socio-Historical Study of Institutionalization in the Pauline and Deutero-Pauline Writings*, SNTSMS 60 (Cambridge: Cambridge University Press, 1988), p. 207.

30.   Philip H. Towner, *The Goal of our Instruction: The Structure of Theology and Ethics in the Pastoral Epistles*, JSNTSup 34 (Sheffield: Sheffield Academic Press, 1989), p. 21. The term 'opponents', while not entirely satisfactory, at least does not endorse the Pastor's view of these people to the same extent as 'false teachers' or 'heretics' does.

are the focus of concern at both the beginning – 'I urge you . . . to remain in Ephesus so that you may instruct certain people not to teach any different doctrine' (1.3) – and the end – 'Avoid the profane chatter and contradictions of what is falsely called knowledge' (6.20) – of 1 Timothy, and warnings against them are prominent in all three epistles.[31] Scholarly attempts to determine their identity from the information the Pastor provides have not enjoyed a great deal of success. As Johnson observes, the combination of elements presented to us here does not match the profile of any known heresy.[32] Indeed, as C.K. Barrett puts it, 'Judaism, legalism, mythology, and gnosis are lumped together in a way that suggests rather that the author was concerned to omit no heresy he had heard of than that he wished, or was able, to analyse, sub-divide, and classify.'[33] This has not stopped some commentators from attempting to put a label on the opposition the Pastorals address; but their efforts are of limited helpfulness at best. Dibelius and Conzelmann's 'Judaizing proto-gnosticism'[34] is still vague and imprecise, while Easton's talk of 'gnosticism in all its protean forms'[35] is just the kind of ready application of that category to all manner of New Testament opponents that Spicq rightly rebukes as 'an abuse of language'.[36]

The difficulty involved in grappling with this question ought not to come as any great surprise. The Pastor is not trying to offer a measured, dispassionate description of those with whom he disagrees; he does not write merely to inform. Instead, he is setting out to prove, by every means available to him, that his opponents are in the wrong, and to call forth from his readers an attitude to them that is utterly unsympathetic. Much of the language he uses is, as Robert Karris has shown, conventional abuse and name-calling that draws on a traditional philosophical schema used to attack the Sophists.[37] Thus the opponents are said to be greedy (1 Tim. 6.5, 9–10; Tit. 1.11), hypocritical (2 Tim. 3.5; Tit. 1.16), engaged in endless and pointless disputes (1 Tim. 1.4, 6–7; 2 Tim. 4.3–4), and guilty of any number of vices (1 Tim. 1.9–10; 2 Tim. 3.2–4) and of targeting gullible women (2 Tim. 3.6–7). Karris' observations on the purpose of such a polemic are especially helpful: 'Perhaps the most significant function of the schema was to demonstrate who had the right to and actually did impart genuine

---

31. See for example 1 Tim. 1.4, 6–7, 9–10; 6.5, 9–10; 2 Tim. 3.2–7; 4.3–4; Tit. 1.11, 16.

32. Johnson, *Letters to Paul's Delegates*, p. 13.

33. C.K. Barrett, 'Pauline Controversies in the Post-Pauline Period', *NTS* 20 (1973/74), pp. 229–45 (240–41).

34. See for example Martin Dibelius and Hans Conzelmann, *The Pastoral Epistles*, ed. Helmut Koester, tr. Philip Buttolph and Adela Yarbro, Hermeneia (Philadelphia: Fortress Press, 1972), p. 3.

35. Easton, *The Pastoral Epistles*, p. 5.

36. Spicq, *Les Epitres pastorales*, p. 111.

37. Robert J. Karris, 'The Background and Significance of the Polemic of the Pastoral Epistles', *JBL* 92 (1973), pp. 549–64.

wisdom and truth.'[38] By discrediting his opponents, the Pastor accrues honour to himself and his own teachings.

In fact, a struggle over teaching appears to be what the Pastorals are all about; as Karris points out, it is only because the opponents are engaging in this activity that the kind of polemic the author uses against them is appropriate.[39] More precisely, this struggle seems to be an inter-Pauline one. There are a number of indications in the Pastorals that the opponents are, or have been, members of the very group to which the author writes. Donelson suggests that '[m]ost likely they would have considered themselves good Paulinists';[40] this is an opinion from which the Pastor would beg very strongly to differ. Timothy is told to instruct them to mend their ways (1 Tim. 1.3), a task it is difficult to imagine him carrying out with any success if he did not have some prior connection with these people, while 1 Tim. 6.10 speaks explicitly of those who have 'wandered away from the faith'. While bringing the opponents back to the fold may be desirable (Tit. 1.13), such a restoration is only a means to the Pastor, not the ultimate end he has in view: 'after a first and second admonition, have nothing more to do with anyone who causes divisions' (Tit. 3.10). If the restoration of order in the community requires that the opponents be permanently excluded from it, this is not too high a price to pay.

In 1 Tim. 4.1–5, the reader learns that the opponents 'forbid marriage and demand abstinence from foods', a call to an ascetic lifestyle that the Pastor contradicts by reminding his readers of the goodness of God's creation. This is the only place where the Pastor engages with his opponents' teaching in any significant way, and it may be that he does so even while being uncomfortably aware that in some respects this teaching comes closer than his own to Paul's position on marriage in 1 Corinthians 7. While the Pastor exerts himself elsewhere in his letters to promote marriage and traditional roles within it for both men and women, here he concentrates exclusively on the issue of food, mindful perhaps that he is after all purporting to write in the name of an apostle who professed a decided, if inconvenient, preference for celibacy. It is the disruptive effects of such a preference as promoted by the opponents that particularly trouble him: according to Tit. 1.11, whole households are being upset. When the household was seen as a microcosm of society as a whole, such disruption was highly unconducive to the church's honour.

The Pastor therefore aims to restore stability and respectability by pro-

---

38.   Karris, 'Background and Significance', p. 556.

39.   Karris, 'Background and Significance', p. 555.

40.   Donelson, *Pseudepigraphy and Ethical Argument*, p. 124. Donelson goes on to write that 'the peculiar direction taken by these people found its inspiration in the Pauline corpus or the Pauline legends'. Perhaps it is only in comparison with the canonical and familiar Pastoral Epistles that the opponents' reading of Paul seems 'peculiar'.

mulgating his own reading of Paul against the unsettling version endorsed by his opponents. As Margaret MacDonald puts it, '[t]he identification of heresy leads to self-definition and to the formulation of objective pronouncements'.[41] 2 Tim. 1.13–14 speaks of a tradition (παραθήκη) handed down from Paul to his co-workers, in which the readers of the Pastorals will share in their turn if they accept the teachings of the letters. The impression given is that of a pre-existent fixed tradition, directly linked to the apostle himself, to which the Pastor is faithful but from which the opponents have deviated; but this impression, while immensely useful to the Pastor, is entirely fictitious. As Donelson points out, the Pastor is in fact 'opposing his creative reading [of Paul] to theirs';[42] he did not have any fixed παραθήκη handed to him ready formed and unalterable, but instead created both the concept and the content himself in the letters that are the topic of the present study.[43] He does want what he has created to be passed on in fixed form, however, and for this reason the teaching of 'sound doctrine' features as one of the most important duties of Timothy (1 Tim. 4.11–16) and Titus (Tit. 2.1), and of the church officials who follow after them.[44]

Because it is supposed to combat the disruptive influence of the opponents, this sound teaching will focus on behaviour: 'I am writing these things to you . . . so that you may know how one ought to conduct oneself in the household of God, the pillar and foundation of the truth' (1 Tim. 3.14–15).[45] It is in the Pastor's community that truth and the presence of God reside; and to retain membership of this community, one must behave in the way that the Pastor prescribes. As Bassler puts it, 'sound teaching and sound behaviour go hand in hand',[46] and the converse is also true. An absolute division between the author and his opponents is thus set up.

1 Timothy 2.9–15: 'I do not permit a woman to teach . . .'

This establishment of a Pauline 'tradition', passed on by suitably qualified teachers and invested with content that upholds the social status quo, has

41. MacDonald, *The Pauline Churches*, p. 173.

42. Donelson, *Pseudepigraphy and Ethical Argument*, p. 125. As Donelson goes on to explain (p. 167), by depicting himself as one who is simply handing on the deposit of sound teaching that he had himself received, the Pastor gives the impression that the origin of the 'traditions' contained in his letters is the very opposite of the highly creative exercise of appropriation in which he is in fact engaged.

43. Donelson, *Pseudepigraphy and Ethical Argument*, p. 165.

44. An ἐπίσκοπος must be an 'apt teacher', 1 Tim. 3.2.

45. Hanson's article 'The Foundation of Truth: 1 Timothy 3.15' (*Studies in the Pastoral Epistles*, pp. 5–20) shows how the language of this verse presents the church as the true dwelling place of God, in place of the temple.

46. Bassler, *1 Timothy, 2 Timothy, Titus*, p. 34.

considerable implications for women. Paul in 1 Corinthians was anxious to control women's participation in the assembly, but for the Pastor, this is not enough: he wants to do away with the problem by forbidding such participation altogether. His situation is such as to demand that the maintenance of Paul's authority (as the Pastor reconstitutes and deploys it) take precedence over adherence to the letter of his instructions.

The Pastor's primary concerns are reiterated at the outset of the chapter in which the infamous passage on women is found. He urges that prayers be made for everyone, including those in positions of authority, 'so that we may lead a quiet [ἡσύχιον] and peaceable life in all godliness and dignity' (1 Tim. 2.2): in other words, a life unlikely to attract censure from outside observers. He then goes on to reassert Paul's (that is to say, his) status as a divinely appointed teacher, who has the authority to issue the instructions which follow: 'I was appointed a herald and an apostle (I am telling the truth, I am not lying), a teacher of the Gentiles in faith and truth' (2.7). Any reader would have to think twice before gainsaying one with such impressive credentials.

Men are addressed briefly in 2.8, but it is clearly women's behaviour that is the overriding concern of the whole passage.[47] While men are ordered to pray, women are treated to a lesson in couture: '[I want] women to adorn [κοσμεῖν] themselves in a fitting manner, with modesty and self-control, not with braided hair and gold or pearls or expensive clothes, but, which is proper for a woman who professes religion, with good works' (2.9–10). Guthrie remarks that these verses show that the author 'was shrewd enough to know that a woman's dress is a mirror of her mind',[48] an idea which, to the Pastor and his contemporaries, may well have had the ring of truth. The vocabulary employed here was extremely common in Graeco-Roman descriptions of feminine virtue. σωφροσύνη was one of the four cardinal virtues of Stoic philosophy, and David Verner's definition helps to explain why this author should advocate it so keenly: 'σωφροσύνη . . . involves the self-control and self-discipline to conduct one's life within the established order *in a way appropriate to one's place within that order.*'[49] Verner goes on to observe that 'αἰδώς and σωφροσύνη are often paired as the virtues of women who exhibit proper self-control in sexual matters. It thus appears that this is the author's emphasis here.'[50]

This concern with sexual propriety also dictates the Pastor's attitude to the ostentatious manner of dress which he forbids. Few, if any, of the

47.   Bassler, *1 Timothy, 2 Timothy, Titus*, p. 56.

48.   Guthrie, *The Pastoral Epistles*, p. 74.

49.   David C. Verner, *The Household of God: The Social World of the Pastoral Epistles*, SBLDS 71 (Chico, Calif.: Scholars Press, 1983), p. 135; my emphasis.

50.   Verner, *The Household of God*, p. 168.

women in his congregation would have had the financial means to appear decked out in gold and pearls, but it is the way of life associated with these things that is the real issue here. Gordon Fee directs the reader to the large body of evidence 'which equated "dressing up" on the part of women with both sexual wantonness and wifely insubordination',[51] evidence for which Juvenal's sixth Satire may stand as a representative:

> There's nothing a woman denies herself, her conscience is nil,
> once she's adorned her neck with that emerald choker, once
> she's weighted down her ear-lobes with vast pearl pendants.
> (What's more insufferable than a wealthy female?)[52]

Juvenal was not alone in his agitation over this kind of female behaviour.[53] High-born 'new women' such as this were an irritating symptom of the disrupted social order of the time of Cicero and Caesar, taking advantage of the situation to claim for themselves 'the indulgence in sexuality of a woman of pleasure'.[54] Such women feature as the inamoratas of prominent poets of the time,[55] but if accounts such as that found in Seneca's letter to his mother are to be believed, their influence was not confined to the sphere of literature:

> Unchastity, the greatest evil of our time, has never classed you with the great majority of women; jewels have not moved you, nor pearls . . . you, who were soundly trained in an old-fashioned and strict household, have not been perverted by the imitation of worse women that leads even the virtuous into pitfalls . . .[56]

51.   Gordon D. Fee, *1 and 2 Timothy, Titus* (Peabody, Mass.: Hendrickson/Carlisle: Paternoster, 1995), p. 71.

52.   Juvenal, *Satires* 6.457–60, in *The Sixteen Satires*, tr. Peter Green (London: Penguin, 1998).

53.   Compare Sallust, *Catiline* 25, where he writes of Sempronia, a married woman with children, that she was 'able to play the lyre and dance more skilfully than an honest woman should, and [had] many other accomplishments which minister to voluptuousness. But there was nothing which she held so cheap as modesty and chastity.' Quoted in Bruce W. Winter, *After Paul Left Corinth: The Influence of Secular Ethics and Social Change* (Grand Rapids and Cambridge: Eerdmans, 2001), p. 124.

54.   Elaine Fantham *et al.*, 'The "New Woman": Representation and Reality', in Elaine Fantham *et al.*, *Women in the Classical World: Image and Text* (New York and Oxford: Oxford University Press, 1994), pp. 280–93 (280).

55.   Fantham *et al.* ('The "New Woman" ', p. 282) points out that these poets often appeared as corresponding 'new men', men who, overcome with passion, voluntarily subordinated themselves to their lovers' dominant personalities. Ovid, for example, may opine scathingly that 'it's so provincial | to object to adulterous wives' – but he himself undergoes agonies at the thought of his mistress showing more affection to her husband than she does to him (Ovid, *Amores* 3.4, 1.4, in *The Erotic Poems*, tr. Peter Green [London: Penguin, 1982]).

56.   Seneca, *Consolation to his Mother* 16.3–5; quoted in Fantham *et al.*, *Women in the Classical World*, p. 301. It may be, of course, that phrases such as 'the great majority of women'

Like Seneca, the Pastor reacts with revulsion to the immorality and social disruption that female finery has come to represent. He therefore urges his female readers to join him in turning his back on such things, and adorn themselves instead with 'good works'.[57] In doing so, they would be following in the footsteps of the likes of Eleazar in 4 Maccabees,[58] who when stripped of his clothes by his torturers 'remained adorned [ἐκκεκοσμημένον] with the gracefulness of his piety' (6.2).[59]

The shift to the imperative μανθανέτω in 2.11 serves to draw special attention to the next section of the passage, a purpose further enhanced by the chiastic structure of vv. 11–12 detected by Bassler:[60]

A. γυνὴ ἐν ἡσυχίᾳ μανθανέτω
    B. ἐν πάσῃ ὑποταγῇ
        C. **διδάσκειν δὲ γυναικὶ οὐκ ἐπιτρέπω**
    B'. οὐδὲ αὐθεντεῖν ἀνδρός [the opposite of ὑποταγη above]
A.' ἀλλ' εἶναι ἐν ἡσυχίᾳ.

This pattern places the emphasis firmly on the prohibition of women from teaching, a prohibition which is absolute; there is no question here of women being allowed to take an active role as long as they veil their heads.[61] The author adopts this position for the same twofold reason he writes the whole correspondence: to combat the influence of his opponents, and thereby to maintain good order and with it his community's honourable reputation. 1 Tim. 5.15 suggests that some women did indeed find the opponents' version of Paul attractive: 'some have already turned away to follow Satan'. However, it is not these defections in themselves that really bother the Pastor, but rather what he perceives to be their underlying cause: the fundamental female predisposition to gullibility and being easily taken in. As Ramsey MacMullen puts it, 'Ardent credulity was presented as a

---

are exaggerations for the purposes of rhetorical effect; nonetheless, even if there were not in fact as many of them as Seneca would have his readers believe, his concern that *any* such women should trouble his society is undeniable.

57. A favourite theme of the Pastoral Epistles; cf. 1 Tim. 5.10; 6.18; 2 Tim. 2.21; 3.17; Tit. 2.14; 3.1, 8, 14.

58. A work which the Pastor appears to have rated highly (see Hanson, 'An Academic Phrase: 1 Timothy 3.16a', in *Studies in the Pastoral Epistles*, pp. 21–28).

59. Eleazar, according to Spicq, resembles the Pastoral Epistles' Christian ideal of piety (*Les Epitres pastorales*, p. 219).

60. Bassler, *1 Timothy, 2 Timothy, Titus*, p. 59.

61. It is true that Paul and the Pastor are dealing with different activities, the former with prophecy, the latter with teaching. However, a case can be made that the two are analogous: just as prophecy occupies a pre-eminent position for Paul (1 Cor. 14.1–5), so does teaching for the Pastor, as I have attempted to demonstrate above. While Paul, however uneasily, permits women to take part in the defining activity of his community, the author of the Pastorals does not.

weakness characteristic of the [female] sex, pagan or Christian',[62] and the Pastor is an enthusiastic subscriber to cultural stereotypes in this respect. Regardless of whether they have actually already 'gone astray after Satan' or not, women simply cannot be trusted with a task as important as sound teaching, especially not when the community's reputation is at stake.

The vocabulary of the verses provides ample evidence of the author's concern to maintain socially acceptable order in male–female relationships. ἡσυχία needs to be understood in relation to the related adjective deployed in 2.2: 'so that we may lead a quiet [ἡσύχιον] and peaceable life'. The idea in both instances is one of quietness in connection with acceptance of society's norms; Luise Schottroff's rendering of ἡσυχία as 'conformity' captures this well.[63] The verb αὐθεντεῖν, meanwhile, refers to an authority which George Knight has shown to be 'a positive concept [that] is in no way regarded as having any overtone of misuse of position or power'.[64] Likewise διδάσκειν, with which αὐθεντεῖν is paired in 2.12, has in itself no negative connotations. The problem for the author is not that women are misusing authority so as to be domineering or overbearing, but rather that they are exercising it at all. As Verner puts it, the Pastor 'regards women who teach in the public assembly as having transgressed the limits of their place as women in the order of things'.[65] In the final verses of the passage, he attempts to reinforce his idea of the order of things by appealing to scripture.

Scripture occupies an important place for the author of the Pastorals. In 2 Tim. 3.14–15, he urges his supposed reader to continue in his faith, remembering 'how from childhood you have known the sacred writings that are able to instruct you for salvation through faith in Jesus Christ'.[66] The human role in this process of instruction becomes clearer in the following v. 16: 'every scripture . . . is useful for teaching, reproof, correction, and training in righteousness'. Any interpreter who takes on the tasks listed can find in the scriptures valuable tools with which to carry them out. At the same time, the designation of God himself as the ultimate source of the scriptures provides a strong disincentive for disregarding any instruction for

---

62.   Ramsey MacMullen, *Christianizing the Roman Empire (AD100–400)* (New Haven and London: Yale University Press, 1984), p. 39; cited in Margaret Y. MacDonald, *Early Christian Women and Pagan Opinion: The Power of the Hysterical Woman* (Cambridge: Cambridge University Press, 1996), p. 2.

63.   Luise Schottroff, *Lydia's Impatient Sisters: A Feminist Social History of Early Christianity* (London: SCM Press, 1995), p. 69.

64.   George W. Knight, 'ΑΥΘΕΝΤΕΩ in Reference to Women in 1 Timothy 2.12', *NTS* 30 (1984), pp. 143–57 (150–51).

65.   Verner, *The Household of God*, p. 169.

66.   Unintentionally, perhaps, the author seems to grant a positive role to two women, Eunice and Lois, Timothy's mother and grandmother, in whom lived first the faith that now lives in Timothy (2 Tim. 1.5).

which the author can find a scriptural warrant; such disobedience becomes tantamount to defying God. Having identified the scriptures as 'God-breathed', the author by invoking them places himself on the side of God in his dealings with the readers of his letter, and thus lays claim to considerable power and authority over them.

This is done in a particularly striking fashion in 1 Tim. 2.13–15, where a very condensed version of the Genesis account of the creation and fall of human beings is used to provide theological justification for the preceding instructions. 'For Adam was formed first, then Eve' (v. 13). Paul in 1 Cor. 11.8–9 also utilized the fact of Adam's prior creation in his argument that women in the assembly should comport themselves in a manner appropriate to the subordinate partner in a hierarchical relationship, just as 'nature' (a highly culturally conditioned term) itself demanded. However, Paul softens the force of this argument from creation somewhat by admitting that 'in the Lord woman is not independent of man or man independent of woman. For just as woman came from man, so man comes through woman; but all things come from God' (1 Cor. 11.11–12). No such mitigation is forthcoming in 1 Timothy; instead, the fact of Adam's prior creation and hence superior status is reinforced with a second bold statement: 'and Adam was not led astray [οὐκ ἠπατήθη], but the woman was utterly led astray [ἐξαπατηθεῖσα] and has become a transgressor [ἐν παραβάσει γέγονεν]' (1 Tim. 2.14).

The reader familiar with Genesis 3 will be struck by this author's exoneration of Adam and his contrasting emphasis on the sole guilt of Eve.[67] In Gen. 3.12, of course, the man does his best to blame his wife for his misconduct as well as her own, while the woman in the following verse makes the confession that 'the serpent deceived [ἠπάτησέν in the LXX] me, and I ate'. However, God is unpersuaded that there is only one culprit, and metes out punishment to the serpent, the woman and the man in turn (Gen. 3.14–19). Similarly, the undisputed Pauline letters leave little doubt as to Adam's culpability: in Rom. 5.12–14, for example, it is Adam who is guilty of transgression (παράβασις), and through whom sin and death came into the world. On what grounds, then, does the Pastor let Adam off the hook? What is the nature of the transgression that has been committed so that only the woman bears the blame?

A.T. Hanson draws attention to the strand of Jewish tradition which understood Eve to have been sexually seduced by the serpent.[68] While the

---

67. Stanley Porter notes that one of the functions of prefixing a preposition to a verb is to preserve but intensify its meaning (*Idioms of the Greek New Testament*, 2nd edn [Sheffield: Sheffield Academic Press, 1994], p. 140).

68. A.T. Hanson, 'Eve's Transgression: 1 Timothy 2.13–15', in *Studies in the Pastoral Epistles*, pp. 65–77.

Hebrew of Gen. 3.13 (הַנָּחָשׁ הִשִּׁיאַנִי וָאֹכֵל) provides little basis for this inter-pretation (the verb נשא bears no such connotations),[69] the rendering of the verse in Greek introduces a degree of ambiguity which makes it possible to argue that the author of the Pastorals did indeed understand Eve's sin as sexual. The verb ἀπατάω, and its more intense form ἐξαπατάω, can be used to refer to seduction as well as straightforward deception. Several uses of these verbs in the New Testament, in circumstances not dissimilar to those of the Pastorals, seem to play on this ambiguity; 2 Cor. 11.1–3 provides a good example. Here, Paul develops a metaphor concerned with sexual con-duct to express his fears over the Corinthians' attraction to certain false teaching. He presents himself as the father of the Corinthians, whom he has promised to present to Christ as a 'chaste virgin', who is anxious lest his charge will be tempted to be unfaithful to Christ 'just as the serpent led Eve astray [ὡς ὁ ὄφις ἐξηπάτησεν Εὕαν]'. Paul's primary concern is that his congregation will be taken in by untruths; but the story of Eve offers a better illustration of how this constitutes betrayal of their 'husband', Christ, if it is assumed that she was *seduced* by the serpent, and thus was unfaithful to her husband, Adam.

In this example the ideas of deception and of sexual seduction are very closely intertwined, and the same is true in 1 Tim. 2.14. The cultural stereo-type of female gullibility has already been mentioned above, and it is hard to deny that the Pastor has it in view here. As Philo, another author with no little interest in Genesis, puts it: 'woman is more accustomed to being deceived than man. For his judgement, like his body, is masculine and cap-able of dissolving or destroying the designs of deception; but the judgement of woman is more feminine, and because of softness she easily gives way and is taken in by plausible falsehoods which resemble the truth.'[70] This kind of belief certainly helps to explain the denial of Adam's deception in 1 Tim. 2.14: by his very nature he ought to have been able to withstand it. The idea that Eve was seduced explains it even better, however, and the Pastor's great anxiety about women's sexual propriety in vv. 9–10 makes it extremely plausible that in v. 14 he does indeed have this idea in mind. This being the case, his use here of the fallibility of Eve as a justification for his prohibition on women's teaching effectively places such teaching on the same moral level as sexual misconduct. Through a slippage of terminology in vv. 13–15 – 'Eve' is formed after Adam; 'the woman' is led astray; 'she' will be saved through childbearing if 'they' continue in faith and love and holiness – Eve comes to stand for all women. If the Pastor's female readers want to avoid Eve's fate and keep themselves from her state of transgression, they must renounce their desire to teach, just as Eve should have renounced the

---

69. Hanson, 'Eve's Transgression', p. 77.
70. Philo, *Quaest. in Gen.* 1.33.

serpent, and devote themselves instead to the traditional household roles of wife and mother. In this way, the all-important responsibility of teaching the tradition is to be placed in the hands of those who are (in the Pastor's opinion) actually capable of carrying it out, and the much-longed-for stability and order are restored to individual households and the church as a whole.

1 Timothy 5.3–16: 'Honour widows who are really widows'

Having thus dealt with women who want to teach, however, the Pastor's female troubles are not over. In 1 Tim. 5.3–16 (a passage Kelly describes as 'surprisingly long'),[71] he is to be found devoting considerable space and effort to widows. This is a group to whom Paul in 1 Corinthians does not have a great deal to say. In 7.8–9, he encourages the unmarried and widows to remain 'as I myself also am' – that is to say, single – unless they lack the self-control necessary for celibacy, in which case they should marry. Again in 7.39–40, while granting that a woman whose husband has died is no longer bound but is free to marry as she wishes, he asserts that 'in my judgement she is more blessed if she remains as she is'. Paul's instructions here certainly give no indication that widows caused him more concern than any other group in the Corinthian community.

The situation in 1 Timothy is rather different. In the Pastor's opinion at least, widows constitute a major problem, a problem which, by means of a diverse array of criteria, he attempts to define out of existence, as will be seen. 'Honour widows who are really widows', he urges at the outset of the passage, thus encouraging the reader to press on with two questions in her mind: Who are the real widows? And what does it mean to honour them? The answers to both these questions evolve as the passage proceeds, producing in the end a definition of 'widowhood' that is highly restrictive and primarily driven, once again, by the dual concerns of combatting the opponents' teaching and appeasing public opinion.

To begin with, the author's intention seems reasonable enough: he appears to want to restrict the church's provision of material support to those widows who really need it. Thus nearly all commentators detect an economic dimension to the verb τιμάω in this instance,[72] even if it does not

---

71.   Kelly, *A Commentary on the Pastoral Epistles*, p. 112.

72.   For example, Bassler, *1 Timothy, 2 Timothy, Titus*, p. 92; Donald Guthrie, *The Pastoral Epistles*, p. 100; Johnson, *Letters to Paul's Delegates*, p. 174; E.F. Scott, *The Pastoral Epistles* (London: Hodder & Stoughton, 1936), p. 58.

imply 'payment' in the same sense as in 5.17.[73] The duty to care for widows was firmly established in Jewish tradition; for example, Deut. 24.19 reads: 'when you reap your harvest in your field and forget a sheaf in the field, you shall not go back to get it; it shall be left for the alien, the orphan and the widow, so that the Lord your God may bless you in all your undertakings'.[74] Acts 6.1 shows that providing for widows also became part of Christian practice.[75] Gordon Fee is therefore correct that the point of the opening verses of our passage in 1 Timothy is not to enjoin care itself – that was already taking place – but rather to set out guidelines as to who should receive it.[76]

Any woman, then, who still has children or grandchildren to support her, even though her husband is dead, is not a 'real' widow, according to this author's definition. Instead of looking to the church, the household of God, for help, 'they should first learn [μανθανέτωσαν] to carry out their religious duty toward their own household and to render payment to their forebears; for this is pleasing to God' (5.4). No subject is supplied for the verb μανθάνω, and Bassler takes advantage of this ambiguity to suggest that it is the 'widows [who] are reminded that their religious duty is first to fulfil their duties to their own families . . . This is promoted as the appropriate way to honor their deceased ancestors'.[77] However, Scott brands such an approach 'too subtle and artificial', observing that the whole context points to the children as the subjects of μανθάνω.[78] As the latter verses of this passage make abundantly clear, the author is indeed anxious that widows should fulfil familial responsibilities; but at this early stage he is still primarily concerned with directing the attitudes of others towards the widows, so Scott's interpretation is to be preferred. Verses 7–8 reiterate the responsibilities of offspring towards their widowed mothers, and make clear how much is at stake: if even unbelievers care for their relatives when they are in need, how can members of the church possibly do any less?

In contrast to those widows who have family members on whom to depend, the real widow 'has been left alone [μεμονωμένη]' – it is this, Knight says, which is the most basic description of the real widow[79] – and 'has put her hope in God' (5.5). The real widow is the one who must look to

---

73. Towner, *The Goal of our Instruction*, p. 183; Verner, *The Household of God*, pp. 162–63. Towner's insistence that the meaning of τιμάω in each case must be deduced from its immediate context is borne out by the use of the verb in yet another sense in 1 Tim. 6.1.

74. See also vv. 20–22, and Exod. 22.22–24; Isa. 1.17.

75. '. . . the Hellenists complained against the Hebrews because their widows were being neglected in the daily distribution of the food'.

76. Fee, *1 and 2 Timothy, Titus*, p. 116.

77. Bassler, *1 Timothy, 2 Timothy, Titus*, p. 95.

78. Scott, *The Pastoral Epistles*, p. 58.

79. Knight, *The Pastoral Epistles*, p. 218.

God because she has no other means of support,[80] and God's help is to be given to her through the church, the household of God,[81] because she has no household of her own. This distinction on the basis of access to material resources is not the only one our author draws, however, and a moral aspect to the designation 'real widow' now begins to emerge. Her dependence on God is no mere sign of desperation, but is instead a fundamental part of a pious life that expresses itself in 'prayers and petitions night and day [ταῖς δεήσεσιν καὶ ταῖς προσευχαῖς νυκτὸς καὶ ἡμέρας]' (5.5). This pious life, of which the author clearly approves,[82] finds its opposite in the existence of the one who, 'living in self-indulgence, is dead even though she lives' (5.6).

In attempting to determine the meaning of this severe phrase, it is unnecessary to go as far as Easton, who readily assumes the very worst: 'widowhood was only too apt to lead to prostitution, all the more because of the sexual tension experienced by young widows. Against this insistent temptation unceasing prayer is the only safeguard.'[83] Guthrie too is persuaded that the idea of widows resorting to 'immoral living' as a means of support was in the author's mind when he used the verb σπαταλάω – a verb for which Guthrie provides the translation 'liveth in pleasure'.[84] The verb does indeed carry connotations of enjoyment and self-indulgence, but the highly distasteful implications of Easton and Guthrie's readings[85] can be avoided if one looks at other instances of its use, for example, Jas 5.5: 'You have lived on the earth in luxury and pleasure [ἐτρυφήσατε ἐπι τῆς γῆς καὶ ἐσπαταλήσατε]; you have fattened your hearts in a day of slaughter.'[86] These parallels suggest that another issue is at stake, to which Johnson draws attention: the verb σπαταλάω is indicative of a lifestyle enabled by wealth.[87] Just such a lifestyle is contrasted to the one to which the Pastor wants his readers to aspire in 1 Tim. 6.17: 'As for those who in the present age are rich, command them not to be haughty, or to set their hopes on the

80. Kelly, *A Commentary on the Pastoral Epistles*, p. 114.

81. Scott, *The Pastoral Epistles*, p. 58.

82. He has 'Paul' himself remember Timothy constantly in his prayers (δεήσεσίν) night and day (νυκτὸς καὶ ἡμέρας) in 2 Tim. 1.3.

83. Easton, *The Pastoral Epistles*, p. 152.

84. Guthrie, *The Pastoral Epistles*, p. 101.

85. In itself, the idea that some widows, out of sheer desperation, may resort to prostitution as a means of support is quite acceptable. However, the (unintended?) implications of Easton and Guthrie's readings that the women might derive some pleasure from this kind of life are rather more objectionable.

86. See also Ezek. 16.49: 'This was the guilt of your sister Sodom: she and her daughters had pride, excess of food, and prosperous ease [LXX ἐν πλησμονῇ ἄρτων καὶ ἐν εὐθησίᾳ ἐσπατάλων], but did not aid the poor and needy'; and Sir. 21.15: 'When an intelligent person hears a wise saying, he praises it and adds to it; when a reveller hears it, he laughs at it [ἤκουσεν ὁ σπαταλῶν καὶ ἀπήρεσεν αὐτῷ] and throws it behind his back.'

87. Johnson, *Letters to Paul's Delegates*, p. 174.

uncertainty of riches, but rather on God' – just as the 'real widow' in 5.5 has done.[88] It would seem that 5.7, 'Give these commands so that they may be above reproach', was written with at least one eye on the widows themselves as well as on their families.[89]

5.9 introduces a new element into the argument: 'let a widow be put on the list'. Does this mean that there was something in the Pastor's community that could be called an order of widows? And how did such an order relate to the 'real' widows discussed in the preceding verses? These questions can best be addressed in the course of examining the contents of the following verses. 'Let a widow be put on the list if she is not less than sixty years old' (5.9a). As Fee and Kelly point out, sixty was the traditional beginning of old age.[90] If financial support is still the issue, why does the author make the enrolment age so high? It becomes increasingly clear as the passage proceeds that its predominant concern is no longer widows' material need, as it was in the opening verses, but is now their moral reputation. Any woman who could meet the requirements the author specifies in 5.9–10 was unlikely to be destitute and in need of the church's help: she had to be 'the wife of one husband, attested for good works, who has brought up children, shown hospitality, washed the feet of the saints, helped the afflicted, and devoted herself to every good work'. These activities are not duties she is to perform, with the church's aid, once she is put on the list, but rather prerequisites of that enrolment that she must have carried out already out of her own resources.[91]

The significance of 'wife of one husband [ἑνὸς ἀνδρὸς γυνή]' has been the subject of some debate. While the literal meaning of the phrase – that a woman has married once, been widowed, and never entered another marital relationship – seems the most obvious one to take,[92] it entails that the younger widows who follow the Pastor's command to remarry in 5.14 effectively debar themselves from ever being enrolled. To Hanson, this is a problem, and he prefers to read ἑνὸς ἀνδρὸς γυνή as prohibiting only divorce and remarriage.[93] However, the contemporary cultural ideal of the *univira*

---

88. In 6.9, the author levels some rather lurid accusations against those who *aspire* to be rich – 'those who want to be rich fall into temptation and are trapped by many senseless and harmful desires that plunge people into ruin and destruction' – but there is no need to assume that he has sexual misconduct in mind in 5.6; as Hanson admits, the Greek there does not require it (*The Pastoral Epistles*, p. 97).

89. Kelly, *A Commentary on the Pastoral Epistles*, p. 114.

90. Fee, *1 and 2 Timothy, Titus*, p. 114; Kelly, *A Commentary on the Pastoral Epistles*, p. 115.

91. Thus Hanson, *The Pastoral Epistles*, p. 98, and Johnson, *Letters to Paul's Delegates*, p. 172.

92. Fee (*1 and 2 Timothy, Titus*, p. 119), Guthrie (*The Pastoral Epistles*, p. 102) and Kelly (*A Commentary on the Pastoral Epistles*, p. 75) all adopt this reading.

93. Hanson, *The Pastoral Epistles*, pp. 77–78.

gives good reason to prefer the literal interpretation. Marjorie Lightman and William Zeisel note that, by the time the Pastorals were written, the term *univira* had gained widespread currency 'to become one of the many pagan epithets for the good wife', and was used to distinguish women who merited it from matrons who had been divorced and remarried.[94] The author is invoking a standard with which his readers would have been familiar.

ἑνὸς ἀνδρὸς γυνή should also sound a recognizable note even for modern readers of the Pastorals, since it is the exact equivalent of a qualification required of those aspiring to the office of ἐπίσκοπος in 3.2: such a one must be μιᾶς γυναικὸς ἄνδρα, the husband of one wife. Other similarities between 5.9–10 and 3.2–7 have been taken by some as evidence that the Pastor is indeed legislating for an office of widows here.[95] However, while there are some common points,[96] the two sets of requirements are in fact rather different in tone; that for the ἐπίσκοπος focuses mainly on the candidate's personal qualities, while that for the widow betrays a much greater interest in the things she has done. More importantly, the office of ἐπίσκοπος carries no age limit; it is open to men of any age, provided they fulfil the other requirements. If there is such a thing as an 'office' of widows, however, the Pastor has just made its pool of potential candidates incredibly small by comparison. In fact, rather than delineating qualifications for an 'office', he seems to be more interested in setting out an ideal version of female Christian behaviour, which all the women in his congregation should aspire to fulfil in their traditional household roles.[97]

With 5.11–13, the reader discovers why the Pastor should be so enthusiastic to promote such an ideal, and why he imposes an age limit of sixty for putting widows on the list. The behaviour of younger widows is causing all manner of problems, not least of which that 'whenever they are drawn away from Christ by their sensuous impulses, they want to marry, incurring condemnation because they broke their first pledge' (5.11–12). It is strange indeed to find this author speaking of a desire to marry in a negative light, and he does so only because the 'pledge' that has been made to Christ is

---

94.   Marjorie Lightman and William Zeisel, 'Univira: An Example of Continuity and Change in Roman Society', *CH* 46 (1977), pp. 19–32 (24, 25).

95.   For example, MacDonald, *The Pauline Churches*, pp. 185–86.

96.   In addition to being married only once, hospitality features on both lists (3.2 and 5.10), as does the raising of children (3.4 and 5.10, though for the would-be ἐπίσκοπος, his dealings with his children are important as an indicator of his ability to exercise authority, while for the widow this activity appears to be an end in itself) and being well spoken of by others (3.7 and 5.10; only in the case of the ἐπίσκοπος is it made explicit that this testimony must come from outsiders).

97.   Indeed, Tit. 2.3–5 makes explicit older women's role in fostering the right kind of behaviour among the younger generation.

such 'that even desire for marriage is infidelity to him'.[98] Knight suggests that the pledge made was one to remain a widow and serve Christ in that capacity:[99] in other words, a vow of celibacy, and just the kind of behaviour that Paul could be understood to be encouraging in 1 Cor. 7.39–40. Because the vow is made to Christ, the Pastor cannot but disapprove of its being broken; but the difficulty of imagining any circumstances in which he would have authorized the taking of such a pledge makes clear that he is dealing here with an already existing organization, not instigated by him, but which he is now desperately anxious to control.

Ill-advised promises aside, these young widows also 'learn to be idle, going around the households, and not only idle but gossips and busybodies [περίεργοι], saying what they ought not to say' (5.13). Gossips get short shrift from Juvenal, who writes mockingly of the kind of woman who

> . . . knows all the news of the world, what's cooking in Thrace
> or China, the secrets of stepson and stepmother
> behind closed doors, who's in love, which gallant is all the rage . . .
>   . . . Such stuff
> she'll unload at street-corners, on anyone she encounters.[100]

Whether or not the young widows were going around the houses in fulfilment of pastoral duties they had taken on themselves, the Pastor is in no doubt that such visits did not represent a worthwhile use of their time. But could 'saying what they ought not to say' indicate a more serious concern here? These young widows were not the only ones who went around households for unwholesome purposes: the opponents are accused of doing so as well (2 Tim. 3.6). The term translated 'busybodies' in 1 Tim. 5.13, περίεργοι, is related to that used in Acts 19.19 for magic acts, περίεργα: might this suggest that the widows were resorting to magic and spells, as Hanson and Kelly suggest?[101] Similarly, the opponents in 2 Tim. 3.8 are compared with Jannes and Jambres, magicians at the court of Pharaoh who opposed Moses, while a few verses later, in 3.13, the author refers to them as 'wicked people and γόητες [who] will go from bad to worse'. γόητες is often translated as 'impostors' or 'charlatans', but in context it seems legitimate to give it its literal meaning of 'magicians'. The young widows and the opponents are thus described in very similar terms, and if 5.15 is to be believed, some of the widows have in fact aligned themselves with the

98.   Easton, *The Pastoral Epistles*, p. 154.
99.   Knight, *The Pastoral Epistles*, p. 222.
100.   Juvenal, *Satires* 6.402–404, 411–12, in *The Sixteen Satires*, tr. Peter Green (London: Penguin, 1998).
101.   Hanson, *The Pastoral Epistles*, p. 99; Kelly, *A Commentary on the Pastoral Epistles*, p. 118.

opponents.[102] It is not necessary to think that either group was actually engaging in 'magical' activity, however, since accusations of such practices were often made in a polemical attempt to discredit those so accused.[103] What can be deduced is that the Pastor was highly troubled by both groups, and perhaps by describing them in such similar terms he hoped to discredit them both by mutual association.

The solution the Pastor prescribes for the problems caused by young widows should by now come as no surprise: 'I would have younger widows marry, bear children, and manage their households, so as to give no opportunity to the enemy to speak ill of us on this account' (1 Tim. 5.14). What young widows are to do is to emulate the lifestyles of those over sixty who already qualify to be put on the list – even though by doing so, they disqualify themselves from ever being so enrolled because they will have been married more than once. If every widow under sixty obeyed the Pastor's command, in time scarcely anyone would be eligible to be enrolled. The Pastor's aim is to stamp the widows' organization out of existence by reasserting socially acceptable values; his concern with outside opinion has now been made quite explicit. Indeed, his aim in this passage as a whole seems to be to limit widows' participation in and reliance on the church to a minimum.[104] The reappearance of the issue of financial support in v. 16, accompanied by a plea that the church not be burdened, serves to confirm that all the diverse regulations concerning who is to be honoured and who is to be enrolled are set out with this single purpose in mind.

Concluding Remarks

Barbara Vaughan did return safely through the Mandelbaum Gate. She married her Qumran archaeologist in the end, because she wanted to, and they 'got along fairly well together ever after'. It is a matter of opinion whether the Pastoral Epistles hold out the prospect of a similarly happy ending. Such is the author's anxiety to appropriate Pauline authority and exercise it in the way that he sees as appropriate to his community's needs that on more than one occasion he sets out practical instructions diametrically opposed to those of the apostle, even as he purports to write in his name. Despite (or perhaps because of) such desperate measures, the Pastorals were, in the short term and of themselves, remarkably unsuccessful in stamping out other readings of and traditions about Paul. In time, however,

---

102. Bassler suggests that the widows' organization provided 'a natural route of defection' ('The Widows' Tale: A Fresh Look at 1 Tim. 5.13–16', *JBL* 103 [1984], pp. 23–41 [37]).

103. Spicq, *Les Epitres pastorales*, p. 105.

104. MacDonald, *The Pauline Churches*, p. 187.

they came to be extremely useful to those who, like Irenaeus, wished to demonstrate the falsity of such other readings, made by people who in his view 'have altogether misunderstood what Paul has spoken'.[105] Barrett goes so far as to suggest that it was only because of the socially acceptable and 'safe' version of Paul given in the Pastorals that the works of the apostle who had provided so much inspiration for the 'heretics' were accepted into the canon;[106] as Walter Bauer puts it, 'the introduction of the pastoral Epistles actually made the collection of Paul's letters ecclesiastically viable for the very first time'.[107] However, the Paul thus preserved, the Paul of the Pastorals, is a rather different figure from the one encountered through the pages of 1 Corinthians read in isolation: in his attitude to certain practical matters, the apostle appears to have been tamed, domesticated, and tailored to fit more closely the mores of the world in which the church now had to survive. Before deciding whether this does indeed represent a 'happy ending', it is necessary now to turn to some other, less well-known readers of Paul, and consider how his teachings on marriage and on women might look through their eyes.

---

105. Irenaeus, *Adv. Haer.* 4.41.4. It has already been noted above that Irenaeus uses a quotation from 1 Timothy (1.4) to open this work.

106. Barrett, 'Pauline Controversies', p. 244.

107. Walter Bauer, *Orthodoxy and Heresy in Earliest Christianity* (London: SCM Press, 1972 [1934]), p. 228.

Part III

NAG HAMMADI

Chapter 5

MARRIAGE IN THE NAG HAMMADI TEXTS

> . . . anything which exists, once it has somehow come into being, can be
> reinterpreted in the service of new intentions . . .
>
> Friedrich Nietzsche, *On the Genealogy of Morals*

Anyone familiar with the traditional stereotype of 'gnostic' ethics might be forgiven for expecting a chapter on 'Marriage in the Nag Hammadi Texts' to be rather short. According to this caricature, the 'gnostics' were either lewd libertines or austere ascetics; and neither of these patterns of behaviour is one in which marriage is likely to figure highly. In order to justify the space I devote to the subject, therefore, it is necessary for me to begin by interrogating this stereotype. Once I have discussed the presentations of 'gnostic' morals to be found both in the accounts of the heresiologists and in modern scholars' interactions with them, and considered the possible motivations for their respective portrayals, I shall then turn to examine the Nag Hammadi texts themselves, focusing especially on the *Gospel of Philip* and the *Exegesis on the Soul*. Since these texts tend not to give straightforward practical instructions in the manner of Paul, but do make considerable use of marriage as a symbol and a metaphor, it will be helpful to pay some attention to *Gos. Phil.*'s reflections on the significance and efficacy of language and images, taking note in so doing of points of similarity to some (post)modern philosophers. Finally, in the course of analysing the use of marital imagery in the selected texts, the question of their relationship to social reality, and to Paul and the deutero-Paulines, can also be addressed. The use of marriage as an image of salvation in *Gos. Phil.* and *Ex. Soul* may be seen as a more thoroughgoing development of a device first seen in the deutero-Pauline Ephesians. However, given the resulting ambiguity and ambivalence of both texts on marriage as a social practice, it is to the authentic Paul of 1 Corinthians that the strongest resemblance can be discerned.

The Stereotype of 'Gnostic' Morality

One of the most problematic aspects of the traditional category of 'gnosticism' has been its skewed portrayal of 'gnostic' morals.[1] The key elements of this caricature are presented in all their glory in the following footnote to Book III of Clement of Alexandria's *Stromateis*, in the *Ante-Nicene Fathers* collection:

> After much consideration, the Editors have deemed it best to give the whole of this Book in Latin. [In the former Book, Clement has shown, not without a decided leaning to chaste celibacy, that marriage is a holy estate, and consistent with the perfect man in Christ. He now enters upon the refutation of the false-gnostics and their licentious tenets. Professing a stricter rule to begin with, and despising the ordinances of the creator, their result was the grossest immorality in practice. The melancholy consequences of an enforced celibacy are, here, all foreseen and foreshown; and this Book, though necessarily offensive to our Christian taste, is most useful as a commentary on monasticism, and the celibacy of priests, in the Western churches. The resolution of the Edinburgh editors to give this Book to scholars *only*, in the Latin, is probably wise . . .][2]

This censorious footnote can be seen as representative of a stereotypical view of 'gnostic' morals which portrays their adherents as *either* ruthlessly ascetic *or* extravagantly libertine (or even, as in the quotation above, both at the same time). As Michael Williams has argued, such characterizations are often based on a grossly oversimplified understanding of 'gnostic' attitudes to the body and to the material world.[3] It is surely unrealistic to expect that 'gnostic' ethics, any more than those of other groups, can be mapped only onto either extreme of the moral spectrum and not onto any point in between.

As I hope to demonstrate below, a careful and attentive reading of the 'gnostic' texts found at Nag Hammadi both requires and reinforces a much more subtle and nuanced approach to the question of 'gnostic' ethics. But why, even before the discovery of the Nag Hammadi library, did the dubious traditional view thrive for so long? What purpose did it serve for those who

---

1. By describing this portrayal with a value-laden term like 'skewed', I am of course betraying my own particular take on the matter. In showing traditional accounts of 'gnostic' morals to be driven by vested interests, I am not claiming to be free of such interests myself, only that mine are different; nor do I expect all my readers to approach these questions from the same perspective as I do. For a lengthier discussion of the importance of context and particular objectives in the writing and reading of texts, see the section in the Introduction on my theoretical approach (pp. 4–7).

2. Alexander Roberts and James Donaldson (eds), *Fathers of the Second Century*, ANF ii (repr. Grand Rapids: Eerdmans, 1971), p. 381 n. 1.

3. Michael Williams, *Rethinking 'Gnosticism': An Argument for Dismantling a Dubious Category* (Princeton: Princeton University Press, 1996), p. 139.

promoted it? Elaine Pagels suggests an answer that is worthy of further consideration when she observes that 'certain patristic scholars still use "gnosticism" as shorthand for all that is false, *a foil for everything genuine and authentic*'.[4] 'Gnosticism', one might say, is the Other of ('orthodox') early Christianity, the opponent against whom the latter is defined. That an idealized vision of the early church is still important today becomes clear in an account Pagels gives elsewhere of a conversation with a German Lutheran professor by whom she was taught at graduate school. Pagels' suggestion to this man that Paul certainly preferred celibacy to marriage (an idea with which I find little fault!) was dismissed by him as 'a complete misunderstanding'.[5] Pagels' professor may be taken as representative of all those who ascribe authority to the New Testament writings, yet to whom marriage and family are of the utmost importance, and who therefore seek to find in Paul's letters (and in the practice of the early church generally) an endorsement of their own position.[6] If 'orthodoxy' is supposed to have taken a moderate, pro-marriage line, then its Other, 'heresy', must in contrast have gravitated towards extreme behaviour of either an ascetic or a libertine variety. This clean-cut division of the sheep from the goats in the early church, while providing a simple model for modern would-be sheep to follow, denies the complexities that characterized the Christian movement in its first centuries, and in so doing gives a false impression of both 'orthodoxy' and 'heresy'.

To raise the spectre of complexity can therefore be profoundly unsettling. When scholars such as Frederik Wisse suggest that differences in doctrine and practice were not necessarily of primary importance in the conflicts between early Christian groups,[7] the resulting effect is a blurring of the boundaries between those groups, so that their previously distinct identities become muddied. What if the 'gnostics' and other Christian groups were

---

4. Elaine Pagels, 'Ritual in the *Gospel of Philip*', in John D. Turner and Anne McGuire (eds), *The Nag Hammadi Library after Fifty Years: Proceedings of the 1995 Society of Biblical Literature Commemoration* (Leiden: E.J. Brill, 1997), pp. 280–91 (280); my emphasis.

5. Cited in Leif E. Vaage and Vincent L. Wimbush, 'Introduction', in Leif E. Vaage and Vincent L. Wimbush (eds), *Asceticism and the New Testament* [New York and London: Routledge, 1999], pp. 1–7 (4).

6. Dale B. Martin also testifies to this phenomenon, and hints at the extent to which it is in fact driven by particular vested interests: 'Since the inception of Protestantism, there has been a broad, concerted attempt to package Paul as a promoter of sex and marriage, in spite of (and in reaction to) most of Christian history' (*The Corinthian Body* [New Haven and London: Yale University Press, 1995], p. 209).

7. 'The real reason for the expulsion of some of the heads of ["gnostic"] "schools" was more likely a conflict with the church authorities over the right to teach than over heresy' (Frederik Wisse, 'Prolegomena to the Study of the New Testament and Gnosis', in A.H.B. Logan and A.J.M Wedderburn [eds], *The New Testament and Gnosis: Essays in Honour of Robert McL. Wilson* [Edinburgh: T. & T. Clark, 1983], pp. 138–45 [139]).

more similar than used to be supposed? What if interpreters do not simply accept the traditional view that the so-called gnostics' anti-cosmic dualism led them to extreme varieties of sexual behaviour, but examine 'gnostic' texts carefully on their own terms? First, they may well find that 'gnostic' ethics are much more interesting and subtle than they have been led to believe. Furthermore, however, it will also be necessary to subject the more familiar, canonical texts to renewed scrutiny; for if the traditional portrayal of 'heresy' has been fundamentally mistaken, then the accompanying ideal version of 'orthodoxy' cannot go unchallenged either.[8] In what follows I shall evaluate both the testimonies of the heresiologists and modern scholars' interactions with them, with the aim of showing how the familiar caricature is both deficient and suspect.

The bipolar view of 'gnostic' ethics is set out with particular clarity in the work of Hans Jonas. Having asserted that '[t]he cardinal feature of gnostic thought is the radical dualism that governs the relationship between God and world, and correspondingly that of man and world',[9] he goes on to demonstrate how this anti-cosmic attitude forms the basis for two contrasting types of conduct. Although he claims that Greek notions of virtue are utterly absent from 'gnostic' thought (because such virtue consists in fulfilling one's duty to one's fellow human being and to the social world as a whole, and anti-cosmists can have no concern with such things),[10] it does

---

8. 'Orthodoxy' and 'heresy' may in fact be treated as one of the fundamental oppositions of Western thought which Jacques Derrida aims to deconstruct. As with other pairs of opposites – light and dark, male and female, and so on – the former term is the good, the ideal, while the latter is its inferior but necessary opposite. Focusing attention on the second term undermines the priority and pre-eminence of the first. To adapt Gayatri Chakravorty Spivak's discussion of 'engineering' and *bricolage* in her preface to Derrida's *Of Grammatology*, 'All knowledge, whether one knows it or not, is a species of [heresy], with its eye on the myth of [orthodoxy]' ('Translator's Preface' to Jacques Derrida, *Of Grammatology* [Baltimore and London: Johns Hopkins University Press, 1976], p. xx). In other words, all knowledge, all the diverse range of ways of talking about the world, is an opinion, a 'taking for oneself', a choice (from the Greek αἱρέομαι), some of which some people seek to elevate to the status of objectively correct belief. 'Orthodoxy', in this abstract universal sense, is a myth which does not really exist. Yet this means that 'heresy' too, as that which is not orthodoxy, does not really exist either: as the concept which brings down the whole dichotomy, it is, to use Spivak's phrase, 'untenable but necessary' (p. xx).

Such a philosophical digression may of course be regarded as an indulgence, but it does no harm to reiterate the point that 'orthodoxy' and 'heresy' are linguistic categories, and that there are other ways of talking about the phenomena they describe. To quote Richard Rorty's dictum, 'The world is out there, but descriptions of the world are not' (*Contingency, Irony, and Solidarity* [Cambridge: Cambridge University Press, 1989], p. 5). The familiar terms (used without scare quotes) are part of a vocabulary which serves the purposes of a particular group, and which may for the sake of other interests be deposed.

9. Hans Jonas, *The Gnostic Religion: The Message of the Alien God and the Beginnings of Christianity* (Boston: Beacon Press, 1958), p. 42.

10. Jonas, *The Gnostic Religion*, p. 267.

not therefore follow that the 'gnostics' have no interest in behaviour at all. On the contrary, their nihilistic worldview leads logically either to a conscious repudiation of the power of the demiurge by wilfully flouting all his decrees, or to the attempt to evade it by means of ascetic abstinence from all the so-called goods of his world. Jonas understands the differences between these two approaches as follows:

> Libertinism was the most insolent expression of the metaphysical revolt, reveling in its own bravado: the utmost contempt for the world consists in dismissing it even as a danger or an adversary. Asceticism acknowledges the world's corrupting power: it takes seriously the danger of contamination and is thus animated more by fear than by contempt.[11]

Even such a painstakingly argued presentation as Jonas' does not eradicate the problems of the 'two extremes' hypothesis. I have already alluded to Williams' argument that the phenomena of 'world-rejection' and 'hatred of the body' upon which the theory is based are rather more complex than those who invoke them tend to recognize.[12] Moreover, the relationship between these supposed attitudes and actual behaviour is rarely straightforward. It is too simplistic to assume that a particular cosmogony must manifest itself in one of two types of action, or to explain a pattern of conduct purely by reference to an underlying mythical system. For example, Marcion, renowned for his rigorous asceticism, was hardly displaying anti-cosmic world-rejection when he travelled to Rome, the capital of the empire, to further his world-encompassing plans.[13] When reading the Nag Hammadi texts, a more subtle approach to the relationship between symbol and social reality must be adopted, and a much wider variety of possible moral lifestyles taken into consideration.

'Libertinism'

Of course, as Giovanni Filoramo points out, '[i]t is a strange fate to be able to speak only through the mouth of one's opponents';[14] but until the

---

11. Jonas, *The Gnostic Religion*, p. 275.

12. Williams, *Rethinking 'Gnosticism'*, ch. 5, 'Anticosmic World-Rejection? or Socio-cultural Accommodation?', and ch. 6, 'Hatred of the Body? or the Perfection of the Human?' As Williams points out, 'it is not so much the mere fact that a given myth seems to say bad things about the physical cosmos that interests us, but what that might imply'. Are the authors of such myths to be thought of as anti-environmentalists, anti-social recluses, political anarchists? If this question remains unanswered, the term 'world-rejection' in itself does not provide a very firm basis for any conclusions about 'gnostic' ethics.

13. Walter Bauer, *Orthodoxy and Heresy in Earliest Christianity* (London: SCM Press, 1972 [1934]), p. 71.

14. Giovanni Filoramo, *A History of Gnosticism*, tr. Anthony Alcock (Oxford: Blackwell, 1990), p. 2.

discovery of the Nag Hammadi library, this was by and large the fate of the so-called gnostics. The heresiologists upon whose accounts earlier gener-ations of scholars had to rely were not primarily motivated by any desire to give a fair and unbiased account of their adversaries. For this reason Henry Chadwick suggests that '[i]t is worth asking ourselves whether or not the gnostics, far from being wild or queer or bizarre or pessimistic, far from having systems that were mere sick men's nightmares and evidence of exces-sive addiction to drugs or sex, were offering the most convincing, normal, sensible answer to the contemporary form of the quest for the meaning of life'.[15] In other words, the reports of Irenaeus and his colleagues ought not to be taken at face value. Nor, however, should they be dismissed out of hand, for while they may not yield much accurate factual information, they (and modern scholars' discussions of them) afford highly valuable insights into questions of group identity and conflict as these relate to the early church.[16]

That the church fathers' accounts contain allegations of lewd and immoral behaviour is not particularly surprising, since such 'slander' was a mainstay of the rhetorical arsenal available to them.[17] Nor should readers be greatly taken aback at the absence from the Nag Hammadi library of any evidence to confirm these reports, although this absence appears to be a source of disenchantment for some, such as Jean Doresse: 'one finds oneself almost disappointed at this, so freely had the heresiologists given us to understand that mysteries of that [licentious] description were common practice in the principal sects!'[18] Those who share Doresse's taste for the exotic would do better to confine themselves to accounts such as that to be found in Epiphanius' *Panarion*, which I intend to examine as a test case of attitudes to the question of 'gnostic' libertinism.

---

15. Henry Chadwick, 'The Domestication of Gnosis', in Bentley Layton (ed.), *The School of Valentinus* (Leiden: E.J. Brill, 1981), pp. 3–16 (4).

16. See my discussion of Henri Tajfel's work on group identity theory in Chapter 3. Like the deutero-Pauline authors in their treatments of their opponents, Irenaeus and his kind attempt to portray 'orthodox' morality in the most flattering light by contrasting it to the utter degeneracy that the 'heretics' are said to display.

17. On this topic Frederik Wisse's cautionary note is worthy of attention: 'Though this claim would have been in most cases untrue, it cannot simply be called slander, since it was not considered possible for a false believer to speak the truth and live a genuinely moral life' ('The Use of Early Christian Literature as Evidence for Inner Diversity and Conflict', in Charles W. Hedrick and Robert Hodgson [eds], *Nag Hammadi, Gnosticism, and Early Christianity* [Pea-body, Mass.: Hendrickson, 1986], pp. 177–90 [185]). Accusations of immorality are not simply barefaced lies told to discredit parties known to be innocent; on the contrary, because these parties are (from the heresiologist's point of view) outsiders, opposed to those whom he pre-sumes to be in the right, they are to his mind wholly guilty from the outset, and can be deemed capable of nothing other than sinful conduct.

18. Jean Doresse, *The Secret Books of the Egyptian Gnostics: An Introduction to the Gnos-tic Coptic Manuscripts Discovered at Chenoboskion*, tr. Philip Mairet (London: Hollis and Carter, 1960), p. 251.

The hapless Epiphanius gives the following account of his experience with the Phibionites:

> I will come now to the place of depth in their deadly story (for they have various false teachings about pleasure). First, they have their women in common . . . The man leaving his wife says to his own wife: Stand up and perform the *agape* with the brother. Then the unfortunates unite with each other, and as I am truly ashamed to say the shameful things that are being done by them, because according to the holy apostle the things that are happening by them are shameful even to mention (Eph. 5.12), nevertheless I will not be ashamed to say those things which they are not ashamed to do, in order that I may cause in every way a horror in those who hear about their shameful practices.[19]

Epiphanius goes on to tell how emissions of semen and menstrual blood are offered up as the body and blood of Christ. After informing his readers that '[t]hey have intercourse with each other but they teach that one may not beget children', he reports what happens if a woman does become pregnant:

> they pull out the embryo in the time when they can reach it with the hand. They take out this unborn child and in a sort of mortar pound it with the pestle and into this mix honey and pepper and other certain spices and myrrh, in order that it may not nauseate them, and then they come together, all this company of swine and dogs, and each communicates with the finger from the bruised child. And after they have finished this cannibalism finally they pray to God, saying, that we did not let the Archon of this desire play with us but collected the mistake of the brother.[20]

The reliability of this gruesome account has been the subject of considerable controversy. That Epiphanius claims to be speaking from first-hand experience is a sufficient guarantee of his credibility for some,[21] but others are less convinced; indeed, G.R.S. Mead argues that 'the moral shock [his experiences] gave him seems to have warped his judgment as a historian in this part of his work; it led him to collect every scrap of evidence of obscenity he could lay his hand on and every gross scandal that had come to his ears, and freely to generalize therefrom'.[22] This raises the important question of what precisely motivated Epiphanius to write as he did, and also the

---

19. Epiphanius, *Panarion* 26.4.1–4; quoted in Stephen Benko, 'The Libertine Gnostic Sect of the Phibionites according to Epiphanius', *VC* 21 (1967), pp. 103–19 (109).

20. Epiphanius, *Panarion* 26.5.5–6; quoted in Benko, 'The Libertine Gnostic Sect of the Phibionites', p. 110.

21. For example Benko, 'The Libertine Gnostic Sect of the Phibionites', p. 111; see also Jorunn Jacobsen Buckley, 'Libertines or Not: Fruit, Bread, Semen and other Bodily Fluids in Gnosticism', *JECS* 2 (1994), pp. 15–31 (16).

22. Cited in Benko, 'The Libertine Gnostic Sect of the Phibionites', p. 111.

related question of why individual modern scholars accept or reject his account.

Williams, carefully reading between the lines, makes a persuasive case that Epiphanius' 'first-hand' evidence is not really as compelling as it may at first appear. In fact, the author of the *Panarion* has not actually witnessed any of the rituals he describes in such detail, but instead has derived his information from books belonging to the group, which he appears to have (deliberately?) misunderstood.[23] Williams contends that the most convincing explanation of the situation is that the non-'orthodox' group with whom Epiphanius spent some time was in fact a circle of ascetics, among whom he had some experience or made some discovery that caused him to revise his initial positive opinion of them.[24] It is the connection between this change of mind and the way in which the group comes to be presented that is particularly interesting. Epiphanius is not the only individual said to have ventured beyond the 'orthodox' pale and come back to tell the story. Irenaeus more than once refers to women who have been 'led astray' by certain sects, only to return to the church full of contrition and tales of their horrific experiences.[25] For anyone like Epiphanius and these women, who wishes to be fully welcomed back into the 'orthodox' fold, it surely makes sense to portray in the worst possible light the 'heretical' group which one has just left, in order to emphasize one's newfound distance from it and the unlikelihood of any return to it. It is also helpful in this scenario for the penitent to give the impression that the members of this group set out ruthlessly to deceive naïve and innocent young Christians; this blackens their reputation even further, and firmly places the blame for defection solely on their shoulders. Concerning the Phibionites, Epiphanius does not simply give the evidence of an insider; he testifies as one who used to be an insider but who has now decided to realign himself with another group. As such, it is difficult to regard his account as reliable.

Yet some scholars do still decide to see Epiphanius as trustworthy, for interesting reasons of their own. Jorunn Jacobsen Buckley attempts to explain how the practices Epiphanius describes might make internal sense, and asks what cosmology and soteriology might accompany such a 'libertine' outlook.[26] Impressed by the fact that the Phibionite ritual lays equal emphasis on male and female bodily fluids, she observes that 'if hierarchy and submission of the female reigns among the Orthodox, it often pays to

---

23. Williams, *Rethinking 'Gnosticism'*, pp. 180–81.
24. Williams, *Rethinking 'Gnosticism'*, p. 182.
25. *Adv. Haer.* 1.6.3, 1.13.5.
26. Buckley, 'Libertines or Not', p. 17. The potential difficulties attending such an enterprise have already been noted above (p. 113).

look for the opposite in heretical circles'.[27] Her modern distaste for ancient 'orthodox' misogyny is easy to understand, but her reasons for seeking a corrective to it primarily in other texts from the same social and cultural milieu are rather less clear. James Goehring similarly betrays modern sensibilities in his treatment of Epiphanius. While recognizing that '[t]he charge of sexual deviance is part of the rhetoric of opposition',[28] he seems to accept the facts of what Epiphanius reports and challenges only his interpretation of them. Goehring argues that the explanation of the behaviour of the women in the group is governed by its author's 'patriarchal conservatism'.[29] Indeed, he almost gives the impression that if Epiphanius had only been a little more open-minded, if he had only understood that the ritual that appalled him was an enactment of the tenets of 'gnostic' theology and not a lust-driven free-for-all, then he would have applauded this lifestyle that offered women some liberation from the usual social constraints. However, I am unconvinced that Epiphanius' description of these practices and his interpretation of them can be separated in this way. It is not his aim merely to 'understand' the Phibionites; rather he sets out unreservedly to discredit and dishonour them, and both description and interpretation are indispensable components of this project.

Any argument for Epiphanius' credibility is not helped by the fact that charges remarkably similar to those he laid against the Phibionites were also brought against 'orthodox' Christians by some of their opponents. The resemblances are such as to suggest a common stock of slanderous charges upon which any could draw at need, and which even if untrue possessed the capacity to wound. Thus Justin enquires of Trypho:

> 'And I ask this: have you also believed concerning us, that we *eat men*; and that after the feast, having extinguished the lights, we *engage in promiscuous concubinage*? Or do you condemn us in this alone, that we adhere to such tenets, and believe in an opinion, untrue, as you think?'
>
> 'This is what we are amazed at,' said Trypho, 'but those things about which the multitude speak are not worthy of belief; for they are most repugnant to human nature.'[30]

Tertullian makes a similar complaint in his *Apology*:

> Monsters of wickedness, we are accused of observing a holy rite in which we *kill a little child and then eat it*; in which, after the feast, we *practice*

---

27. Buckley, 'Libertines or Not', p. 19.

28. James E. Goehring, 'Libertine or Liberated: Women in the So-called Libertine Gnostic Communities', in David Scholer (ed.), *Women in Early Christianity*, Studies in Early Christianity 14 (New York and London: Garland, 1993), pp. 183–98 (186).

29. Goehring, 'Libertine or Liberated', p. 195.

30. Justin, *Dialogue with Trypho* 10. The italics in this and the following quotations from primary sources indicate similarities with the *Panarion*.

incest, the dogs – our pimps, forsooth, overturning the lights and getting us the shamelessness of darkness for our *impious lusts.* This is what is constantly laid to our charge, and yet you take no pains to elicit the truth of what we have been so long accused.[31]

He dismisses the charges because they are nothing more than rumour, an evil thing that is by nature mendacious. Of course, one would not expect these early Christian apologists to accept the accusations made against them, nor is it surprising that they lay similar indictments against their own enemies; but to find the same double standards displayed by supposedly 'objective' modern commentators is a little disappointing. As Williams remarks, 'rumors that we find unbelievable with regard to "orthodox" Christians are somehow supposed to be quite believable in the case of "gnostics" '.[32]

The treatment of a piece of anti-Christian polemic cited in the work of the apologist Minucius Felix will serve as an example of this phenomenon. In *Octavius* he records the following remarks:

They recognize each other by *secret marks and signs;*[33] hardly have they met when they love each other, throughout the world uniting in the practice of a veritable religion of lusts. Indiscriminately they call each other *brother and sister,* thus turning even ordinary *fornication into incest . . .* [F]lushed with the banquet after *. . . feasting,* they begin to burn with incestuous passions . . . the light is overturned and extinguished, and with it common knowledge of their actions; in the shameless dark with unspeakable lust they *copulate in random unions,* all equally being guilty of incest, some by deed, but everyone by complicity.[34]

Margaret MacDonald, who cites this passage, understands it to be directed against Christians in general, and uses it as evidence for the importance of women's role in how the early church was perceived by outsiders.[35] However, Stephen Benko, noting as I have done the similarities between this excerpt from *Octavius* and Epiphanius' *Panarion,* explains these similarities not by reference to a common stock of rhetorical weapons, but rather by arguing that the two sources in fact refer to the same group:

We must come to the painful recognition of the fact that the charges of the pagans against the Christians involving immoral sexual rites and

---

31. Tertullian, *Apol.* 7.

32. Williams, *Rethinking 'Gnosticism'*, p. 183.

33. Epiphanius also speaks of some kind of special distinguishing handshake (*Panarion* 26.4).

34. Minucius Felix, *Octavius* 8.8; cited in Margaret Y. MacDonald, *Early Christian Women and Pagan Opinion: The Power of the Hysterical Woman* (Cambridge: Cambridge University Press, 1996), p. 60.

35. MacDonald, *Early Christian Women,* pp. 60–61.

murdering of children were not at all unfounded. . . . A non-Christian quite naturally could not make any distinction between orthodox Christianity and Gnosticism and the malpractices of the libertine gnostics were held against all Christians indiscriminately.[36]

Underlying this argument are a number of erroneous assumptions. First, Benko appears to be unaware that there could be any cause for laying a charge of immoral behaviour other than its being true. If an accusation has been made, then someone is culpable. Secondly, 'real' Christians could never be the guilty party; only 'gnostic' Christians (whose entitlement to the epithet is dubious at best) could possibly be responsible for such acts.[37] This presupposition is based on the neat division of early Christians into groups of heroes and villains which I attempted to deconstruct earlier in this section. However, Benko's third assumption – that outsiders 'naturally' could not distinguish between these two groups – seriously undermines the notion of any such unproblematic division between them. If outsiders (whom there is no reason to think were particularly dense or unobservant) were unable to tell the difference, then how distinct could 'orthodox' and 'heretical' Christians in fact have been? Either orgiastic sex and baby-eating were much more common practices in the church than anyone has hitherto supposed, or the 'gnostics' are just as likely to be victims of vicious rumours as their 'orthodox' counterparts.

'Asceticism'

These allegations of libertinism represent only one side of the caricature of 'gnostic' morals. It is also necessary to consider the question of 'gnostic' asceticism, and here the situation is a little more complex. Far from disapproving of ascetic practices as they did of more hedonistic behaviours, the heresiologists in many respects aspired to such a lifestyle themselves. Before analysing the effect this has on their arguments, however, it is pertinent to ask exactly what the reader ought to understand by 'asceticism'. As far as it is used in the conventional way to denote sexual abstinence and self-denial, Richard Valantasis finds the term unhelpful for the task of interpreting texts, and sets out to redefine it in a more fruitful manner. He suggests that '[t]he presence or absence of an agenda *to reformulate or refashion the self* provides the key to whether (or not) a text is ascetical'.[38] In other words, it is

---

36. Benko, 'The Libertine Gnostic Sect of the Phibionites', p. 114.

37. Buckley also discusses how presuppositions about 'Christianity' and 'Gnosticism' influence decisions concerning the truth of charges of sexual immorality ('Libertines or Not', p. 16).

38. Richard Valantasis, 'Is the Gospel of Thomas Ascetical? Revisiting an Old Problem with a New Theory', *JECS* 7 (1999), pp. 55–81 (61); my emphasis.

not the mere mention of sexual abstinence that makes a text ascetical, but rather the role ascribed to such abstinence in the formation of a new identity. Furthermore, practices not traditionally thought of as 'ascetical' may also contribute to this new identity and in doing so become worthy of the epithet.[39]

Valantasis' reference to identity serves as a reminder of the heresiologists' need to differentiate themselves in a positive way from their 'gnostic' Other. As I noted in the preceding paragraph, they too adopted some ascetic practices as part of their distinctive Christian identity. Tertullian, for example, exhorts his readers on more than one occasion to refrain from second marriages: 'whether it be for the sake of the flesh, or of the world, or of posterity, that marriage is undertaken, nothing of all these "necessities" affects the servants of God, so as to prevent my deeming it enough to have once for all yielded to some one of them, and by one marriage appeased concupiscence of this kind'.[40] The only reason he does not forbid marriage altogether is because it is a divine ordinance;[41] following Paul, he laments the dangers of desire that make marriage necessary, and views children as a source of anxiety and distraction.[42]

Because they themselves value ascetic practices positively, then, 'orthodox' writers cannot discredit their 'heretical' opponents simply by accusing them of adopting such practices too; more subtle charges have to be brought. Thus Clement of Alexandria attacks the Marcionites' continence because it has the wrong basis, namely 'hatred of the Creator'; he also attacks the inconsistency of his opponents' self-denial (they reject marriage, but partake of food, drink and air, which are also the gifts of God).[43] Irenaeus cleverly disparages the so-called gnostics' failure to live up to the standards they profess, writing of those 'who pretend at first to live in all modesty with [women] as with sisters, [but who] have in course of time been revealed in their true colours, when the sister has been found with child by her [pretended] brother'.[44] Not only do the 'gnostics' engage in immoral behaviour, they are liars as well. (A more charitable onlooker may interpret events rather differently, reckoning that the occasional appearance of issue

39.   Valantasis, 'Is the Gospel of Thomas Ascetical?', p. 65.

40.   Tertullian, *Ad Uxor.* 5; see also *De Exhor. Cast.* 12 and *De Monogamia* 16.

41.   Some 'gnostic' authors, subscribing to a form of biblical demiurgical myth according to which the world and its institutions derived not from the true God but from a lesser being, felt no such compunction. For example, the author of the *Testimony of Truth* insists that 'the defilement of the Law is manifest . . . The Law commands [one] to take a husband [or] to take a wife, and to beget, to multiply like the sand of the sea' (29.26–30.5). By contrast, the man who knows the God of truth 'has subdued desire in every [way] within himself' (41.12–13).

42.   Tertullian, *Ad Uxor.* 2, 4, 5.

43.   Clement of Alexandria, *Stromateis* 3.12, 37.

44.   Irenaeus, *Adv. Haer.* 1.6.3.

from such relationships does not expose the whole enterprise as a pretence, but represents only a temporary failure of self-control on the part of individuals who are making a genuine effort.[45])

Many texts in the Nag Hammadi library itself do appear to encourage an ascetic position (which, as I have shown, was not the case with libertinism); a few examples will suffice here. The *Book of Thomas the Contender Writing to the Perfect* (*Thom. Cont.*) is dominated by imagery depicting sexual desire as fire. Those whom its author regards as outsiders are said to be no better than beasts, and are 'deprived of [the kingdom] since they love the sweetness of the fire and are servants of death and rush to the works of corruption' (141.29–31).[46] By contrast, 'Everyone who seeks the truth from true wisdom will make himself wings so as to fly, fleeing the lust that scorches the spirits of men' (140.1–4). Lest the reader still be unsure what is required of him, words attributed to the Saviour himself make the matter quite clear: 'Woe to you who love intimacy with womankind and polluted intercourse with them!' (144.8–10) Unlike another writer who once likened desire to a burning fire,[47] this author sets out his position without the slightest hint of ambiguity. The *Teachings of Silvanus* conveys a similar idea with similar imagery, though in a slightly more measured tone: 'Protect yourself lest you are burned by the fires of fornication. . . . If you cast out of yourself the desire whose devices are many, you will release yourself from the sins of lust' (105.8–9, 22–25).

On the basis of texts such as these, Wisse asserts that '[i]f there is a unity at all in the [Nag Hammadi] Library it must be found not in doctrine but in the ethical stance of the tractates'.[48] Admittedly, the ethical stance of *Thom. Cont.* is fairly unambiguous, but by no means all the Nag Hammadi documents set out their position so clearly; other texts are rather less direct in their approach. The *Authoritative Teaching*, for example, uses objects typically eschewed by ascetic practice, such as food, as images of the snares of the devil, sources of mortal danger for the soul: 'For [he places] many foods before our eyes, (things) which belong to this world. He wishes to make us desire one of them and to taste only a little, so that he may seize us with his hidden poison and bring us out of freedom and take us into slavery' (30.10–20). Such unwholesome 'foods' include 'love of money, pride, vanity, envy that rivals another envy, beauty of body, fraudulence . . . ignorance and ease' (31.2–7).

45. Williams, *Rethinking 'Gnosticism'*, p. 148.

46. This and all subsequent quotations from Nag Hammadi texts are taken from James M. Robinson (ed.), *The Nag Hammadi Library in English*, 3rd edn (New York: HarperCollins, 1988).

47. Paul, of course, in 1 Corinthians 7.

48. Frederik Wisse, 'The Nag Hammadi Library and the Heresiologists', *VC* 25 (1971), pp. 205–23 (220).

Drawing conclusions about actual practice from such mesmerizing imagery is no simple matter. It is not implausible that the author of the *Authoritative Teaching* is encouraging his readers to adopt renunciatory practices; but it is by no means certain either. A similar difficulty is presented by many other tractates, including *Gos. Phil.* and *Ex. Soul*, which will be discussed in the following sections. As Williams points out, any evidence for an ascetic position is 'often more implicit than explicit',[49] and it seems no more reasonable to assume that a particular cosmogony or anthropogony results in asceticism than in libertinism. Buckley rightly observes that an assumption that ascetic forms of 'gnosticism' are the norm has (potentially distorting) implications for how the Nag Hammadi texts are read,[50] so it is therefore my intention to bear in mind that underlying them may be much more subtle and complex moral reflections than have hitherto been recognized.

'Truth in types and images': The Gospel of Philip *on Language and Imagery*

Neither *Gos. Phil.* nor *Ex. Soul* dispenses unequivocal practical advice on marriage and celibacy in the manner of Paul and the other New Testament authors who write in his name. However, the use of marriage as an image of salvation, which was first observed in Ephesians, has in these documents been adopted in a wholesale manner. This means that a sophisticated approach will be required when comparing these Nag Hammadi texts with their canonical counterparts, since (to reiterate once again) the relationship between symbol and social reality is not always straightforward.[51] But not only does *Gos. Phil.* deploy marital imagery, it also contains substantial reflections on the efficacy of human language and symbols at conveying divine realities, and it is by discussing these that I propose to begin this section.

The twenty-first-century reader could almost read into the following words an adumbration of structuralism: 'Light and darkness, life and death, right and left, are brothers of one another. They are inseparable. Because of

---

49.   Williams, *Rethinking 'Gnosticism'*, p. 140.

50.   Buckley, 'Libertines or Not', p. 15 n. 2.

51.   Williams' advice on approaching gendered imagery in the Nag Hammadi texts is also pertinent to this discussion of marriage, suitable adaptations being made to the questions he proposes: To what extent does a text use marital imagery? Is such imagery used for the sake of its marital character, or for some other reason? What is the relationship between the roles depicted in the imagery and the author's perspective on social marital roles? ('Variety in Gnostic Perspectives on Gender', in Karen L. King [ed.], *Images of the Feminine in Gnosticism* [Philadelphia: Fortress Press, 1988], pp. 2–22 [4].)

this neither are the good good, nor the evil evil, nor is life life, nor death death' (53.14–19). Anachronistic though it may be to draw attention to it, the apparent similarity to Ferdinand de Saussure's definition of the linguistic sign, in which the relationship between signifier and signified is arbitrary, and opposing terms are endowed with meaning primarily in relation to one another,[52] is striking. However, it goes a little too far to describe this excerpt, as Schuyler Brown does, as 'an extraordinary anticipation of Derrida'.[53] For the passage continues: 'For this reason each one [of these opposites] will dissolve into its earliest origin. But those who are exalted above the world are indissoluble, eternal' (53.20–23). In other words, the author of *Gos. Phil.*, unlike Derrida, envisages a place where the play of signifiers stops, a location other than this world where language works differently.

Gos. Phil.'s understanding of the way in which language functions in this world is developed in the following paragraph: 'Names given to the worldly are very deceptive [Ⲙ̄ⲠⲖⲀⲚⲎ], for they divert our thoughts from what is correct [ⲚⲉⲦⲤⲘⲟⲚⲦ] to what is incorrect [ⲉⲚⲉⲦⲤⲘⲟⲚⲦ ⲀⲚ]. Thus one who hears the word "God" does not perceive what is correct [ⲠⲉⲦⲤⲘⲟⲚⲦ], but perceives what is incorrect [Ⲙ̄ⲠⲉⲦⲤⲘⲟⲚⲦ ⲀⲚ]' (53.23–26). Buckley suggests that the Coptic words in brackets ought to be translated 'erring', 'stable' and 'unstable' respectively, because 'the "stable" entities, like Truth or Jesus, on their Pleromatic level possess one, immutable identity – an ineffable reality necessarily modified, on earth, by "names", "types and images." '[54] It is this ineffable reality that is *Gos. Phil.*'s primary concern, and in comparison with it worldly instability is evaluated negatively. But because names used in the world derive their meaning primarily in relation to one another, the utterance of a name directs the mind not to its heavenly referent (which is stable) but instead to other earthly names (which are unstable); and in this, according to *Gos. Phil.*, they err. The 'name above all things' is the one which is not uttered in the world (54.5–7) and which therefore is not subject to its vicissitudes.

What, then, is the origin of this state of affairs? From where did the crudely hewn tool that is language come? Flawed and misleading though it may be, it is also necessary, and was bestowed as a divine gift: 'truth brought names into existence in the world for our sakes because it is not possible to learn it without these names' (54.13–15). The author then goes on to

---

52. Ferdinand de Saussure, *Course in General Linguistics*, ed. and tr. Roy Harris (London: Duckworth, 1983), pp. 67–70.

53. Schuyler Brown, ' "Begotten, Not Created": The Gnostic Use of Language in Jungian Perspective', in Robert Segal (ed.), *The Allure of Gnosticism: The Gnostic Experience in Jungian Psychology and Contemporary Culture* (Chicago and La Salle, Ill.: Open Court, 1995), pp. 70–83 (77).

54. Jorunn Jacobsen Buckley, 'Conceptual Models and Polemical Issues in the Gospel of Philip', in *ANRW* II.25.5 (1988), pp. 4167–94 (4173).

describe how the archons, in their efforts to keep human beings under their thrall, 'took the name of those that are good and gave it to those that are not good' (54.18–26). Is this intended to explain language's inadequacy and potential to deceive? If the archons had not interfered, would names serve as perfect reflections of the realities they represent? This seems unlikely. Readers are told at a later point that '[t]he world came into being through a mistake', for the one who created it failed to achieve his desire of making it imperishable and immortal (75.2–9). This unstable, ever-changing world is thus qualitatively different from the immutable divine realm, and the language used in it can only ever conform to the conditions of its environment. In the same way Jesus himself appeared to all people 'not . . . as he was, but in the manner in which [they would] be able to see him' (57.29–32). Language is always already imperfect; the archons' interference can only exacerbate an existing situation.

But the rulers' nefarious meddling is not the end of the story, for they then proceed to reassign the names they have displaced to their original purposes, seemingly hoping in this way to gain control over human beings through language (54.26–31). However, as shortly becomes clear, the archons' apparent power is delusory, for 'the holy spirit in secret was accomplishing everything through them as it wished. Truth, which existed since the beginning, is sown everywhere' (55.17–20). Here it does begin to seem appropriate to invoke Derrida, in particular his declaration that 'there is nothing outside the text.' This claim, as Rorty reads it, is primarily intended to debunk any kind of correspondence theory of reality, according to which language is a means of accurately representing the world and objects in it.[55] When the archons seek to use language to misrepresent such objects, they are undone, for they fail to see the implications of the names' divine origin, and thus are blind to the power that the supreme God is able to exercise over them through these names, which awaken human beings to knowledge of their true nature. Seeking to manipulate language to their own ends, the archons are instead overcome by it. The rulers of this world, albeit unwittingly, become agents of divine truth.

All this hints at a close and complex relationship between the divine, truth, and language that will repay closer attention. (Perhaps not coincidentally, it also reflects what Einar Thomassen calls a 'relatively optimistic cosmology'[56] on the part of the author of *Gos. Phil.*, which may come as something of a surprise to those accustomed to thinking in terms of a gnostic 'anti-cosmic attitude'.) Some interesting parallels to these aspects of

55. Richard Rorty, 'Philosophy as a Kind of Writing: An Essay on Derrida', in Richard Rorty, *Consequences of Pragmatism* (Minneapolis: University of Minnesota Press, 1982), pp. 90–109 (97).

56. Einar Thomassen, 'How Valentinian is *The Gospel of Philip?*', in Turner and McGuire (eds), *The Nag Hammadi Library After Fifty Years*, pp. 251–79 (273).

Gos. Phil. may be found in another Nag Hammadi document: *The Thunder: Perfect Mind.* This text is presented as a revelation discourse by a female figure, Thunder, who 'is allegorized as Perfect Mind, meaning the extension of the divine into the world':[57] a role, I want to suggest, which is analogous to that of the divinely bestowed names in *Gos. Phil.* Thunder's opening words testify to her divine origin: 'I was sent forth from the power, and I have come to those who reflect on me, and I have been found among those who seek after me' (13.1–5). However, they also hint at her ambiguous status and awareness of the possibility of negative responses to it: 'do not banish me from your sight. And do not make your voice hate me, nor your hearing. Do not be ignorant of me anywhere or at any time. Be on your guard!' (13.9–15)

Gos. Phil.'s account of language as consisting in pairs of opposites (53.14–19) is mirrored in Thunder's description of herself in a series of coupled contradictory terms: the first and last, the honoured and the scorned, the whore and the holy one, and so on (13.16–27). She repeatedly insists that a simplistic response is not adequate to the complex, multivalent phenomenon that she/language is: 'You who deny me, confess me, and you who confess me, deny me. You who tell the truth about me, lie about me, and you who have lied about me, tell the truth about me' (14.18–22). Like language, Thunder conveys the divine reality, but must adapt herself to the world into which she has come; she is indispensable, but flawed. Thus 'I am the one whom you have despised, and you reflect upon me' (16.29–31). The paradoxical reaction of revulsion and fascination is appropriate to the stimulus.

Thunder's discourse gives rise to a question which must also be asked of *Gos. Phil.*: how far can one distinguish this 'extension of the divine into the world', the language which the supreme being gives, from the divine reality in itself? When Thunder declares that 'I am the one who alone exists, and I have no one who will judge me' (21.18–20), her claims to uniqueness and transcendence suggest a fundamental unity between the divine (to whom such attributes naturally belong) and the means by which it is made manifest in the world (which also here lay claim to them). But what of the stability and unity of the divine realm, in contrast to the unstable, fragmented earthly sphere? Thunder leaves the reader only with an impression of the polyvalent wildness of the divine language: '[I am] control and the uncontrollable. I am the union and the dissolution' (19.9–11). The divine entry into the world in the form of names topples the divisions between apparent and hidden, human and divine, to enable human beings to acquire

---

57. Douglas M. Parrott, introduction to *The Thunder: Perfect Mind*, in Robinson (ed.), *The Nag Hammadi Library in English*, p. 296.

salvific knowledge.[58] Rorty has suggested that '[t]o drop the idea of languages as representations ... would be to de-divinize the world',[59] since '[t]he suggestion that truth, as well as the world, is out there is a legacy of an age in which the world was seen as the creation of a being who had a language of his own'.[60] But when God puts language into the world in the way depicted in *Gos. Phil.* and *Thunder*, making it subject to the world's contingencies and inconsistencies, perhaps then one ought to speak not of divinizing the world, but rather of 'linguifying' the divine: God himself has entered the interminable play of signs.

The author of *Gos. Phil.*, of course, is unlikely to have seen things this way, or indeed to have been aware that his thought might have these consequences. As noted above, he speaks with approval of the indissoluble and eternal character of those exalted above the world (53.21–23). Some modern interpreters, too, wish to find in his text a more reliable mediator of divine realities than language appears to be, and look to the following passage for aid: 'Truth did not come into the world naked, but it came in types and images. The world will not receive truth in any other way' (67.9–12). Despite the similarities between these lines on images and those describing names (54.13–15), Pagels insists that there is a fundamental difference between the two: 'while Philip's discussion of *names* is equivocal and ambivalent, when he discusses "types and images" – the sacramental elements – he does not equivocate'.[61] While types and images share in names' ambivalence insofar as both have a hidden as well as a manifest element,[62] names only teach truth (and have the potential to teach error), but types and images 'convey' it.[63] Pagels uses the term 'convey' more than once without explaining exactly what she means by it, or how it differs from the way in which names 'teach'. Even granting her assumption that 'types and images' are the sacramental elements, precisely how bread, wine, oil and so on become these elements without the use of language – without being redescribed, as Rorty would put it – is unclear. By leaving this question unanswered, she fails to convince the reader that her proposed distinction between 'names' and 'images' should be upheld. In the following examination of the bridal chamber, therefore, I shall assume that this 'image' holds just as much richly ambiguous potential as the 'names' which have formed the main focus of discussion in this section.

---

58.   Jorunn Jacobsen Buckley, 'A Cult-Mystery in *The Gospel of Philip*', *JBL* 99 (1980), pp. 569–81 (576).

59.   Richard Rorty, *Contingency, Irony, and Solidarity* (Cambridge: Cambridge University Press, 1989), p. 21.

60.   Rorty, *Contingency, Irony, and Solidarity*, p. 5.

61.   Pagels, 'Ritual', p. 288; emphasis in original.

62.   Pagels, 'Ritual', p. 287.

63.   Pagels, 'Ritual', p. 288.

'The mystery of marriage' in the Gospel of Philip

'Great is the mystery of marriage! For [without] it the world would [not exist]' (*Gos. Phil.* 64.31–33). This declaration is reminiscent of the fundamental importance ascribed to marriage by Musonius Rufus for the welfare of the city and the whole human race.[64] That the author of *Gos. Phil.* accords marriage such a prominent place in his text also serves as another reminder that so-called gnosticism's anti-cosmism has been somewhat exaggerated. Without wishing at this stage to draw any conclusions about the author's preferred moral practice, his decision to make extensive use of marital imagery to represent crucial theological tenets is in itself significant.

Robin McL. Wilson suggests that Eph. 5.32 – 'This is a great mystery, and I am applying it to Christ and the church' – may have been the source for all of *Gos. Phil.*'s speculation concerning the bridal chamber.[65] Unlike Ephesians, however, *Gos. Phil.*'s positive use of marital imagery does not occur in the context of a household code; nor does it go hand in hand with a wholehearted endorsement of the practice of earthly marriage. The two texts do share an interest in Adam and Eve and the relevance of these two archetypal figures for their respective readers' situations, but *Gos. Phil.* goes further than its suggested source by explicitly asserting that the purpose of Christ's coming was to restore the primal androgyne rent apart in humankind's earliest days:

> If the woman had not separated from the man, she should not die with the man. His separation became the beginning of death. Because of this Christ came to repair the separation which was from the beginning and again unite the two, and to give life to those who died as a result of the separation and unite them. But the woman is united to her husband in the bridal chamber. (70.9–18)

Why does separation result in death? An earlier passage in *Gos. Phil.* seems to echo another tractate from Codex 2 which may suggest an answer. 61.5–10 reads as follows: 'First adultery came into being, afterward murder. And he [Cain] was begotten in adultery, for he was the child of the serpent. So he became a murderer, just like his father, and he killed his brother.' This sounds rather like a more succinct version of the reading of the opening chapters of Genesis which is found in the *Hypostasis of the Archons*.[66] According to this text, the separation of the spiritual Eve from Adam (when

---

64. Musonius Rufus 14, in Cora E. Lutz, 'Musonius Rufus "The Roman Socrates" ', *Yale Classical Studies* 10 (1947), pp. 3–147 (93).

65. R. McL. Wilson, 'The New Testament in the Nag Hammadi Gospel of Philip', *NTS* 9 (1962/63), pp. 291–94 (292).

66. This tractate will be discussed in detail in the following chapter. The passage of *Hyp. Arch.* relevant to this discussion is 89.3–91.30.

the archons open up his side, *Hyp. Arch.* 89.3–17) launches a series of events which culminates in the carnal Eve's separation from her husband Adam, the result of which is a murderous offspring, Cain, understood to be the archons' son (91.11–30). The problem, then, is Eve's adultery (a term which is not to be narrowly defined: '[i]ndeed every act of sexual intercourse which has occurred between those unlike one another is adultery', *Gos. Phil.* 61.10–12); and if adultery is the problem, then a form of monogamous marriage – the bridal chamber (ⲡⲛⲩⲙⲫⲱⲛ) – is the solution: 'When Eve was still in Adam death did not exist. When she was separated from him death came into being. If he enters again and attains his former self, death will be no more' (68.22–26).

65.1–26 describes the restoration of the unity between man and woman in the bridal chamber, which serves to protect them both from the lascivious advances of sexually predatory evil spirits that beset solitary individuals. The passage culminates with a reiterated declaration of the inviolability of the united couple: 'But if they [the evil spirits] see the man and his wife sitting beside one another, the female cannot come into the man, nor can the male come into the woman. So if the image and the angel are reunited with one another, neither can any venture to go in to the man or the woman' (65.19–26).

If one may put the question crudely, how exactly does this process work? Thomassen offers some interesting reflections on *Gos. Phil.*'s 'soteriology of symbolic parallelism'.[67] He suggests that two joinings are here closely inter-related: the joining of the human and the angel in the bridal chamber, and that of this ritual act itself with its model, the redemption of the redeemer.[68] This linking of the bridal chamber with Jesus' baptism in the Jordan is certainly not without justification, for *Gos. Phil.* applies the same term, ⲙⲩⲥⲧⲏⲣⲓⲟⲛ, to them both (64.32 and 71.4). Jesus, because he 'came down' to earthly existence, himself requires the redemption of which he is also the agent, and it is on these grounds that the designation of him as '(female) virgin' (ⲧⲡⲁⲣⲑⲉⲛⲟⲥ) can be explained: 'Jesus . . . as the model of the saved human, represents the female part in the union, *and* . . . as the saving mani-festation of the fullness of the Father, and the personified unity of all the angels, he is the male bridegroom in the bridal chamber.'[69] The pivotal events of Jesus' life are the basis and guarantee of the ritual which is intended to actualize their effects in the lives of a group of believers many decades later.

---

67.   Thomassen, 'How Valentinian is *The Gospel of Philip*?', p. 262.

68.   Thomassen, 'How Valentinian is *The Gospel of Philip*?', p. 263.

69.   Thomassen, 'How Valentinian is *The Gospel of Philip*?', p. 263, emphasis in original. It should not come as a great surprise that the flawed and dependent human being requiring salvation is presented as female. However, it is interesting that Thomassen (intentionally?) has Jesus only 'representing' the female bride, while he simply 'is' the male bridegroom!

How then does the ritual actually achieve the desired results? Thomassen explains by means of a paradox: 'What takes place in ritual is desired to be something real (rebirth and resurrection), but this reality is only achieved by eliminating the reality of the physical acts performed in the ritual and by affirming the reality of the non-physical symbolism of which these acts are the bearers.'[70] In what sense can 'rebirth and resurrection' be said to be 'something real' in the same way that physical acts are 'real'? The situation is not such a philosophical conundrum as Thomassen seems to make out. The physical acts which form the basic constituents of a ritual can come to signify something else by being described in a new vocabulary. To reiterate the point made previously in relation to Pagels, sacrament cannot be separated from language, for it is ultimately language that gives it its efficacy. As *Gos. Phil.* itself makes clear, however, language is not an easy thing to control, and even fundamentally important rituals can only ever be imperfect vehicles: 'The mysteries of truth are revealed, though in type and image. . . . [W]e shall go in there by means of lowly types and forms of weakness. They are lowly indeed when compared with the perfect glory' (84.20–21; 85.14–16).

At last, then, one may ask about the relationship of the bridal chamber to marriage in the ordinary sense. What position does the author of *Gos. Phil.* take on the debate over marriage and celibacy that so exercised his contemporaries? Pagels suggests that, because of his view on language which was discussed above, he simply refuses to engage in this and other current controversies.[71] Her theory appears to be borne out by *Gos. Phil.*'s treatment of the argument over the resurrection of the flesh, with regard to which the author asserts that both the believers and the deniers are at fault. To believe in the resurrection of human flesh is to fail to recognize that ' "flesh [and blood shall] not inherit the kingdom [of God]". What is this which will not inherit? This which is on us' (56.32–57.1). On the other hand, to deny the resurrection of the 'flesh' is to deny the life imparted by the flesh and blood which are Jesus' word and the holy spirit (57.6–7). Simply to assert or deny the proposition that the flesh will be raised is to fail to take into account the subtleties of language use and the way in which the meaning of words changes depending upon the context in which they are employed. In fact, the question of the resurrection is inseparable from the words in which it is expressed: 'whatever you shall say, you say nothing outside the flesh. It is necessary to rise in this flesh, since everything exists in it' (57.16–19). To speak and to rise, to inhabit language and to be saved, become conflated.

---

70. Thomassen, 'How Valentinian is *The Gospel of Philip*?', p. 264.
71. Elaine Pagels, 'The "Mystery of Marriage" in the *Gospel of Philip* Revisited', in Birger A. Pearson (ed.), *The Future of Early Christianity* (Minneapolis: Fortress Press, 1991), pp. 442–54 (449).

After such a treatment of one controversial question, readers should not expect a straightforward answer to any other.

Unsurprisingly, this has not stopped scholars trying to find such an answer; equally unsurprisingly, there is a lack of consensus as to what it should be. Is *Gos. Phil.* pro-marriage? No, argues Schenke, insisting that the ritual acts of the bridal chamber had nothing to do with actual marriage; yes, contends Quispel, asserting on the contrary that such rites presuppose it.[72] It is – of course – possible to adduce evidence from the text for both of these positions. Buckley is one who adopts the latter stance, contending that the application of the significant term 'mystery' (ⲙⲩⲥⲧⲏⲣⲓⲟⲛ) to worldly marriage, even if it is not the 'true mystery' (82.2–6), still suggests a not wholly negative view.[73] Indeed, she asserts elsewhere that 'earthly union seems to mark the first, *required* step before one may enter into the "spiritual" union'.[74] Commenting on the passage concerned with warding off the advances of evil spirits (65.1–26), she concludes that ' "spiritual" power asserts itself exclusively in earthly marriage'.[75] If Buckley's interpretation is correct, then it is by means of their sexual relationship that husband and wife defend themselves from the incubi and succubae.

Buckley's reading makes *Gos. Phil.* concur closely with Paul's instructions in 1 Corinthians 7, in which he advocates marriage as a remedy for sexual immorality and urges married couples to engage in sexual relations with one another. However, while the author of *Gos. Phil.* does share Paul's concern that untoward sexual misconduct be avoided (though as noted above, *Gos. Phil.*'s notion of 'adultery' may be rather different), unlike Paul he characterizes worldly marriage in which sexual intercourse takes place as the 'marriage of defilement' (ⲡⲅⲁⲙⲟⲥ ⲙ̄ⲡⲭⲱϩⲙ), and contrasts it with another, superior kind of marriage:

> No [one can] know when [the husband] and the wife have intercourse with one another except the two of them. Indeed, marriage in the world is a mystery for those who have taken a wife. If there is a hidden quality to the marriage of defilement, how much more is the undefiled marriage a true mystery! It is not fleshly but pure. It belongs not to desire but to the will. It belongs not to darkness or the night but to the day and the light. (81.34–82.10)

In addition, the bridal chamber is said to be only for free men and virgins (ⲛ̄ⲉⲗⲉⲩⲑⲉⲣⲟⲥ ⲙⲛ̄ ϩⲛ̄ⲡⲁⲣⲑⲉⲛⲟⲥ, 69.1–4). Bearing these considerations in

---

72. Pagels, 'The "Mystery of Marriage" ', pp. 442–43.

73. Jorunn Jacobsen Buckley, ' "The Holy Spirit is a Double Name": Holy Spirit, Mary, and Sophia in the *Gospel of Philip*', in King (ed.), *Images of the Feminine in Gnosticism*, pp. 211–27 (224).

74. Buckley, 'A Cult-Mystery in *The Gospel of Philip*', p. 572, emphasis in original.

75. Buckley, 'A Cult-Mystery in *The Gospel of Philip*', p. 572.

mind, Williams offers a somewhat different conception of the means by which the evil spirits are warded off. He notes that (unlike Paul in 1 Corinthians 7), the author mentions only the *pairing* of the man and woman and says nothing about a sexual relationship between them; the reader is told only that they sit beside one another (65.20–21). Williams thus argues that this companionship of man and woman is sufficient to ward off the seductive spirits, and proposes that it is spiritual marriage, free from the defiling element of sexual intercourse, which *Gos. Phil.* as a whole is intended to endorse.[76] Given the testimony to such practice to be found in the writings of the church fathers,[77] this is certainly a plausible contention.

When one wishes to make comparisons between the attitudes to marriage displayed in *Gos. Phil.* and in other texts, it is especially tempting finally to come down (with due humility and caution, naturally) in favour of one of these two interpretations. It is worth bearing in mind Pagels' legitimate point that if the author of *Gos. Phil.* did in fact have a preference for one type of conduct over another, one might expect to find it more clearly stated in his text.[78] But as she goes on to argue, he probably never meant to adopt one stance over another in the first place; on the contrary, she says, he 'intend[ed] to reject entirely the question concerning sexual practice, the same question that contemporary scholars have been trying to use the text to answer'.[79] How one aligns oneself with regard to the 'marriage of defilement' appears to be a matter of choice which readers must make for themselves. While it may be fitting to destroy the flesh (ϣϣⲉ ⲉⲧⲁⲕⲟ ⲛ̄ⲧⲥⲁⲣⲝ̄, 82.29), it is not essential. Instead, a moderate attitude is encouraged: 'Fear not the flesh nor love it. If you [sg.] fear it, it will gain mastery over you. If you love it, it will swallow and paralyse you' (66.4–6). Pagels observes that 'Although the apostle Paul strongly urged celibacy upon his converts, but added that marriage is, nevertheless, "not sin" and is certainly preferable to promiscuity (1 Cor. 7.1–10), few Christians in the following generations could tolerate such ambivalence.'[80] In the author of the *Gospel of Philip*, perhaps, there is at least one other who could. Might one find a second in the writer of the *Exegesis on the Soul*?

---

76. Williams, *Rethinking 'Gnosticism'*, pp. 148–50.
77. For example, Tertullian, *De Exhor. Cast.* 12, *De Monogamia* 16; Clement of Alexandria, *Stromateis* 6.100.
78. Pagels, 'The "Mystery of Marriage" ', p. 446.
79. Pagels, 'The "Mystery of Marriage" ', p. 444.
80. Pagels, 'The "Mystery of Marriage" ', pp. 446–47.

Marriage as Salvation in the Exegesis on the Soul

This relatively short, but dense and rich, tractate recounts the tale of the origin, fall, suffering and redemption of the soul. The soul is gendered female, and is presented in the character of her divine father's only daughter, 'virgin [ογπαρθενοc] and in form androgynous' (127.24). But both of these characteristics are lost when she falls down into a body (thus becoming gendered) and enters 'this life' and is set upon by 'robbers' who, by force or other means, seduce her and steal her virginity from her (127.25–32). A woeful picture is painted of the naïve soul's desperate attempts to find some measure of safety and security; she prostitutes herself (αcπορνεγε) to all comers, 'considering each one she was about to embrace to be her husband' (128.3–4). But without exception they deceive and exploit her, 'pretending to be faithful, true husbands' (128.14) while being in reality 'wanton, unfaithful adulterers' (128.5), who abandon her and leave her with nothing but 'dumb, blind and sickly' offspring (128.23–25).[81] Forsaken and alone, the soul is utterly helpless, until she remembers her divine origins, repents of her actions and beseeches her father to restore her again. Her pleas are not in vain, for '[w]hen he sees her in such a state, then he will count her worthy of his mercy upon her, for many are the afflictions that have come upon her because she abandoned her house' (128.26–129.5). In contrast to the carnal world, the father's house offers the soul a place of purity.[82]

This account of the soul's journey is followed by a number of lengthy quotations from the prophets Jeremiah, Hosea and Ezekiel. The author takes passages that the majority of modern interpreters understand as descriptions of God's relationship with Israel, and interprets them in the light of the story he has just told. William Robinson attempts to argue that these excerpts 'are not integral to the narrative but are catchword insertions, interruptions which in most cases have not influenced their present contexts'.[83] This is not the impression given, however, by the way in which the author himself introduces his scriptural extracts: 'Now concerning the prostitution of the soul the holy spirit prophesies in many places . . .' (129.5–7). In other words, the author deploys these quotations in order to make it clear that his discussion of his central theme is neither groundless nor untrustworthy, but instead has the support of the highest possible authority; they thus perform a very important function in his text. Robin McL. Wilson is compelled to note that this 'work thus reveals a somewhat deeper

---

81.   *Gos. Phil.* 61.6–10 also testifies to the belief that adulterous relationships do not result in desirable progeny.

82.   As William C. Robinson observes, the idea of this contrast was by no means unique to *Ex. Soul* ('The Exegesis on the Soul', *NovT* 12 [1970], pp. 102–17 [111]). A similar notion is encountered in, for example, Philo, *Deus Imm.* 136–37.

83.   Robinson, 'The Exegesis on the Soul', p. 104.

interest in, and more intensive study of, the Old Testament than the Gnostics are commonly given credit for'.[84]

It is not only the Old Testament that this author is interested in. *Ex. Soul* also incorporates two quotations from the Pauline corpus,[85] which, as Wisse observes, do nothing less than give 'apostolic sanction to the whole exegetical enterprise' of the tractate.[86] The goal of this enterprise is set out following the author's citation of Ezek. 16.23–26, when he asks what 'the sons of Egypt, men great of flesh' means (130.21–22). He immediately proceeds to answer his own question, making clear that the 'robbers' who beset the soul in his opening account are not to be understood solely or narrowly in sexual terms; instead, they represent every aspect of the soul's unfortunate involvement in earthly life, including her interest in food and clothing 'and the other external nonsense surrounding the body – the things she thinks she needs' (130.26–28). In other words, the author is not concerned merely with ⲧⲡⲟⲣⲛⲓⲁ ⲙ̄ⲡⲥⲱⲙⲁ (translated by Robinson as 'prostitution of the body'), but with the more fundamental and wide-ranging problem of ⲧⲡⲟⲣⲛⲓⲁ ⲛ̄ⲧϥⲩⲭⲏ ('prostitution of the soul'). The term conventionally used for sexual immorality has become a synecdoche for all inappropriate involvement in the world, casting such involvement in the same negative light as prostitution; and it is the quotations taken from the Pauline correspondence that allow this step to be made. Taking 1 Cor. 5.9–10 and Eph. 6.12 in conjunction with one another, the author of *Ex. Soul* seeks to convince his readers that Paul's command not to associate with πόρνοις ('prostitutes') is not to be understood merely in terms of 'flesh and blood' – that is to say, in its literal, conventional sense – but rather in terms of the struggle 'against the world rulers of this darkness and the spirits of wickedness' (131.11–13). Sexual immorality may be the world's defining characteristic, and as such an appropriate metaphor for the soul's involvement in worldly things, but it is still only a symptom, not the disease itself.[87]

What remedy does the author propose for this disease? In 131.19–22 the reader learns that, when the father perceives the soul's weeping repentance, 'he will make her womb turn from the external domain and will turn it again

---

84.   Robert McL. Wilson, 'Old Testament Exegesis in the Gnostic Exegesis on the Soul', in Martin Krause (ed.), *Essays on the Nag Hammadi Texts in Honour of Pahor Labib* (Leiden: E.J. Brill, 1975), pp. 217–24 (222). The notion that all 'gnostic' dealings with scripture took the form of perverse 'protest exegesis' will be dealt with more thoroughly in the following chapter.

85.   1 Cor. 5.9–10, at 131.2–8, and Eph. 6.12, at 131.9–13.

86.   Frederik Wisse, 'On Exegeting "The Exegesis on the Soul" ', in Jacques-E. Ménard (ed.), *Les textes de Nag Hammadi*, Nag Hammadi Studies 7 (Leiden: E.J. Brill, 1975), pp. 68–81 (72).

87.   Contra Robinson's argument that 'sexuality *in itself* is the soul's plight' ('Introduction' to the *Exegesis on the Soul*, in Bentley Layton [ed.], *Nag Hammadi Codex II, 2–7*, ii, Nag Hammadi Studies 21 [Leiden: E.J. Brill, 1989], pp. 136–41 [137]; my emphasis).

inward, so that the soul will regain her proper character'. In her fallen state, 'the womb of the soul is around the outside like the male genitalia' (131.24–26), but this is not how things ought to be. Just as there would be something seriously amiss with a human female whose womb was on the outside, so also the soul's misplaced organ, representing her involvement with the world, is indicative of a significant problem. The solution in both cases is a restoration of inwardness: just as the womb ought to be inside the body, the soul, like an honourable woman, should eschew entanglement with the affairs of the world.[88] This re-establishment of the correct inward-looking attitude has an immediate cleansing effect; external pollutions are removed, enabling the soul 'to regain the [newness] of her former nature and to turn herself back again' (131.35–132.1).

After such dishonourable behaviour, for the soul to be taken back into her father's house is remarkable enough; but the restoration of her virginity (her 'former nature') is not the end of the story. While during her initial sojourn in this life the soul sought for a faithful, true husband without success, now the father provides her with just such a partner (132.7–9). Cleansed and beautified, the bride awaits the arrival of her bridegroom, dreaming of him 'like a woman in love with a man' (132.22–23). Clearly this is no ordinary union – the man is 'her brother, the firstborn' – but the reader may nonetheless find it striking that marriage is used as an image of redemption here. After all, as I have argued in Chapter 1, marriage, fundamental to the status quo, could be seen as the ultimate investment in the life of the world, and therefore not an institution of which one might expect the author of *Ex. Soul* to have a particularly high opinion.

As if aware of this point, the author goes on to assert that 'that marriage is not like the carnal marriage [Ⲙ̄ⲡⲅⲀⲘⲞⲤ Ⲛ̄ⲤⲀⲢⲔⲓⲔⲞⲤ]' (132.27–28) – not least in the respect that in the union he is discussing, physical desire is left behind (132.31–32). Furthermore, it becomes clear that this marriage of the soul is a complicated business, and any attempt to fathom its relationship to social reality will not be straightforward. With the citation of the Genesis creation account (133.1–3), the story of the soul's fall and separation from her bridegroom becomes intermingled with that of the fall of Eve and her leading Adam astray into disobedience to the divine commands. The 'marriage' the author describes both reunites the primal androgyne and rejoins the soul to 'her true love, her real master' (a hierarchical view of the union which is backed up by a quotation from Eph. 5.23 in 133.8–10).[89] The story

88.   Bruce J. Malina, *The New Testament World: Insights from Cultural Anthropology* (Louisville, Ky.: Westminster/John Knox Press, 1993), p. 49. Female spaces and things 'face toward the inside, with a sort of invisible magnet of social pressure turning females inward, toward their space in the house or the village. . . . [A]ll things remaining on the inside are female.'

89.   The superior position of the masculine partner appears to be at least one worldly custom that the author of *Ex. Soul* is content to leave in place.

of the soul in its entirety seems intended to serve a dual purpose: on the one hand, it is a myth of origins, explaining the general human condition of alienation from God; on the other, it is a metaphorical depiction of the situation of each individual member of the author's audience, designed to inform them how to restore their connection with the divine. So what is the relationship of this myth to social reality? How, especially with regard to marriage, does this author want his readers to act?

When the author turns to speak to his readers directly, he does so with the following words: '[i]t is therefore fitting to pray to the father and to call on him with all our soul ... repenting for the life we lived' (135.4–9). This attention-catching shift to the second-person address indicates that the repentance here called for is the focal point of the text. Wisse (who, it will be remembered, has suggested elsewhere that an ascetic outlook may be the unifying characteristic of the Nag Hammadi library)[90] insists that this repentance can only express itself through celibacy.[91] Yet must this necessarily be the case? *Ex. Soul*, according to Robinson, 'revels in condemning sex'.[92] Certainly, there can be little doubt that the rapacious sexual exploitation to which the soul is subjected by the worldly 'robbers' in the opening paragraphs of the tractate are viewed by the author with the utmost disapproval. But marriage – even 'carnal marriage' – is not the same thing as πορνεία, and Paul himself, in the same letter from which the author of *Ex. Soul* quotes, recommends the former as a protection against the latter.

Ex. Soul makes no such explicit recommendation; but it is surely noteworthy that the soul's restoration from her defilement is not considered complete until she is united with the bridegroom. Elsewhere too it is marriage that is used to represent the soul's true home, in contrast to other sexual temptations that might induce her to leave it. The author quotes Helen's lament from the *Odyssey* (4.261–64): 'It is Aphrodite who deceived me and brought me out of my village. My only daughter I left behind me, and my good, understanding, handsome husband' (137.2–5); it is to this house that she longs to return (137.1). If *Ex. Soul* nowhere expressly encourages 'carnal marriage', neither is it condemned outright. It might be concluded, then, that while the author insists on the need to repent and uses marital imagery to encourage his readers to do so, he refrains from expressing any explicit preference for marriage or celibacy in practice. As in *Gos. Phil.*, it is left to readers to make up their own minds on this matter.

---

90. See n. 48 above.
91. Wisse, 'On Exegeting "The Exegesis on the Soul" ', p. 78.
92. Robinson, 'The Exegesis on the Soul', p. 105.

Concluding Remarks

This examination of *Gos. Phil.* and *Ex. Soul* has shown that the question of 'gnostic' morals is a great deal more complex (and interesting) than the traditional stereotype would have one believe. The deployment of marriage as an image of salvation is taken much further in these texts than it was in Ephesians, and as a result the relationship between marriage and social reality is more difficult to discern. Insofar as both these tractates display an ambivalent attitude to earthly marriage, they resemble Paul in 1 Corinthians 7; but whereas the ambivalence of Paul's letter derives primarily from his attempt to issue different instructions to different groups of people at the same time, in the Nag Hammadi texts it arises from an apparent reluctance to set down any practical instructions on the matter at all. As I shall show in the next chapter, a similar situation prevails when attempting to unravel 'gnostic' attitudes to women.

Chapter 6

WOMEN AND FEMININE IMAGERY IN THE NAG
HAMMADI TEXTS

> ... that mystery of a woman's soul, so sacred even in its pollution.
>
> Nathaniel Hawthorne, *The Scarlet Letter*

With these dozen words, Nathaniel Hawthorne effectively sums up the
complexities involved in the interpretation of any text in which feminine
imagery is prominent. 'Woman'[1] is a mystery, a bundle of contradictions; to
refer to her, and for readers to ascribe meaning to that reference, is no
straightforward matter. *The Scarlet Letter* as a whole provides a rich illustration of this phenomenon. Set in a Puritan settlement in seventeenth-
century New England, the novel's central character is a young woman
named Hester Prynne, who has been found guilty of adultery after conceiv-
ing and giving birth to a child in the absence of her husband. Yet Hawthorne's view of his heroine is far from one-dimensional. Depicting Hester
standing on the pillory with her illegitimate child in her arms, the author
surprises his readers with the suggestion that the watching townsfolk might
be reminded, by the sinner's beauty and mien, of none other than the Virgin
Mary – although he swiftly goes on to clarify that such a reminder should be
'only by contrast'. Nonetheless, as the novel progresses, Hester appears to
become more deserving of such a favourable comparison as, through her
charitable works, she gradually wins back the town's respect. In the openness with which she acknowledges her guilt and the fortitude with which she
bears her punishment, she stands in stark contrast to the town's authority
figures, whose hypocrisy and hidden sins have been laid bare to the novel's
readers (the governor's sister indulges in witchcraft; and the adored young

---

1. I refer here not to individual, actual women but rather to the category 'Woman' that has
characterized much of Western thought. Daphne Hampson provides a useful overview (with
particular reference to the Judaeo-Christian tradition) in *After Christianity* (London: SCM
Press, 1996), pp. 169–73. She shows how the category has drawn together contradictory notions
of femininity – morally pure motherhood on the one hand, degenerate sexuality on the other –
not with the interests of women themselves in mind, but rather the needs of the masculine
subject: 'woman is represented with reference to what man is – which is what it is to be a slave'
(p. 173). Recognition of the category's pervasiveness and power (and, therefore, the need to
engage with it critically) is not tantamount to accepting its validity.

minister, Arthur Dimmesdale, is in fact the secret father of Hester's child). Like the townsfolk, the reader can never forget Hester's original sin – the scarlet letter is always there on her breast as a reminder to her and everyone else – but in time that symbol takes on other significances as well, becoming a token of her good deeds, even imparting a kind of holiness in a way similar to a cross on a nun's bosom. Female 'sacredness' and 'pollution' are both embodied in one woman.

Yet Hawthorne does not write about Hester Prynne primarily in order to say something about actual women. Instead he uses the character to expose the harshness and hypocrisy of a community which he would condemn – a group of people so strict and restrained that, on their annual holiday, they 'appeared scarcely more grave than most other communities at a period of general affliction'. In 'gnostic' and heresiological texts too, feminine imagery is deployed for a variety of purposes and, as was the case with the marital imagery discussed in the previous chapter, its relationship to social reality is not always straightforward. Unlike 1 Corinthians or the Pastoral Epistles, the Nag Hammadi texts on which I shall focus in this chapter do not set out explicit practical instructions for female conduct. However, this does not leave me completely lacking in grounds for comparison. The *Hypostasis of the Archons* (like many other tractates) shows a great deal of interest in the same Genesis accounts that both Paul and the Pastor use to justify their teachings, while the *Gospel of Thomas* incorporates intriguing reflections on the fate of traditional gender roles in the believer's new life. It is certainly not my aim here to argue that either one of these texts takes a 'better' position on gender issues than the Pastoral Epistles, and is therefore to be preferred by modern readers who have a concern for such things. What they do offer is a *different* approach to the topic, and in so doing they provide a context in which it is necessary for the Pastorals (and Paul himself) to be re-evaluated. Once again it can be seen that there is always more than one way to read a text.

Women and 'Heresy'

My adoption of this relatively cautious approach may surprise those who are accustomed to think of the 'gnostics' as particularly friendly to women. In one of her early works Elaine Pagels, noting the extensive use of feminine imagery for the divine in 'gnostic' texts, argues that this counts as evidence which 'clearly indicates a correlation between religious theory and social practice', and that, among some 'gnostic' groups, women were considered equal to men.[2] The difficulties already encountered in the preceding chapter

---

2. Elaine Pagels, *The Gnostic Gospels* (Harmondsworth: Penguin, 1990 [1979]), p. 81. She does go on to admit that this observation is not universally applicable – not because feminine

in inferring practical advice from the use of marital imagery should act as a warning against accepting such a conclusion too readily. Yet some of the heresiologists' accounts also testify to women taking a prominent role in 'heretical' circles. Tertullian exclaims: 'These heretical women – how audacious they are! They have no modesty; they are bold enough to teach, to engage in argument, to enact exorcisms, to undertake cures, and, it may be, even to baptize!'[3] Irenaeus, meanwhile, describes the women in Marcus' circle who are encouraged to take part in ritual and to prophesy, though he is cynical in the extreme about Marcus' motivation for these inclusive practices. 'He devotes himself to women,' notes Irenaeus, 'especially those who are well-bred, and elegantly attired, and of great wealth'. What is worse, he bids women prophesy only to further his attempts to seduce them.[4] Yet, as noted in the previous chapter, Jorunn Jacobsen Buckley has attempted to put a positive spin on practices even more shocking than these; to reiterate her assessment of the Phibionite ritual described by Epiphanius: 'if hierarchy and submission of the female reigns among the Orthodox, it often pays to look for the opposite in heretical circles'.[5]

How is one to assess all this evidence? Daniel Hoffman, in his attempt to overturn the position adopted by Pagels in *The Gnostic Gospels*, does note that plentiful though feminine imagery may be in 'gnostic' texts, it includes few direct accounts of social situation.[6] This does not prevent him, however, from making much of the negative aspects of such imagery, and arguing on this basis that women were unlikely to have had high status or religious roles equal to men in 'gnostic' circles.[7] By contrast, he attempts to show that Irenaeus and Tertullian had (for their time) a high regard for women; in his discussion of Marcus and the women in his circle, for example, Irenaeus supposedly is motivated not by misogyny, but by concern for the deluded females whom the charlatan has taken in.[8]

But when Hoffman insists that the extreme lengths to which Irenaeus was

---

imagery does not always result in 'feminist' social practice, but rather on the grounds that some 'heretical' circles that still retained masculine imagery for God also permitted women to hold leadership positions.

3. Tertullian, *Praescr.* 41.

4. Irenaeus, *Adv. Haer.* 1.13.2–4.

5. Jorunn Jacobsen Buckley, 'Libertines or Not: Fruit, Bread, Semen and other Bodily Fluids in Gnosticism', *JECS* 2 (1994), pp. 15–31 (17).

6. Daniel L. Hoffman, *The Status of Women and Gnosticism in Irenaeus and Tertullian*, Studies in Women and Religion 36 (Lewiston, NY: Edwin Mellen, 1995), p. 27.

7. Hoffman, *The Status of Women and Gnosticism*, p. 23. Joseph R. Hoffman similarly argues that 'gnostic' myth correlates with social reality in a way unfavourable to women, because of its negative view of creation and the female figure's role in it: '[s]he is the enfigurement of the primordial accident' ('De Statu Feminarum: The Correlation between Gnostic Theory and Social Practice', *Eglise et Théologie* 14 [1983], pp. 293–304 [302]).

8. Hoffman, *The Status of Women and Gnosticism*, pp. 99, 108.

prepared to go in his efforts to deny the validity of 'gnostic' beliefs would not necessarily affect his portrayal of women in the 'gnostic' groups,[9] he fails to convince. Why would someone this determined to discredit his opponents refrain from depicting the women associated with them in a negative light, when to do so would so easily advance his cause? In his desire to find only positive things in Irenaeus and Tertullian's treatment of women, Hoffman betrays his own vested interests. These interests appear to strike a chord with those of Craig Evans, who provides the foreword for Hoffman's book and takes the opportunity thus provided to warn against the twin dangers of 'deconstructionism on the one hand and politically correct agendas on the other'.[10] Dismissing Pagels' work as the product of the latter of these two evils, he praises Hoffman for showing 'that the heresiologists Tertullian and Irenaeus recognized and praised the personal qualities and ecclesial contributions of Christian women'.[11] The implied conclusion is that there ought then to be no need for Buckley or anyone else to look to 'heretical' sources to find a positive evaluation of women in early Christianity.

If modern readings of the heresiological accounts are governed by vested interests such as these, it would be naïve indeed to expect the accounts themselves to be free from them. As Gérard Vallée has observed, Irenaeus and his colleagues do not simply provide objective information; instead, 'the data are decisively placed within an interpretative scheme that colours them'.[12] Like Hawthorne's portrayal of Hester Prynne, the heresiologists' depiction of 'heretical' women is motivated by a concern with something greater than the women themselves, and a further remark of Vallée's provides the clue as to what this might be. Irenaeus, he notes, wrote at a time (*c.* 180 CE) 'when the heretic/orthodox polarization does not seem to have been clear'; in fact, it was Irenaeus himself who established insurmountable boundaries between the two fronts.[13]

Virginia Burrus has shown that the heresiologists' portrayal of women made a vital contribution to the setting up of these boundaries. The 'heretical' woman, nearly always sexually promiscuous and indifferent to male authority, is the threatening counterpart to the demure and submissive 'orthodox' virgin; the former represents a community which has uncontrolled boundaries (and is therefore open to all manner of contamination), while the latter in contrast signifies a group whose boundaries are secure

9. Hoffman, *The Status of Women and Gnosticism*, p. 112.

10. Craig A. Evans, 'Foreword' to Hoffman, *The Status of Women and Gnosticism*, p. i.

11. Evans, 'Foreword', p. i.

12. Gérard Vallée, *A Study in Anti-Gnostic Polemics: Irenaeus, Hippolytus, and Epiphanius*, Studies in Christianity and Judaism 1 (Waterloo, Ont.: Wilfrid Laurier University Press, 1981), p. 4.

13. Vallée, *A Study in Anti-Gnostic Polemics*, p. 11.

(and which is therefore pure and unsullied).[14] How much either of these images has to do with actual women is, of course, open to question. While it may be tempting to glorify 'heretical' women as some feminist scholars have done,[15] such an approach does little to help the interpreter dig beneath the surface of the ancient writers' rhetorical concerns. It is therefore my aim in what follows to read the 'gnostic' texts without any assumption that they will be particularly favourable to women, and to attempt to blur the boundaries between supposedly permissive 'heresy' and restrictive 'ortho-doxy'. Given the cultural distance separating texts belonging to both these categories from modern readers, it would be surprising indeed to find ideas truly congenial to a twenty-first-century feminist viewpoint in any of them.

Reading Genesis in the Hypostasis of the Archons

The *Hypostasis of the Archons* presents to the reader what Philip Alexander describes as 'a highly erudite exegesis of Genesis 1–6, albeit from an unusual hermeneutical standpoint'.[16] This text's interaction with the Old Testament account is much more extensive than that found in the Pastoral Epistles and, in comparison with them, its interpretative stance is indeed 'unusual' and bold. What makes its reading of Genesis so striking? *Hyp. Arch.* pro-vides an excellent example of what Michael Williams calls the 'biblical demiurgical traditions', that is to say 'all those that ascribe the creation and management of the cosmos to some lower entity or entities, distinct from the highest God'.[17] So when the author of *Hyp. Arch.* reads the creation accounts with the assumption that the actions and words which Genesis ascribes to God should instead be attributed to the chief archon or ruler of this world, these actions and words (and those of the story's other main characters) take on a significance rather different from that which they carried in their original context.

The tractate opens with the author declaring his intention to answer his reader's question about the 'reality of the authorities [ⲟⲨⲠⲞⲤⲦⲀⲤⲒⲤ

---

14. Virginia Burrus, 'The Heretical Woman as Symbol in Alexander, Athanasius, Epipha-nius, and Jerome', *HTR* 84 (1991), pp. 229–48 (232).

15. Burrus offers the example of Carol Christ. I would suggest that Pagels and Buckley, in the works cited so far in this chapter, cannot be counted completely blameless in this regard either.

16. Philip Alexander, 'Jewish Elements in Gnosticism and Magic c. CE 70–c. CE 270', in William Horbury, W.D. Davies and John Sturdy (eds), *The Cambridge History of Judaism*, iii (Cambridge: Cambridge University Press, 1999), pp. 1052–78 (1058).

17. Michael A. Williams, *Rethinking 'Gnosticism': An Argument for Dismantling a Dubious Category* (Princeton: Princeton University Press, 1996), p. 51.

ⲚⲈⲌⲞⲨⲤⲒⲀ]', the same 'authorities of the darkness' and 'of the universe' to whom 'the great apostle' referred in his letters to the Colossians and the Ephesians (86.20–27).[18] From the outset, the reader is permitted to enjoy her own superiority to these beings, as they, and in particular their chief, display their ignorance of facts of which the reader is already well aware, not least their own derivative status and the limitations of their power. The chief archon's claim that 'It is I who am God; there is none [apart from me]' (86.30–31) receives an immediate rebuttal from the voice from incorruptibility: 'You are mistaken, Samael . . . god of the blind' (87.1–4). That this is a female voice becomes clear a few lines later, when the author speaks of incorruptibility looking down at 'her image [ⲀⲠⲈⲤⲒⲚⲈ]' in the waters (87.13). Not for the last time, an authoritative female voice is shown to get the better of the hapless male archons.

After such a beginning, the reader cannot be greatly surprised when the archons' attempt to create a human being does not go entirely to plan. They make a man of sorts, 'but they could not make him arise because of their powerlessness' (88.5–6).[19] It is instead the spirit from the father that enables Adam to become a living soul (88.13–15). With these circumstances in the background, the archons' command to Adam not to eat the fruit from the tree of knowledge becomes, as Alexander recognizes, highly ironic.[20] Elaborating the scene for his readers' benefit, the author notes that 'by the father's will, they said this in such a way that he might (in fact) eat, and that Adam might [not] regard them as would a man of an exclusively material nature' (88.34–89.3). In this version of the account, it is no longer the eating of the fruit, but rather the command not to do so that is portrayed as problematic, because partaking of the fruit confers awareness and understanding. Not only are these attributes which are highly valued throughout the text as characteristic of the 'children of the light' (97.14), they are qualities in which the archons yet again show themselves to be lacking. They

---

18.   It would appear that the author of *Hyp. Arch.* takes these letters to be authentic; but it is helpful to his argument to do so. That Paul is described as 'inspired by the spirit of the father of truth' (86.20–21) may be taken as an indication that this author understands himself to be in continuity with the Pauline tradition, different though his reading of Genesis might be from those found in 1 Corinthians or the Pastorals.

19.   Williams notes that the ability to stand upright was 'a feature commonly regarded in the ancient world as distinctly human', setting people apart from animals (*Rethinking 'Gnosticism'*, p. 128). The archons' failure here is therefore a significant one.

20.   Philip S. Alexander, 'The Fall into Knowledge: The Garden of Eden/Paradise in Gnostic Literature', in Paul Morris and Deborah Sawyer (eds), *A Walk in the Garden: Biblical, Iconographical and Literary Images of Eden*, JSOTSup 136 (Sheffield: JSOT Press, 1992), pp. 91–104 (95). It is also noteworthy that the words of the original command in Gen. 2.16–17 have here been augmented with a prohibition on touching the fruit, so that they now concur exactly with the reply the woman gives to the snake when she is asked what the archon said to her (90.3–4).

understand neither the true nature of the human being whom they address, nor the effect on him that their command will in fact have.

The archons' next actions too will have unforeseen consequences. Putting Adam into a deep sleep and opening up his side, they inadvertently create the spirit-endowed woman (ⲧⲥϩⲓⲙⲉ ⲙ̄ⲡⲛⲉⲩⲙⲁⲧⲓⲕⲏ), whom Adam greets thus: 'It is you who have given me life; you will be called "Mother of the Living" ' (89.3–15). She seems to make a similarly striking impression on the archons, though their response is much less appropriate: 'they became enamoured of her . . . and pursued her', attempting to rape her (89.21–22). (Unlike 1 Timothy, it is not the serpent that is associated with seduction in this text.) Their attempts are futile, however, as she escapes their clutches by turning herself into a tree,[21] leaving before them only 'her shadowy reflection resembling herself' (89.26). Although one may, like the spirit-endowed woman, laugh at the witlessness of the archons and the ease with which they are thwarted, Karen L. King offers an interpretation of this event which shows why modern feminist interpreters may not find such a ready ally in *Hyp. Arch.* as they might hope. The woman does escape the rape, explains King, but only at the cost of withdrawal from her own body, something that might be described by a modern psychiatrist as 'a severe case of dissociation and psychic disruption'.[22]

The archons' folly becomes ever more apparent as the narrative progresses. Having tried to keep Adam firmly in the dark (the 'deep sleep' into which they put him is glossed by the author as 'Ignorance' in 89.7), they have succeeded only in furthering his enlightenment. The 'female spiritual principle [ⲧⲡⲛⲉⲩⲙⲁⲧⲓⲕⲏ]' returns in the form of the snake (89.31), who is twice designated 'the instructor [ⲡⲣⲉϥⲧⲁⲙⲟ]' (89.32; 90.5). Resulting as it

---

21.   This image of the woman turning herself into a tree is one rich in associations. First, one may be reminded of Daphne being transformed into a laurel to escape the amorous clutches of Apollo (Ovid, *Metamorphoses* 1.545–52; cited in Karen L. King, 'Ridicule and Rape, Rule and Rebellion: The Hypostasis of the Archons', in James E. Goehring *et al.* [eds], *Gnosticism and the Early Christian World: In Honor of James M. Robinson* [Sonoma, Calif.: Polebridge, 1990], pp. 3–24 [12]). Secondly, there is Pagels' interesting suggestion that the archons' failure to recognize the spirit-endowed woman's true nature mirrors the failure of the 'rulers of this world' to understand God's wisdom in 1 Cor. 2.6–8, wisdom being likened to a 'tree of life' in Prov. 3.18 ('Exegesis and Exposition of the Genesis Creation Accounts in Selected Texts from Nag Hammadi', in Charles W. Hedrick and Robert Hodgson [eds], *Nag Hammadi, Gnosticism, and Early Christianity* [Peabody, Mass.: Hendrickson, 1986], pp. 257–85 [271]). Finally, Alexander draws attention to the series of Aramaic puns which serve to connect the spiritual Eve to the tree of knowledge (understood by some early commentators to be identical to the tree of life) and to the snake ('The Fall into Knowledge', pp. 97–98).

22.   King, 'Ridicule and Rape', p. 14. While this is a valid concern for modern readers, the author of *Hyp. Arch.* was presumably not greatly interested in the question of a woman's relationship to her body, and in the world of the text itself the spirit-endowed woman's tactics are evaluated positively.

does in Adam and Eve disobeying the archons' command and eating the fruit, 'this act of spiritual instruction is simultaneously an act of insubordination', as Anne McGuire points out.[23] As I showed in Chapter 4, female teaching activity was associated with insubordination in 1 Timothy as well, and both were evaluated negatively. In *Hyp. Arch.*, however, the teaching and the resulting act of defiance are shown to have positive results, since the command that is transgressed was issued by beings unworthy of obedience. Adam and Eve eat the fruit and gain awareness, not merely that they are naked in the physical sense as in Gen. 3.7, but that 'they were naked of the spiritual element' (90.17). As the author predicted (89.1–3) and as the reader has been expecting, they attain the knowledge of their true nature which the archons would have kept from them. Once again, an authoritative female voice has thwarted the archons' plans.

Subtle adaptations of the description of the creator's actions in Gen. 3.4–5 serve to emphasize the archons' jealousy of and inferiority to the human beings they have created. When the chief archon calls out to Adam asking where he is, the author of *Hyp. Arch.* adds an explanatory note – 'for he did not understand what had happened' (90.20–21) – to help his readers draw what he believes to be the right conclusion. The archons punish the man and woman for disobeying their command, but the one who curses Eve is described as 'arrogant' (90.29), and the author construes the punishment in decidedly negative terms: 'they threw mankind into great distraction and into a life of toil, so that their mankind might be occupied by worldly affairs, and might not have the opportunity of being devoted to the holy spirit' (91.7–11). The goal which the archons failed to achieve with their original command – keeping mankind divided from his true origins – they now seek to accomplish by means of this penalty.

The first consequence of this unfavourable set of circumstances is the birth of Cain, who (as in Gen. 4.1–16) turns out to be something of a problem child, eventually killing his own brother. In *Hyp. Arch.*, this extreme unpleasantness is put down to Cain's parentage: 91.11–12 appears to suggest that he was fathered by the archons.[24] It thus seems unlikely that the author of *Hyp. Arch.* subscribes to the idea of salvation through childbearing found in 1 Tim. 2.15. However, it is not legitimate to assume that he held an entirely negative attitude toward human reproduction; Eve's daughter Norea is described as 'an assistance for *many generations* of mankind'

---

23.   Anne McGuire, 'Virginity and Subversion: Norea against the Powers in the *Hypostasis of the Archons*', in Karen L. King (ed.), *Images of the Feminine in Gnosticism* (Philadelphia: Fortress Press, 1988), pp. 239–58 (246).

24.   'Now afterwards, she bore Cain, their son [ⲡⲟⲩϣⲏⲣⲉ]'. Presumably this is the result of the archons' defilement of the carnal Eve, the 'shadowy reflection' left behind by the spirit-endowed woman, in 89.27.

(92.1), after whose birth 'mankind began to *multiply and improve*' (92.3–4; my emphasis).

Yet these consequences are attributed to the fact that Norea herself is 'the virgin whom the forces did not defile' (92.2–3). In this she differs from the carnal Eve, but resembles her true mother, the spiritual Eve; and like her Norea too gets the better of the archons and exposes their foolishness yet again. Having learned nothing from their failure with the mother, they try to seduce the daughter, only to meet with an equal lack of success. For the third time a female voice exerts its authority over them, as Norea says: 'It is you who are the rulers of the darkness; you are accursed. And you did not know my mother; instead it was your female counterpart that you knew. For I am not your descendant; rather it is from the world above that I come' (92.22–26).[25] As McGuire explains, Norea thus 'escapes the clutches of their acquisitive and domineering power by renaming them ("Rulers of Darkness"[26]) and renaming herself as one who is "from the World Above" '.[27]

On its own, however, even this Rortian piece of redescription is not enough to save Norea, and she must call on the divine for protection. At her bidding the great angel, Eleleth, comes down from the heavens, and the rulers of unrighteousness withdraw from her (92.32–93.8).[28] It is at this point that the text changes in form to a revelation dialogue, the author speaking in the first person as he presents himself as the recipient of the angel Eleleth's authoritative disclosures, perhaps even identifying himself with Norea as he does so. For readers who share the worldview of this text, Norea serves as a model, and they can understand themselves as her children: 'You, together with your offspring, are from the primeval father; from above, out of the imperishable light, their souls are come' (96.19–22). Since they have the same origin, they, like her, can overcome the archons, who may indeed be 'real', but whose reality is limited and impaired.

So what is the purpose of the gendered nature of this imagery? Repeatedly throughout *Hyp. Arch.* readers have witnessed the archons (characterized male) overcome by the power of authoritative female voices, identified with the world above. Do these feminine victories set an agenda for social

---

25. Norea's voice is not always so effective; when she asks Noah to let her on to the ark, he refuses. She does, however, have other means of exerting her will, 'and when he would not let her, she blew upon the ark and caused it to be consumed by fire' (92.14–18).

26. In fact this epithet (ⲚⲀⲢⲬⲰⲚ ⲘⲠⲔⲀⲔⲈ) is very similar to that which the author takes from Col. 1.13 at the outset of the text (ⲚⲈⲜⲞⲨⲤⲒⲀ ⲘⲠⲔⲀⲔⲈ, 86.22). The point is that it is Norea who is telling the archons what they are, rather than the other way round; their attempt to define her ('your mother Eve came to us', 92.20–21) is by contrast flawed and unsuccessful.

27. McGuire, 'Virginity and Subversion', p. 252.

28. This 'paternal intervention' is identified by King as the second pattern for female success offered by this text, the first being the division of the self discussed above ('Ridicule and Rape', p. 11).

change outside the world of the text? Karen King, for one, argues that *Hyp. Arch.* advances no such plan; on the contrary, it confirms the prevailing social constructions of gender.[29] While the female figures in the text triumph over the archons, they are themselves ultimately dependent on and subordinate to higher male authorities. Incorruptibility, whose voice exposes the folly of the chief archon's solipsistic tendencies, acts 'by the father's will' to bring the entirety into union with the light (87.22–23), while Norea is ultimately dependent on the intervention of her divine father to ensure that she remains 'the virgin whom the forces did not defile' (93.1–2).

Nevertheless, even if traditional constructions of gender do remain in place, it cannot be denied that the author of *Hyp. Arch.* deploys them in a particularly striking and effective fashion. What better way to demonstrate the foolishness and inadequacies of the rulers of this (patriarchal) world than to have them outwitted by a woman?[30] To those who might seek one, *Hyp. Arch.* offers no simple corrective to the stance adopted in the Pastoral Epistles; there are no explicit directions here for women to teach, or to free themselves from familial obligations.[31] However, by offering a very different reading of Genesis from those found in 1 Corinthians and 1 Timothy, *Hyp. Arch.* effectively undermines the scriptural justification used by Paul and by the Pastor to authorize their instructions on women's behaviour, and in doing so leads the reader to look at those instructions in a new light.

'Protest Exegesis'?

In the reading of Genesis just discussed, there are numerous elements that may well surprise readers familiar only with the 'orthodox' presentation of the story. The God of Genesis has been transformed into the villain of the piece; the serpent, by contrast, has become a positively valued revealer-figure; and the eating of the fruit no longer represents human beings' fall from grace, but rather their acquisition of divine knowledge. When centuries of ('orthodox') Christian scholarship, literature and art have made the traditional interpretation of this story feel obvious and self-evident, *Hyp. Arch.*'s version may well appear shocking, preposterous even, in comparison. Alexander, for example, levels at its author the dual charge of rebelliousness and eisegesis, arguing that he 'systematically reverses the values of the earlier text' and 'exploit[s] it as a source of words and images

---

29. King, 'Ridicule and Rape', p. 21.

30. One is reminded in this regard of the similarly effective (and entertaining) story of Judith and her triumph over Holofernes.

31. Norea's virginal status is important, but it appears to make her an exception to other people; see 91.35–92.3.

with which to clothe fundamentally alien ideas'.[32] But can such accusations be convincingly proved?

Before answering this question, it should be noted that *Hyp. Arch.* is not the only text in the dock. A similar charge has been levelled against all 'gnostic' interpretation of scripture by a number of modern scholars, for whom Kurt Rudolph may stand as representative:

> This [allegorical] method of exegesis is in Gnosis a chief means of producing one's own ideas under the cloak of the older literature – above all the sacred and the canonical. What contortionist's tricks were performed in the process we shall see at various points. We may frankly speak of a 'protest exegesis' in so far as it runs counter to the external text and the traditional interpretation.[33]

In a similar vein, Birger Pearson finds it easy to identify the basic principle of 'gnostic' hermeneutics as one of revolt.[34] However, with Williams,[35] I wish to argue that this evaluation is seriously flawed. To describe the methods and results of 'gnostic' readings as perverse or rebellious betrays a belief in the normative status of 'orthodox' interpretative practice which is itself problematic. As Wisse has pointed out, in the early Christian centuries there were no established standards for the interpretation of scripture, and therefore no grounds for saying that one side or the other has got it right.[36] More fundamentally, from a pragmatist's point of view, the apparent normativity of any hermeneutical standpoint does not mean that that standpoint is therefore 'correct', but only that it is at present familiar and conventional. As Stanley Fish puts it, 'there is no single way of reading that is correct and natural, only "ways of reading" that are the extensions of community perspectives'.[37]

The pragmatist always wishes to emphasize the importance of context, and in this regard Michael Williams offers a valuable observation. He notes that the particularly 'rebellious' components of 'gnostic' readings of Genesis, such as that found in *Hyp. Arch.*, 'tend almost always to involve

---

32.   Alexander, 'The Fall into Knowledge', pp. 100–101.

33.   Kurt Rudolph, *Gnosis: The Nature and History of Gnosticism*, tr. R. McL. Wilson (San Francisco: Harper & Row, 1987), p. 54.

34.   Birger A. Pearson, 'Some Observations on Gnostic Hermeneutics', in Wendy Doniger O'Flaherty (ed.), *The Critical Study of Sacred Texts* (Berkeley: Graduate Theological Union, 1979), pp. 243–56 (253).

35.   See Williams, *Rethinking 'Gnosticism'*, ch. 3, 'Protest Exegesis? or Hermeneutical Problem-Solving?', pp. 54–79.

36.   Frederik Wisse, 'The Use of Early Christian Literature as Evidence for Inner Diversity and Conflict', in Charles W. Hedrick and Robert Hodgson (eds), *Nag Hammadi, Gnosticism, and Early Christianity* (Peabody, Mass.: Hendrickson, 1986), pp. 177–90 (186).

37.   Stanley Fish, *Is There a Text in This Class? The Authority of Interpretive Communities* (Cambridge, Mass. and London: Harvard University Press, 1980), p. 16.

passages or elements from Jewish Scripture that were notorious "difficulties" '.[38] In other words, 'gnostic' interpretations are not merely the perverse outcome of a desire to be controversial; instead, they ought to be recognized as just some of the many serious attempts to deal with what was a set of generally recognized problems in their time. To view them in this context casts them in a rather different light. An account of just some of the issues in question is provided by the author of the *Testimony of Truth*:

> But of what sort is this God? First [he] maliciously refused Adam from eating of the tree of knowledge. And secondly he said, 'Adam, where are you?' God does not have foreknowledge; (otherwise), would he not know from the beginning? [And] afterwards he said, 'Let us cast him [out] of this place, lest he eat of the tree of life and live for ever.' Surely he has shown himself to be a malicious grudger. (47.14–30)

Williams notes that the type of concern expressed here is probably pre-Christian.[39] That 'gnostic' writers were not the only ones to be troubled by the impression the Genesis account can give of a God lacking in foresight and subject to petty jealousies is confirmed by the writings of Philo. He addresses himself to the problem of divine envy, arguing that God 'often employs ambiguous things and expressions' for the sake of communicating with human beings in a way they might understand, while insisting more than once that God could never actually be subject to such an unworthy emotion as jealousy.[40] Clement of Alexandria also insists that any apparent attribution in the scriptures of anthropomorphic traits to God must always be subject to allegorical rather than literal interpretation.[41] The contrived or awkward feel of some other attempts to deal with problematic elements of Genesis not only indicates the degree of concern with which these difficulties were generally regarded,[42] but also gives the unbiased observer cause to wonder whether, on occasion, the 'gnostic' solutions might not make more sense.

The overarching stereotype of 'protest exegesis' also gives the impression that all 'gnostic' authors interpret Genesis (and other texts) in the same way. As a survey of the Nag Hammadi texts themselves reveals, this impression is erroneous; the readings offered by the various tractates are in fact diverse,

38.   Williams, *Rethinking 'Gnosticism'*, p. 63.

39.   Williams, *Rethinking 'Gnosticism'*, p. 70.

40.   Philo, *Quaest. in Gen.* 1.55.

41.   Clement of Alexandria, *Stromateis* 5.68.3.

42.   For example, Williams draws attention to the Pseudo-Clementine writings, in which problems of the type under discussion here are treated as corruptions of the original text (*Rethinking 'Gnosticism'*, p. 66) – a strategy not dissimilar to that of the commentators who (albeit for understandable reasons) judge 1 Cor. 14.34–35 to be inauthentic, in spite of textual evidence to the contrary, as discussed in Chapter 2.

and this being the case, it is hard to see how they can count as evidence for one all-encompassing 'gnostic attitude' of rebellion. A few examples must suffice here to illustrate the point. While some texts, such as *On the Origin of the World*[43] and the *Apocryphon of John*[44], share *Hyp. Arch.*'s positive re-evaluation of the eating of the fruit, others adopt an approach to this event more akin to the traditional interpretation. Thus for example the *Tripartite Tractate* informs the reader that the serpent 'made [man] transgress the command, so that he would die. And he was expelled from every enjoyment of that place [i.e. Paradise]' (107.15–18). There is no reference here to the eating of the fruit bestowing enlightenment or any other benefits. Looking beyond the stories of creation and fall, it can be seen that 'gnostic' opinion is similarly divided on Noah. He fares badly in *Hyp. Arch.* because of his negative response to the heroine Norea,[45] but figures in a much better light in *Apoc. John*, where he serves as a messenger of the light of the fore-knowledge (29.1–4). This familiarly positive evaluation of Noah is found in the same tractate as an apparently favourable assessment of Adam and Eve's eating of the fruit. If a thoroughgoing reversal of values is not even maintained through one text, how much less likely is a consistent approach across the whole body of 'gnostic' literature?

Alexander in fact recognizes this diversity of 'gnostic' sources, but he then proceeds to construe the lack of a consistent 'gnostic' view on Genesis as evidence for their indulgence in eisegesis (a negative concept in his vocabulary).[46] He thus gives the impression of believing that had 'gnostic' interpreters only drawn their ideas from the text rather than their own diverse imaginations, they would then have been more or less in agreement on its meaning. Such a belief betrays adherence to a theory of reading rather different from the one I have adopted in this book, and in accordance with which one could insist that adjudicators of different readings cannot simply appeal to 'the text', 'since that is the very "object" in dispute'.[47]

---

43. 'Now Eve had confidence in the words of the instructor. She gazed at the tree and saw that it was beautiful and appetising, and liked it; she took some of its fruit and ate it; and she gave some also to her husband, and he too ate it. Then their intellect became open. For when they had eaten, the light of acquaintance had shone upon them' (*Orig. World* 119.6–13). That *Orig. World* should resemble *Hyp. Arch.* in this respect is not surprising, since there is a close relationship between the two texts, probably based on shared source material (Hans-Gebhard Bethke, introduction to *On the Origin of the World*, in James M. Robinson [ed.], *The Nag Hammadi Library in English* [New York: HarperCollins, 1990], p. 171).

44. In *Apoc. John* 22.9, the Saviour asserts that it was he who brought it about that Adam and Eve ate the fruit. While the actual eating is thus evaluated positively, in this text the serpent's role in events is not (22.12–15).

45. See n. 25 above.

46. Alexander, 'The Fall into Knowledge', p. 100.

47. The Bible and Culture Collective, *The Postmodern Bible* (New Haven and London: Yale University Press, 1995), p. 55.

Meaning is not some deposit in the text that interpreters must attempt to mine; it rather arises out of an active engagement between reader and text, in which the influence of the reader's own point of view and particular aims is inescapable. Recent experiments in autobiographical biblical criticism have made this particularly clear; in fact, it is one of the express aims of this practice 'to raise personal voices in biblical studies precisely so that we all might be more aware of how we can bring critical understanding to bear upon the ordinariness and interestedness of all our readings'.[48] Perhaps this means that every interpretation, wittingly or otherwise, is an act of eisegesis. If this is so, then the term cannot simply be used to label the products of 'gnostic' hermeneutical enterprises; it applies with equal force to 'orthodox', and indeed modern, interpretations as well.

Male and Female in the Gospel of Thomas

In 1 Cor. 11.2–16, Paul instructed women prophesying in the assembly to cover their heads with a veil, the symbol of submission, so as to maintain the divinely ordained hierarchical relationship between men and women. The attitude to this relationship taken by the *Gospel of Thomas* appears to be in sharp contrast to that of Paul; here, the reader finds Jesus teaching his disciples to 'make the male and the female one and the same, so that the male not be male nor the female female' (logion 22), and even avowing that 'every woman who will make herself male will enter the kingdom of heaven' (logion 114). Certainly in the popular imagination *Gos. Thom.* has something of a reputation as a radical text with the potential to shake the establishment to its foundations;[49] it is necessary to ask, however, whether (at least as far as its treatment of gender is concerned) this reputation is deserved.

Gilles Quispel correctly points out that the way in which *Gos. Thom.* is categorized – whether that be as 'gnostic', 'encratite', or something else entirely – has an effect on how it is translated and read.[50] As Richard

---

48. Jeffrey L. Staley, 'What is Critical about Autobiographical (Biblical) Criticism?', in Ingrid Rosa Kitzberger (ed.), *Autobiographical Biblical Criticism: Between Text and Self* (Leiden: Deo, 2002), pp. 12–33 (19–20).

49. For example, the plot of the recent film *Stigmata* (1999), directed by Rupert Wainwright, centres on the Vatican's suppression of an ancient gospel, supposedly written by Jesus himself, and clearly based on *Gos. Thom.* (the line 'Split a piece of wood, and I am there. Lift up the stone, and you will find me there' [logion 77] recurs throughout the film). This document appears to represent such a danger to traditional church authority that it must be kept secret at all costs.

50. Gilles Quispel, 'The *Gospel of Thomas* Revisited', in Bernard Barc (ed.), *Colloque Internationale sur les Textes de Nag Hammadi*, Bibliothèque Copte de Nag Hammadi Études 1 (Québec: Les Presses de l'Université Laval/Louvain: Editions Peeters, 1981), pp. 218–66 (221).

Valantasis notes, the Nag Hammadi texts are 'very frequently translated by modern authors so as to make [them] sound exotic and peculiar',[51] due primarily to these translators' conceptions of 'gnosticism'. This question of categorization is itself subject to the influences of prejudices and presuppositions, as Quispel's own attempt to answer it makes plain. Insisting that 'sound scholarship' vindicates both 'the trustworthiness of our [*sic*] gospels and . . . the value of Thomas',[52] he rejects categorizations of *Gos. Thom.* either as some kind of antecedent to Q (since this would compromise the priority of the canonical gospels), or as 'gnostic' (since that designation tends to be deployed in a pejorative fashion and would devalue *Gos. Thom.*).[53] Instead, he declares the tractate to be the work of an author who was 'an encratite, rejecting women, wine and meat, and therefore taught that only bachelors could go to heaven'.[54] That this decision represents entirely 'sound scholarship', however, is called into question by Stevan Davies, who points out the unlikelihood of any encratite subscribing to a view such as that expressed in logion 14: 'If you fast you will bring sin upon yourselves.'[55] While some scholars do find in *Gos. Thom.* an attitude of sexual renunciation,[56] Jorunn Jacobsen Buckley disputes this as well, asserting instead that while the text 'deplores the division into genders, it does not repudiate sexuality as such'.[57]

Davies would thus appear to be correct when he argues that '[i]t is possible to read a negative view of sexuality into Thomas but the question then is of the degree of encratite orientation of the person doing the reading'.[58] One is reminded once again of Fish's observation that evidence 'is always a function of what it is to be evidence for';[59] in other words, the answers that a reader finds in a text depend very much upon the questions that she is asking. As for the question of whether *Gos. Thom.* is a 'gnostic' text, Davies explains very effectively how 'gnostic' traits too can be found in the tractate

51. Richard Valantasis, *The Gospel of Thomas* (London and New York: Routledge, 1997), p. xii.

52. Quispel, 'The *Gospel of Thomas* Revisited', p. 232.

53. Quispel, 'The *Gospel of Thomas* Revisited', p. 220.

54. Quispel, 'The *Gospel of Thomas* Revisited', p. 234.

55. Stevan L. Davies, *The Gospel of Thomas and Christian Wisdom* (New York: Seabury Press, 1983), p. 21.

56. Marvin W. Meyer ('Making Mary Male: The Categories "Male" and "Female" in the Gospel of Thomas', *NTS* 31 [1985], pp. 554–70) speaks of *Gos. Thom.*'s 'generally ascetic, world-renouncing message' (554), while A.F.J. Klijn ('The "Single One" in the Gospel of Thomas', *JBL* 81 [1962], pp. 271–78) concludes that 'the preaching of "oneness" results in rejecting marriage' (273).

57. Jorunn Jacobsen Buckley, *Female Fault and Fulfilment in Gnosticism* (Chapel Hill, NC and London: University of North Carolina Press, 1986), p. 134.

58. Davies, *The Gospel of Thomas and Christian Wisdom*, p. 21.

59. Fish, *Is There a Text in This Class?*, p. 272.

if those are what the reader is looking for – despite the fact that, in Davies' own view, 'for the most part Thomas is not gnostic at all'.[60] It is not my goal here to come down in favour of one or other of these traditional designations of *Gos. Thom.*; I only wish to draw attention to the debate, so as to bring into the open the various presuppositions that may influence different interpreters' readings of the text. Valantasis also chooses to set aside the familiar ways of categorizing this tractate, and instead explores the question of how 'these sayings work at constructing a new and alternative subjectivity'[61] in their readers. I propose to adopt a similar approach here and ask how logia 22 and 114 might contribute to this overall purpose of the text.

In fact, according to Valantasis, '[m]ore than any other saying, Saying 22 most specifically constructs the new subjectivity promulgated by this Gospel'.[62] The disciples have asked Jesus how they will enter the kingdom, and he explains to them:

> When you make the two one, and when you make the inside like the outside and the outside like the inside, and the above like the below, and when you make the male and the female one and the same [ⲙ̄ⲫⲟⲟⲩⲧ ⲙ̄ⲛ ⲧⲥⲓⲙⲉ ⲙ̄ⲡⲓⲟⲩⲁ], so that the male not be male nor the female female; and you fashion eyes in place of an eye, and a hand in place of a hand, and a foot in place of a foot, and a likeness in place of a likeness; then will you enter [the kingdom].

The restoration of a singular and unified self overcomes the fundamental problem of division referred to earlier in the text, in logion 11: 'On the day when you were one you became two. But when you become two, what will you do?' But what implications does this have for the categories of male and female? As Buckley notes, there appear to be three different types of change in view in logion 22. The inside is to be made like (ⲛ̄ⲟⲉ) the outside, and vice versa; this, according to Buckley, does not imply full identification, but rather that the two entities become interchangeable.[63] Meanwhile, new body parts are to be fashioned in place of (ⲉⲡⲙⲁ) the old as if, as Valantasis explains, the believer's body were that of a baby, growing up in a different way and being nurtured by a different parent.[64]

In one type of change, then, the opposed terms continue to co-exist in a newly configured relationship; in another, one term (the new eye, hand and foot) supersedes and negates the other (the old eye, and so on). Does one of these models provide a fit analogy for the fate of male and female, or does this third pairing follow yet another pattern? Meyer suggests that it might,

---

60. Davies, *The Gospel of Thomas and Christian Wisdom*, p. 27.
61. Valantasis, *The Gospel of Thomas*, p. 12.
62. Valantasis, *The Gospel of Thomas*, p. 96.
63. Buckley, *Female Fault*, p. 90.
64. Valantasis, *The Gospel of Thomas*, p. 95.

namely that of the abolition of both the opposed terms: becoming a 'single one' takes place 'by means of the mutual elimination of sexual character-istics rather than the hermaphroditic manifestation of complete sexual fea-tures'.[65] Valantasis' thinking may be said to follow similar lines, since although in his view 'the new person . . . creates a "single one" from the male and the female', this does not produce some kind of hermaphrodite being, but rather 'destroys the categories male and female so that they no longer function as valid distinctions'.[66] Yet plausible though these positions may appear in relation to logion 22, the words of logion 114 appear to cast a rather different light on the situation. I therefore propose to suspend judge-ment on the question of the relationship of male and female in *Gos. Thom.* until I have examined the contents of this most well-known of its sayings.

Logion 114 certainly does not give the initial impression that male and female are 'one and the same'. It begins with the words of Simon Peter: 'Let Mary leave us, for women are not worthy of life.' While Jesus defends the right of Mary, and of all women, to be included in salvation, he does so in a way which leaves Simon Peter's low opinion of femininity unchallenged: 'I myself shall lead her in order to make her male [ⲚϨⲞⲞⲨⲦ], so that she too may become a living spirit resembling you males. For every woman who will make herself male will enter the kingdom of heaven.' The relationship between the passive and active forms of the transformation need not trouble the reader unduly. A similar pairing can be found in *Ex. Soul* where, a few lines after referring to the womb of the soul being turned inward by the father (131.19–21), the author speaks of the same organ turning itself inward (131.28). In both texts, the language used serves to indicate the mutual responsibility of the one doing the saving and the one being saved.[67] Just as the father responds to the soul's repentance and brings about in her a change she could not have accomplished by herself, so Jesus will 'make male' any woman who is first prepared to follow him. As Antti Marjanen points out, both active and passive versions 'emphasize the transformation of a woman';[68] whoever is said to take the active role in the process, the final outcome is the same.

What the process of being 'made male' might actually mean requires some unpacking. Marjanen offers three possible explanations, of which I propose to examine the first two in greater depth: concrete male imperson-ation; restoration of the primal androgyne; and a movement from the 'feminine' physical, earthly arena to the 'masculine' spiritual, heavenly

65. Meyer, 'Making Mary Male', p. 560.

66. Valantasis, *The Gospel of Thomas*, p. 96.

67. Buckley, *Female Fault*, p. 102.

68. Antti Marjanen, *The Woman Jesus Loved: Mary Magdalene in the Nag Hammadi Library and Related Documents*, Nag Hammadi and Manichean Studies 40 (Leiden: E.J. Brill, 1996), p. 47.

sphere.[69] Examples of the first of these can be found in the Apocryphal Acts, perhaps most famously in the person of Thecla. Having 'listened day and night to the discourse of virginity, as proclaimed by Paul', this formerly respectable young woman causes consternation to her mother and distress to her fiancé by breaking off her engagement and devoting herself to the apostle. Her actions are perceived to be so socially disruptive that she is sentenced to death, but she escapes execution by miraculous means, and goes to Paul and declares, 'I will cut my hair off and follow you wherever you go.' When she has once again evaded death, she baptizes herself, declares her belief in God, and is hailed by all the women in the city. The reader's last glimpse of this audacious heroine sees her 'wearing a mantle that she had altered so as to make a man's cloak', and being commissioned by Paul to 'go, and teach the word of God', a task which she fulfils with great success.

This story is certainly notable for creating a very different image of Paul from that constructed by the Pastoral Epistles;[70] but does the phenomenon it describes offer an adequate explanation of *Gos. Thom.*'s concept of being 'made male'? Buckley, for one, reckons not, since this kind of male imper-sonation is not the same as the full transformation which *Gos. Thom.* seems to require.[71] To this one might add that the cutting of her hair and the fashioning of the man's cloak are both actions Thecla performs for herself; while God does intervene to save her from death, there is no hint in this story of the divine involvement in being 'made male' that is so crucial in *Gos. Thom.* What, then, of alternative understandings of this phrase?

The second interpretation of being 'made male' to which Marjanen refers is that of the restoration of the primal androgyne. While the modern reader may initially struggle with the idea that making a female male equates to androgyny (it does, after all, seem a little one-sided), placed in context the

---

69. Marjanen, *The Woman Jesus Loved*, p. 48. This final explanation is developed by Meyer, 'Making Mary Male', pp. 565–66. These associations of femininity and masculinity are in fact at work to a large extent in the idea of androgyny, as I hope to show in the ensuing discussion. Meyer's argument that the 'gnostics' understood all human beings to be involved in 'femaleness' does not cancel out the negative implications for actual women of the use of feminine imagery to describe an undesirable state of being.

70. As shown in Chapter 4, this image of the apostle was sufficiently distasteful to Tertul-lian that he denounced as a forgery the work that promulgated it (*De Bap.* 17). Dennis Ronald MacDonald has suggested that the Pastorals were in fact written for the express purpose of counteracting the image of Paul found in just such stories as these, told and passed on by women (*The Legend and the Apostle: The Battle for Paul in Story and Canon* [Philadelphia: Westminster Press, 1983], p. 14). As my arguments in Chapter 4 demonstrate, however, there were sufficient reasons for the Pastor to attempt to direct female behaviour as he did without it being necessary for the reader to assume that he was familiar with the Apocryphal Acts or the traditions underlying them.

71. Buckley, *Female Fault*, p. 86.

suggestion is not so odd. As shown in Chapter 2, 'the androgyne myth is not antiquity's answer to androcentrism; it is but one manifestation of it'.[72] Elizabeth Castelli therefore explains that movement between the genders cannot be reciprocal; the point is specifically for the female to become male, and not vice versa.[73] She illustrates her argument from Philo's allegorical interpretation of Noah and his family's entry to and exit from the ark:

> [W]hen the purification is completed ... then it becomes the man to collect his scattered forces together, not in order that masculine counsels may be rendered effeminate by softness, but that the female race, that is to say, the outward senses, may clothe themselves with the vigour of the male ... so that, from this time forth they may cherish, in all things, sentiments of wisdom, and honour, and justice, and courage, and, in one word, honour.[74]

A more succinct assertion elsewhere shows why this must be the case: 'as the male always has the precedence, the female falls short, and is inferior in rank'.[75]

According to the ancient understanding of androgyny, then, one might say that the problem to be overcome was not so much the existence of two genders as it was the existence of the feminine gender in particular. If logion 114 was written with this concept in mind, then Mary's (or any woman's) being 'made male' might be understood as a reinstatement of the androgynous state of the first human, Adam, who 'was neither gender but consisted of both male and female. . . . This *Man* appeared in the male form as Adam with woman concealed inside of him.'[76] So, as Buckley argues, the term 'male' (ϩⲟⲟⲩⲧ) in *Gos. Thom.* has a dual significance: 'while referring to the male as opposed to female, *at the same time* [it] indicates the male as a singular, autonomous term', the unified being which will become a living spirit.[77] In this way, then, the notion of being 'made male' – despite, or even because of, its one-sided approach – can be understood to be consistent with the idea of male and female becoming 'one and the same' encountered in logion 22. This works best if one construes this becoming 'one and the same' not as the abolition of both terms envisaged by Meyer and Valantasis,

---

72.   D.R. MacDonald, *There Is No Male and Female: The Fate of a Dominical Saying in Paul and Gnosticism*, HDR 20 (Philadelphia: Fortress Press, 1987), p. 101.

73.   Elizabeth Castelli, ' "I Will Make Mary Male": Pieties of the Body and Gender Transformation of Christian Women in Late Antiquity', in Julia Epstein and Kristina Straub (eds), *Body Guards: The Cultural Politics of Gender Ambiguity* (New York and London: Routledge, 1991), pp. 29–49 (32).

74.   Philo, *Quaest. in Gen.* 2.49; cited in Castelli, ' "I Will Make Mary Male" ', p. 32.

75.   Philo, *Fug.* 51.

76.   April D. De Conick, *Seek to See Him: Ascent and Vision Mysticism in the Gospel of Thomas*, Supplements to *VC* 33 (Leiden: Brill, 1996), p. 19; her emphasis.

77.   Buckley, *Female Fault*, p. 94; her emphasis.

but rather as the superseding and negating of one term by the other (that is to say, of the female by the male), thus following a similar pattern of change to that of the new eye, hand and foot being fashioned 'in place of' the old.

This theory that logion 114 has the restoration of the primal androgyne in mind would be even more convincing if the author of the saying had used ⲣⲱⲙⲉ (the Coptic term carrying the dual sense of man and generic human being) here instead of ϩⲟⲟⲩⲧ (meaning male only).[78] It is the former word that is used of Adam before the creation of Eve in *Hyp. Arch.* 88.12 and 15; similarly, both the Hebrew and Greek texts of Genesis employ the equivalent generic terms (אָדָם and ἄνθρωπος respectively) in Gen. 2.15 and the following verses when Adam is alone, only introducing the specifically male terms (אִישׁ and ἀνήρ) in 2.24 once the woman has been formed from his rib, producing two kinds of human beings rather than one. That notwithstanding, it is still neither surprising nor implausible to find expressed in *Gos. Thom.* 114 a perception that has persisted in Western thought till modern times, when Simone de Beauvoir encapsulated it in these words: 'She [woman] is defined and differentiated with reference to man and not he with reference to her; she is the incidental, the inessential as opposed to the essential. He is the Subject, he is the Absolute – she is the Other.'[79]

Yet just as the insights of postmodern thought show how this perception can be overturned,[80] so also the idea of being made male can itself, contrary to first impressions, have a destabilizing effect on traditional categories. Castelli explains the complexities of the situation well: ' "Becoming male" marks . . . the transcendence of gendered differences, but it does so only by reinscribing the traditional gender hierarchies of male over female, masculine over feminine; the possibility that women can "become male", paradoxically however, also reveals the tenuousness and malleability of the naturalized categories of male and female.'[81] While the idea that women must become male and not the other way round reinforces traditional notions of male superiority, the suggestion that women can somehow change their gender identity in this way actually undermines the conventional divisions. Thus, as Castelli goes on to observe, texts like *Gos. Thom.* 114 'do not simply rearticulate the hegemonic gendered order, nor do

78.   As in fact is the case in the *Gospel of Mary*, where male and female disciples alike are said to have been made ⲣⲱⲙⲉ rather than ϩⲟⲟⲩⲧ (9.20, 18.16), as Marjanen observes (*The Woman Jesus Loved*, p. 51).

79.   Simone de Beauvoir, *The Second Sex*, ed. and tr. H.M. Parshley (London: Picador, 1988), p. 16.

80.   See n. 8 in Chapter 5 above on the deconstruction of opposed pairs of terms like 'male' and 'female'.

81.   Castelli, ' "I Will Make Mary Male" ', p. 33.

they simply deconstruct it; rather, they stretch its boundaries and, if only for a moment, call it into question'.[82]

Mary Magdalene in the Gospel of Thomas *and Other 'Gnostic' Texts*

The cautionary phrase 'if only for a moment' should give the reader pause for thought; *Gos. Thom.* may not provide a straightforward endorsement of the status quo, but it cannot on those grounds be hailed as an ally of the feminist cause without further questions being asked. One of those questions pertains to Mary, the catalyst for Simon Peter and Jesus' interchange in logion 114. How is she portrayed in *Gos. Thom.* and other texts, and what clues (if any) might this portrayal provide to the author's attitude to women?

Of the six named members of Jesus' circle in *Gos. Thom.*, two are women: one is Salome, the other Mary Magdalene.[83] As Marjanen observes, both of them are depicted as ones who understand, but not quite enough.[84] Thus in logion 21, the reader finds Mary present in the group of Jesus' followers and able to address questions to him, but still needing to know 'Whom are your disciples like?' Mary features more prominently and even more favourably in the *Dialogue of the Saviour*,[85] where she, along with Judas and Matthew, is privy to a special revelation from the Son of Man (134.24–136.5), and where she is described not as a person still in need of enlightenment, but rather as 'a woman who had understood completely' (139.12–13). Yet as with *Gos. Thom.*, in this tractate too the important role ascribed to Mary Magdalene is found juxtaposed to some strikingly negative uses of feminine imagery. While logion 114 records Simon Peter's assertion that 'women are

---

82.　Castelli, ' "I Will Make Mary Male" ', p. 33.

83.　Of course, as the canonical gospels make plain, there was more than one Mary in Jesus' life. However, Marjanen justifies his identification of the one in *Gos. Thom.* as Mary Magdalene by pointing out that she is the only Mary who appears in 'gnostic' literature in such a polemic context as that found in logion 114: the tension between her and Simon Peter that is in evidence in this saying is also a prominent theme in the *Gospel of Mary*, as I shall presently show. Marjanen also notes that the form of the name used to refer to Mary Magdalene (ⲘⲀⲢⲒⲀⲘ) is different from that employed to designate Jesus' mother (ⲘⲀⲢⲒⲀ) (Marjanen, *The Woman Jesus Loved*, p. 39).

84.　Antti Marjanen, 'Women Disciples in the *Gospel of Thomas*', in Risto Uro (ed.), *Thomas at the Crossroads: Essays on the Gospel of Thomas* (Edinburgh: T&T Clark, 1998), pp. 89–106 (92). One should add that this description applies equally well to most of the male disciples in the tractate, with the exception of Thomas, who is the recipient of special revelation (logion 13).

85.　A tractate which Quispel suggests has strong links with *Gos. Thom.*, on the basis of the use of the term ⲘⲟⲛⲀⲭⲟⲥ in both these texts and nowhere else in 'gnostic' works ('The *Gospel of Thomas* Revisited', p. 223).

not worthy of life' (an assertion left uncontradicted by Jesus, even though he mitigates its consequences), *Dial. Sav.* 144.18–20 urges its readers to ' "pray in the place where there is [no woman]" . . . meaning, "Destroy the works of womanhood" '. The prominent position accorded to one named woman, it would seem, does little to reverse the conventionally negative attitude to femininity in general that allows such statements as these to be made.

The other main element of *Gos. Thom.*'s portrayal of Mary – the tension between her and Simon Peter – is similarly found in a more expansive form in another 'gnostic' text: the *Gospel of Mary*. Here, when the disciples are grieving and confused in the wake of Jesus' departure, Mary acts as their leader, telling them, 'Do not weep and not grieve or be irresolute, for his grace will be entirely with you and will protect you' (9.14–18). At first Peter appears to accept this situation, acknowledging that Jesus loved her 'more than the rest of women', and asking her to 'tell us the words of the Saviour which you remember – which you know [but] we do not, nor have we heard them' (10.3–6). However, when she has done so, Andrew asserts his disbelief that the Saviour could have uttered the 'strange ideas' (17.15) Mary has just shared with them, and Peter agrees, directing his scepticism explicitly towards Mary's gender: 'Did he really speak with a woman without our knowledge (and) not openly? Are we to turn about and all listen to her? Did he prefer her to us?' (17.18–22) The reader familiar with present-day feminine stereotypes will not be surprised to find that on hearing this, Mary begins to cry. Levi, however, comes to her defence and issues to Peter an apparently unanswerable challenge: 'if the Saviour made her worthy, who are you to reject her?' (18.10–12)

In this text at least, it is almost certain that there is more at stake in the rivalry between Peter and Mary than the right of women to teach or assume leadership positions. Mary figures in this gospel that bears her name not just as a woman, but as disciple and teacher *par excellence*. Her gender provides Peter with an easy target, but the main thrust of his attack is directed at the reliability of her words. Peter's response to Mary's revelation is thus analogous to 'orthodox' writers' responses to claims that others outside their number might be able to interpret the scriptures or receive authoritative revelations from God; Irenaeus, for example, dismisses such others just as readily as Peter dismisses Mary, asserting that '[t]hese men falsify the oracles of God, and prove themselves evil interpreters of the good word of revelation'.[86]

Might Peter similarly represent the attitudes of the 'orthodox' church in *Gos. Thom.*? If he does, it is in a rather different way, since his negative attitude to Mary Magdalene in this text does appear to be provoked primarily by her gender rather than by any words she has uttered. It is possible,

---

86. Irenaeus, *Adv. Haer.* 1, preface.

therefore, that Peter does here represent restrictive 'orthodox' attitudes to women from which the author of this tractate wishes to distance himself.[87] Nevertheless, as Marjanen points out, '[a]lthough advocating Mary's and all women's right to attain salvation in terms equal to their male colleagues within the circle of disciples and the kingdom, Jesus [in logion 114] does it by using a language which devalues women'.[88] Mary may be offered the chance to become a disciple in the full Thomasine sense of the word (logion 21), but she cannot do so as a woman; instead, she must 'become male'. The foundations laid in Paul's first letter to the Corinthians for a division between conventional female gender roles and the pursuit of religious leadership have ultimately been left undisturbed, even if *Gos. Thom.*, unlike the Pastorals, appears to encourage women to prioritize the latter over the former.

87. Though Marjanen suggests that Peter may be better understood here as representing a particular kind of ascetic viewpoint where male celibates see women as a threat ('Women Disciples', p. 105).

88. Marjanen, *The Woman Jesus Loved*, p. 51.

Conclusion

REDESCRIBING PAUL

> Reading texts is a matter of reading them in the light of other texts,
> people, obsessions, bits of information, or what have you, and then seeing
> what happens.
>
> Richard Rorty, *Philosophy and Social Hope*

At the end of this particular exercise in reading texts, it is appropriate to
look back and see what has in fact happened – and not happened. In Part I,
I attempted to show that Paul in 1 Corinthians promotes the teaching on
women and marriage that is most helpful to him in furthering his aims in his
particular context. These aims are both personal – he is always anxious to
secure his own authority over his readers – and more widely concerned with
the community as a whole – he wishes to secure its boundaries and establish
a firm and distinctive group identity, even if this is to be at the cost of the
individual aspirations of some of its (female) members. In trying to balance
what he sees as best for different groups within his community, he at times
appears to be promoting two contradictory behaviours at the same time,
and thus (unwittingly) provides a wealth of inspiration for the many interpreters who come after him, with all their diverse objectives and concerns.

Paul's interest in exercising authority over others was something that was
shared by the deutero-Pauline authors who write in his name. Writing for a
new situation after the apostle's death, however, their aims and purposes
were necessarily different from his, and so they adapt the Pauline teachings
on women and marriage to meet new goals, necessarily losing much of the
apostle's ambiguity in the process. In the case of both these areas of concern, there are indications in the deutero-Pauline texts that other appropriations of Paul were in fact current; there would seem to be yet further needs
and circumstances he was being called upon to address. Already, the attentive reader can find clues that, however much they may have wanted to, the
deutero-Pauline authors do not have the final word on Paul.

Such a suspicion has been shown to be more than confirmed when the
reader turns to the Nag Hammadi library. Although none of the 'gnostic'
texts studied here claim to be written by Paul himself, their interest in and
regard for him is made apparent more than once (*Hyp. Arch.* 86.21–22; *Ex.
Soul* 131.2–13). They do not offer the interpreter simple or direct correctives

to the positions on women and marriage taken by the canonical texts, but a serious engagement with them does cause her to look again at the more familiar writings with a new perspective. For example, the interpretation of Genesis offered by *Hyp. Arch.*, so different from that of Paul or the Pastor, serves to undermine the apparently solid scriptural foundation for 1 Corinthians' and 1 Timothy's teaching on women. Or again, by developing the use of marriage as an image of salvation to the extent that it does and demonstrating the complexities involved in relating such an image to social reality, *Gos. Phil.* calls into question the straightforward and unproblematic endorsement of marriage found in the letter to the Ephesians. The sophistication of the reflections of this tractate in particular eloquently debunks the traditional stereotype of 'gnostic' reading as perverse protest exegesis.

However – as *Gos. Thom.*'s deployment of feminine imagery perhaps makes especially clear – these are all texts of their time and place, a time and place that is very different from that of modern readers. As already noted, none of them provides a simple or easy corrective to what might be deemed (by feminist readers not least) the undesirable aspects of the canonical texts. However, the thoroughgoing critique of the category of 'gnosticism' mounted by Michael Williams does not leave these canonical texts untouched. 'Orthodoxy' and 'heresy' are two sides of the same coin: if the latter category is dismantled, then the former must fall down with it. The New Testament texts have a history – they have played a formative role in western civilization – and the difficulties they present must still be grappled with; but the texts of the Nag Hammadi library, freed from the distorting constraints of the category 'gnosticism' as it is traditionally understood, can help readers to see them in a radically new light; the canonical texts' position of privilege is no longer beyond question.

Stanley Fish has observed that in the 'opposition between the merely historical and the transcendent one finds the essence of canonicity'.[1] By drawing attention to the importance of context, and to the vital role played by the presuppositions and vested interests of individuals and communities in both the writing and reading of texts – in short, by focusing on the unavoidable contingency of all human endeavours – it is my hope that this project may make some contribution to the dilution of this essence. The attainment of this goal can only be further advanced by continuing to read early Christian documents alongside and in relation to all the diverse range of other texts, ancient and modern, sacred and profane, that have arisen in the culture the canon has helped to shape.

---

1. Stanley Fish, *The Trouble with Principle* (Cambridge, Mass. and London: Harvard University Press, 1999), p. 47.

BIBLIOGRAPHY

Abrams, M.H., 'How To Do Things with Texts', *Partisan Review* 46 (1979), pp. 566–88.

Alexander, Loveday, ' "Better to Marry than to Burn": St. Paul and the Greek Novel', in Ronald F. Hock, J. Bradley Chance and Judith Perkins (eds), *Ancient Fiction and Early Christian Narrative*, SBL Symposium Series 6 (Atlanta: Scholars Press, 1998), pp. 235–56.

Alexander, Philip S., 'The Fall into Knowledge: The Garden of Eden/Paradise in Gnostic Literature', in Paul Morris and Deborah Sawyer (eds), *A Walk in the Garden: Biblical, Iconographical and Literary Images of Eden*, JSOTSup 136 (Sheffield: JSOT Press, 1992), pp. 91–104.

—'Jewish Elements in Gnosticism and Magic c. CE 70–c. CE 270', in William Horbury, W.D. Davies and John Sturdy (eds), *The Cambridge History of Judaism*, iii (Cambridge: Cambridge University Press, 1999), pp. 1052–78.

Anderson, Janice Capel, and Staley, Jeffrey L. (eds), *Taking it Personally: Autobiographical Biblical Criticism*, *Semeia* 72 (Missoula, Mont.: Scholars Press, 1995).

Austin, J.L., *How To Do Things with Words*, ed. J.O. Urmson and Marina Sbisà (Oxford: Clarendon Press, 1975).

Balch, David L., '1 Cor. 7.32–35 and Stoic Debates about Marriage, Anxiety, and Distraction', *JBL* 102 (1983), pp. 429–39.

Barrett, C.K., *A Commentary on the First Epistle to the Corinthians* (London: A. & C. Black, 1968).

—'Pauline Controversies in the Post-Pauline Period', *NTS* 20 (1973/74), pp. 229–45.

Barth, Markus, *Colossians*, tr. Astrid B. Beck, AB 34B (New York: Doubleday, 1994).

—*Ephesians*, AB 34A (Garden City, NY: Doubleday, 1974).

Barthes, Roland, 'The Death of the Author', in Lodge (ed.), *Modern Criticism and Theory: A Reader*, pp. 167–72.

Barton, Stephen G., 'Paul's Sense of Place: An Anthropological Approach to Community Formation in Corinth', *NTS* 32 (1986), pp. 225–46.

Bassler, Jouette M., *1 Timothy, 2 Timothy, Titus* (Nashville: Abingdon, 1996).

—'The Widows' Tale: A Fresh Look at 1 Tim. 5.3–16', *JBL* 103 (1984), pp. 23–41.

Bauer, Walter, *Orthodoxy and Heresy in Earliest Christianity* (London: SCM Press, 1972 [1934]).

de Beauvoir, Simone, *The Second Sex*, ed. and tr. H.M. Parshley (London: Picador, 1988).

BeDuhn, Jason David, ' "Because of the Angels": Unveiling Paul's Anthropology in 1 Corinthians 11', *JBL* 118 (1999), pp. 295–320.

Beker, J. Christiaan, *Heirs of Paul: Paul's Legacy in the New Testament and in the Church Today* (Edinburgh: T&T Clark, 1992).

Benko, Stephen, 'The Libertine Gnostic Sect of the Phibionites according to Epiphanius', *VC* 21 (1967), pp. 103–19.

Best, Ernest, *Ephesians*, New Testament Guides (Sheffield: JSOT Press, 1993).

The Bible and Culture Collective, *The Postmodern Bible* (New Haven and London: Yale University Press, 1995).

Blass, F., and Debrunner, A., *A Greek Grammar of the New Testament and Other Early Christian Literature*, tr. and revd Robert W. Funk (Cambridge: Cambridge University Press/Chicago: University of Chicago Press, 1961).

de Boer, Martinus C., 'Images of Paul in the Post-Apostolic Period', *CBQ* 42 (1980), pp. 359–80.

Booth, Wayne C., *The Company We Keep: An Ethics of Fiction* (Berkeley and London: University of California Press, 1988).

Boyarin, Daniel, *A Radical Jew: Paul and the Politics of Identity* (Berkeley: University of California Press, 1994).

Brett, Mark G., 'Four or Five Things To Do With Texts: A Taxonomy of Interpretative Interests', in Clines, Fowl and Porter (eds), *The Bible in Three Dimensions*, pp. 357–77.

Brooke, George J., 'Between Qumran and Corinth: Embroidered Allusions to Women's Authority', in James R. Davila (ed.), *The Dead Sea Scrolls as Background to Postbiblical Judaism and Early Christianity*, Studies on the Texts of the Desert of Judah 46 (Leiden and Boston: Brill, 2003), pp. 157–76.

Brooten, Bernadette J., 'Response to "Corinthian Veils and Gnostic Androgynes" by Dennis Ronald MacDonald', in King (ed.), *Images of the Feminine in Gnosticism*, pp. 293–96.

Brown, Peter, *The Body and Society: Men, Women and Sexual Renunication in Early Christianity* (London: Faber & Faber, 1988).

Brown, Schuyler, ' "Begotten, Not Created": The Gnostic Use of Language in Jungian Perspective', in Robert Segal (ed.), *The Allure of Gnosticism: The Gnostic Experience in Jungian Psychology and Contemporary Culture* (Chicago and La Salle, Ill.: Open Court, 1995), pp. 70–83.

Bruce, F.F., *1 and 2 Corinthians*, NCB (London: Oliphants, 1971).

Buckley, Jorunn Jacobsen, 'Conceptual Models and Polemical Issues in the Gospel of Philip', in *ANRW* II.25.5 (1988), pp. 4167–94.

—'A Cult-Mystery in *The Gospel of Philip*', *JBL* 99 (1980), pp. 569–81.

—*Female Fault and Fulfilment in Gnosticism* (Chapel Hill, NC and London: University of North Carolina Press, 1986).

—' "The Holy Spirit is a Double Name": Holy Spirit, Mary, and Sophia in the *Gospel of Philip*', in King (ed.), *Images of the Feminine in Gnosticism*, pp. 211–27.

—'Libertines or Not: Fruit, Bread, Semen and other Bodily Fluids in Gnosticism', *JECS* 2 (1994), pp. 15–31.

Burrus, Virginia, 'The Heretical Woman as Symbol in Alexander, Athanasius, Epiphanius, and Jerome', *HTR* 84 (1991), pp. 229–48.

Caputo, John D., *More Radical Hermeneutics: On Not Knowing Who We Are* (Bloomington and Indianapolis: Indiana University Press, 2000).

Castelli, Elizabeth, *Imitating Paul: A Discourse of Power* (Westminster/John Knox Press, 1991).

—' "I Will Make Mary Male": Pieties of the Body and Gender Transformation of Christian Women in Late Antiquity', in Julia Epstein and Kristina Straub (eds), *Body Guards: The Cultural Politics of Gender Ambiguity* (New York and London: Routledge, 1991), pp. 29–49.

—'Paul on Women and Gender', in Kraemer and D'Angelo (eds), *Women and Christian Origins*, pp. 221–35.

Chadwick, Henry, 'The Domestication of Gnosis', in Bentley Layton (ed.), *The Rediscovery of Gnosticism*, i: *The School of Valentinus* (Leiden: E.J. Brill, 1981), pp. 3–16.

Clines, David J.A., Fowl, Stephen E., and Porter, Stanley E. (eds), *The Bible in Three Dimensions: Essays in Celebration of Forty Years of Biblical Studies in the University of Sheffield* (Sheffield: JSOT Press, 1990).

Conzelmann, Hans, *1 Corinthians*, tr. J.W. Leitch, Hermeneia (Philadelphia: Fortress Press, 1975).

Cooper, Kate, *The Virgin and the Bride: Idealized Womanhood in Late Antiquity* (Cambridge, Mass. and London: Harvard University Press, 1996).

Cope, Lamar, '1 Corinthians 11:2–16: One Step Further', *JBL* 97 (1978), pp. 435–36.

Cotter, Wendy, 'Women's Authority Roles in Paul's Churches: Countercultural or Conventional?', *NovT* 36 (1994), pp. 350–72.

Cox Miller, Patricia, 'In Praise of Nonsense', in A.H. Armstrong (ed.), *Classical Mediterranean Spirituality: Egyptian Greek, Roman* (London: Routledge and Kegan Paul, 1986), pp. 481–505.

Culler, Jonathan, *On Deconstruction: Theory and Criticism after Structuralism* (London: Routledge, 1989).

D'Angelo, Mary Rose, 'Veils, Virgins, and the Tongues of Men and Angels: Women's Heads in Early Christianity', in Eilberg-Schwartz and Doniger (eds), *Off With Her Head!*, pp. 131–64.

Davies, Margaret, *The Pastoral Epistles*, New Testament Guides (Sheffield: Sheffield Academic Press, 1996).

Davies, Stevan L., *The Gospel of Thomas and Christian Wisdom* (New York: Seabury Press, 1983).

De Conick, April D., *Seek To See Him: Ascent and Vision Mysticism in the Gospel of Thomas*, Supplements to *VC* 33 (Leiden: Brill, 1996).

Desjardins, Michel, *Sin in Valentinianism*, SBLDS 108 (Atlanta: Scholars Press, 1990).

Dibelius, Martin, and Conzelmann, Hans, *The Pastoral Epistles*, ed. Helmut Koester, tr. Philip Buttolph and Adela Yarbro, Hermeneia (Philadelphia: Fortress Press, 1972).

Dodd, Brian, *Paul's Paradigmatic 'I': Personal Example as Literary Strategy*, JSNTSup 177 (Sheffield: Sheffield Academic Press, 1999).

Donelson, Lewis R., *Pseudepigraphy and Ethical Argument in the Pastoral Epistles* (Tübingen: J.C.B. Mohr [Paul Siebeck], 1986).

Doresse, Jean, *The Secret Books of the Egyptian Gnostics: An Introduction to the Gnostic Coptic Manuscripts Discovered at Chenoboskion*, tr. Philip Mairet (London: Hollis and Carter, 1960).

Downing, F. Gerald, *Strangely Familiar* (Manchester: F. Gerald Downing, 1985).

Dunn, J.D.G., *1 Corinthians*, New Testament Guides (Sheffield: Sheffield Academic Press, 1995).

—'The "Body" in Colossians', in Thomas S. Schmidt and Moisés Silva (eds), *To Tell the Mystery: Essays on New Testament Eschatology in Honor of Robert H. Gundry* (Sheffield: JSOT Press, 1994), pp. 163–81.

—*The Epistles to the Colossians and to Philemon: A Commentary on the Greek Text*, NIGTC (Grand Rapids: Eerdmans/Carlisle: Paternoster, 1996).

Easton, Burton Scott, *The Pastoral Epistles: Introduction, Translation, Commentary and Word Studies* (London: SCM Press, 1948).

Eggins, Suzanne, *An Introduction to Systemic Functional Linguistics* (London: Pinter, 1994).

Eilberg-Schwartz, Howard, and Doniger, Wendy (eds), *Off With Her Head! The Denial of Women's Identity in Myth, Religion, and Culture* (Berkeley: University of California Press, 1995).

Fantham, Elaine, *et al.*, *Women in the Classical World: Image and Text* (New York and Oxford: Oxford University Press, 1994).

Fee, Gordon D., *1 and 2 Timothy, Titus* (Peabody, Mass.: Hendrickson/Carlisle: Paternoster, 1995).

—*The First Epistle to the Corinthians*, NICNT (Grand Rapids: Eerdmans, 1987).

Feuillet, A., 'L'homme "gloire de Dieu" et la femme "gloire de l'Homme" (1 Cor. 11.7b)', *RB* 81 (1974), pp. 161–82.

Filoramo, Giovanni, *A History of Gnosticism*, tr. Anthony Alcock (Oxford: Blackwell, 1990).

Fish, Stanley, *Is There a Text in This Class? The Authority of Interpretive Communities* (Cambridge, Mass. and London: Harvard University Press, 1980).

—*The Trouble with Principle* (Cambridge, Mass. and London: Harvard University Press, 1999).

Fitzmyer, J.A., 'A Feature of Qumran Angelology and the Angels of 1 Cor. XI. 10', *NTS* 4 (1957/58), pp. 48–58.

—'Another Look at ΚΕΦΑΛΗ in 1 Corinthians 11.3', *NTS* 35 (1989), pp. 503–11.

Foucault, Michel, 'What is an Author?', in Lodge (ed.), *Modern Criticism and Theory: A Reader*, pp. 197–210.

—*The Will to Knowledge*, tr. Robert Hurley (Harmondsworth: Penguin, 1998).

Fowl, Stephen, 'The Ethics of Interpretation, or What's Left Over after the Elimination of Meaning', in Clines, Fowl and Porter (eds), *The Bible in Three Dimensions*, pp. 379–98.

Gamble, Harry Y., *Books and Readers in the Early Church: A History of Early Christian Texts* (New Haven and London: Yale University Press, 1995).

García Martínez, Florentino, *The Dead Sea Scrolls Translated: The Qumran Texts in*

English, tr. Wilfred G.E. Watson, 2nd edn (Leiden: Brill/Grand Rapids: Eerdmans, 1996).

Garnsey, Peter, and Saller, Richard, *The Roman Empire: Economy, Society and Culture* (London: Duckworth, 1987).

Goehring, James E., 'Libertine or Liberated: Women in the So-called Libertine Gnostic Communities', in David Scholer (ed.), *Women in Early Christianity*, Studies in Early Christianity 14 (New York and London: Garland, 1993), pp. 183–98.

Grant, Robert M., 'Two Gnostic Gospels', *JBL* 79 (1960), pp. 1–11.

Guthrie, Donald, *The Pastoral Epistles: An Introduction and Commentary* (Leicester: Inter-Varsity Press, 1957).

Hampson, Daphne, *After Christianity* (London: SCM Press, 1996).

Hanson, Anthony Tyrrell, *The Pastoral Epistles*, NCB (Grand Rapids: Eerdmans/London: Marshall, Morgan & Scott, 1982).

—*Studies in the Pastoral Epistles* (London: SPCK, 1968).

Harrison, P.N., *Paulines and Pastorals* (London: Villiers, 1964).

—*The Problem of the Pastoral Epistles* (London: Oxford University Press, 1921).

Hartman, L., 'Some Unorthodox Thoughts on the "Household-Code Form" ', in Jacob Neusner *et al.* (eds), *The Social World of Formative Christianity and Judaism* (Philadelphia: Fortress Press, 1988), pp. 219–32.

Hawthorne, Nathaniel, *The Scarlet Letter* (Harmondsworth: Penguin, 1994 [1850]).

Hedrick, Charles W., and Hodgson, Robert (eds), *Nag Hammadi, Gnosticism, and Early Christianity* (Peabody, Mass.: Hendrickson, 1986).

Hirsch, E.D., *The Aims of Interpretation* (Chicago and London: University of Chicago Press, 1976).

—*Validity in Interpretation* (New Haven and London: Yale University Press, 1967).

Hoffman, Daniel L., *The Status of Women and Gnosticism in Irenaeus and Tertullian*, Studies in Women and Religion 36 (Lewiston, NY: Edwin Mellen, 1995).

Hoffman, Joseph R., 'De Statu Feminarum: The Correlation between Gnostic Theory and Social Practice', *Eglise et Théologie* 14 (1983), pp. 293–304.

Holmberg, Bengt, *Paul and Power: The Structure of Authority in the Primitive Church as Reflected in the Pauline Epistles* (Lund: CKW Gleerup, 1978).

Hooker, M.D., 'Authority on her Head: An Examination of 1 Cor. XI. 10', *NTS* 10 (1963/64), pp. 410–16.

—'Were There False Teachers in Colossae?', in Barnabas Lindars and Stephen Smalley (eds), *Christ and Spirit in the New Testament: Studies in Honour of C.D.F. Moule* (Cambridge: Cambridge University Press, 1973), pp. 315–31.

Horrell, David G., *The Social Ethos of the Corinthian Correspondence: Interests and Ideology from 1 Corinthians to 1 Clement* (Edinburgh: T&T Clark, 1996).

Houlden, J.L., *The Pastoral Epistles: 1 and 2 Timothy, Titus* (London: SCM Press/Philadelphia: Trinity Press International, 1989).

Irigaray, Luce, 'Equal to Whom?', in Naomi Schor and Elizabeth Weed (eds.), *The Essential Difference* (Bloomington, Ind. and Indianapolis: Indiana University Press, 1994), pp. 63–81.

Jervis, L. Ann, '1 Corinthians 14.34–35: A Reconsideration of Paul's Limitation of the Free Speech of Some Corinthian Women', *JSNT* 58 (1995), pp. 51–74.

—' "But I Want You to Know . . .": Paul's Midrashic Intertextual Response to the Corinthian Worshipers (1 Corinthians 11.2–16)', *JBL* 112 (1993), pp. 231–46.

Johnson, Luke Timothy, *Letters to Paul's Delegates: 1 Timothy, 2 Timothy, Titus*, The New Testament in Context (Valley Forge, Penn.: Trinity Press International, 1996).

Jonas, Hans, *The Gnostic Religion: The Message of the Alien God and the Beginnings of Christianity* (Boston: Beacon Press, 1958).

Karris, Robert J., 'The Background and Significance of the Polemic of the Pastoral Epistles', *JBL* 92 (1973), pp. 549–64.

Kelly, J.N.D., *A Commentary on the Pastoral Epistles* (London: A. & C. Black, 1963).

Kiley, Mark, *Colossians as Pseudepigraphy* (Sheffield: JSOT Press, 1986).

King, Karen L., 'Ridicule and Rape, Rule and Rebellion: The Hypostasis of the Archons', in James E. Goehring *et al.* (eds), *Gnosticism and the Early Christian World* (Sonoma, Calif.: Polebridge, 1990), pp. 3–24.

King, Karen L. (ed.), *Images of the Feminine in Gnosticism* (Philadelphia: Fortress Press, 1988).

Kitzberger, Ingrid Rosa (ed.), *Autobiographical Biblical Criticism: Between Text and Self* (Leiden: Deo, 2002).

Klijn, A.F.J., 'The "Single One" in the Gospel of Thomas', *JBL* 81 (1962), pp. 271–78.

Knight, George W., 'ΑΥΘΕΝΤΕΩ in Reference to Women in 1 Timothy 2.12', *NTS* 30 (1984), pp. 143–57.

—*The Pastoral Epistles: A Commentary on the Greek Text*, NIGTC (Grand Rapids: Eerdmans/Carlisle: Paternoster, 1992).

Kraemer, Ross Shepard, *Her Share of the Blessings: Women's Religions among Pagans, Jews, and Christians in the Greco-Roman World* (Oxford and New York: Oxford University Press, 1992).

—'Response' to Anne McGuire, 'Virginity and Subversion', in King (ed.), *Images of the Feminine in Gnosticism*, pp. 259–64.

Kraemer, Ross Shepard, and D'Angelo, Mary Rose (eds), *Women and Christian Origins* (New York and Oxford: Oxford University Press, 1999), pp. 221–35.

Lambdin, Thomas O., *Introduction to Sahidic Coptic* (Macon, Ga.: Mercer University Press, 1983).

Laughery, G.J., 'Paul: Anti-Marriage? Anti-Sex? Ascetic? A Dialogue with 1 Corinthians 7.1–40', *EvQ* 69 (1997), pp. 109–28.

Layton, Bentley, 'The Riddle of the Thunder (NHC VI, 2): The Function of Paradox in a Gnostic Text from Nag Hammadi', in Hedrick and Hodgson (eds), *Nag Hammadi, Gnosticism, and Early Christianity*, pp. 37–54.

Layton, Bentley (ed.), *The Gnostic Scriptures: A New Translation with Annotations and Introductions* (London: SCM Press, 1987).

—*Nag Hammadi Codex II, 2–7*, 2 vols (Leiden: E.J. Brill, 1989).

Leech, Geoffrey, *Principles of Pragmatics* (London and New York: Longman, 1983).

Levine, Molly Myerowitz, 'The Gendered Grammar of Ancient Mediterranean Hair', in Eilberg-Schwartz and Doniger (eds), *Off With Her Head!*, pp. 76–130.

Lightman, Marjorie, and Zeisel, William, 'Univira: An Example of Continuity and Change in Roman Society', *CH* 46 (1977), pp. 19–32.

Lincoln, Andrew T., *Ephesians*, WBC 42 (Dallas: Word, 1990).

——— 'The Use of the OT in Ephesians', *JSNT* 14 (1982), pp. 16–57.

Lincoln, Andrew T., and Wedderburn, A.J.M., *The Theology of the Later Pauline Letters* (Cambridge: Cambridge University Press, 1993).

Lodge, David (ed.), *Modern Criticism and Theory: A Reader* (London and New York: Longman, 1988).

Lohse, Eduard, *Colossians and Philemon*, tr. W.R. Poehlmann and R.J. Karris, Hermeneia (Philadelphia: Fortress Press, 1971).

Lüdemann, Gerd, *Heretics: The Other Side of Early Christianity*, tr. John Bowden (London: SCM Press, 1996).

Lutz, Cora E., 'Musonius Rufus "The Roman Socrates" ', *Yale Classical Studies* 10 (1947), pp. 3–147.

MacDonald, Dennis Ronald, 'Corinthian Veils and Gnostic Androgynes', in King (ed.), *Images of the Feminine in Gnosticism*, pp. 276–92.

—*The Legend and the Apostle: The Battle for Paul in Story and Canon* (Philadelphia: Westminster Press, 1983).

—*There Is No Male and Female: The Fate of a Dominical Saying in Paul and Gnosticism*, HDR 20 (Philadelphia: Fortress Press, 1987).

MacDonald, Margaret Y., 'Citizens of Heaven and Earth: Asceticism and Social Integration in Colossians and Ephesians', in Leif E. Vaage and Vincent L. Wimbush (eds.), *Asceticism and the New Testament* (New York and London: Routledge, 1999), pp. 269–98.

—*Early Christian Women and Pagan Opinion: The Power of the Hysterical Woman* (Cambridge: Cambridge University Press, 1996).

—*The Pauline Churches: A Socio-Historical Study of Institutionalization in the Pauline and Deutero-Pauline Writings*, SNTSMS 60 (Cambridge: Cambridge University Press, 1988).

—'Reading Real Women through the Undisputed Letters of Paul', in Kraemer and D'Angelo (eds), *Women and Christian Origins*, pp. 199–220.

MacRae, George W., 'The *Ego*-Proclamation in Gnostic Sources', in Ernst Bammel (ed.), *The Trial of Jesus: Cambridge Studies in Honour of C.F.D. Moule* (London: SCM Press, 1970), pp. 122–34.

Mahé, Jean-Pierre, 'Le sens des symboles sexuels dans quelques textes hermétiques et gnostiques', in Ménard (ed.), *Les textes de Nag Hammadi*, pp. 123–45.

Malina, Bruce J., *The New Testament World: Insights from Cultural Anthropology*, revd edn (Louisville, Ky.: Westminster/John Knox Press, 1993).

Marjanen, Antti, 'Is *Thomas* a Gnostic Gospel?', in Uro (ed.), *Thomas at the Crossroads*, pp. 107–39.

—*The Woman Jesus Loved: Mary Magdalene in the Nag Hammadi Library and Related Documents*, Nag Hammadi and Manichean Studies 40 (Leiden: E.J. Brill, 1996).

—'Women Disciples in the *Gospel of Thomas*', in Uro (ed.), *Thomas at the Crossroads*, pp. 89–106.

Martin, Dale B., *The Corinthian Body* (New Haven and London: Yale University Press, 1995).

Matlock, R. Barry, *Unveiling the Apocalyptic Paul: Paul's Interpreters and the Rhetoric of Criticism*, JSNTSup 127 (Sheffield: Sheffield Academic Press, 1996).

McGuire, Anne, 'Virginity and Subversion: Norea against the Powers in the *Hypostasis of the Archons*', in King (ed.), *Images of the Feminine in Gnosticism*, pp. 239–58.

Meade, David G., *Pseudonymity and Canon* (Tübingen: Mohr, 1986).

Meeks, Wayne A., *The First Urban Christians: The Social World of the Apostle Paul* (New Haven and London: Yale University Press, 1983).

—'The Image of the Androgyne: Some Uses of a Symbol in Earliest Christianity', *HR* 13 (1973/74), pp. 165–208.

—' "To Walk Worthily of the Lord": Moral Formation in the Pauline School Exemplified by the Letter to Colossians', in Eleanore Stump and Thomas P. Flint (eds.), *Hermes and Athena: Biblical Exegesis and Philosophical Theology* (Notre Dame, Ind.: University of Notre Dame Press, 1993), pp. 37–58.

Meier, John P., 'On the Veiling of Hermeneutics (1 Corinthians 11.2–16)', *CBQ* 40 (1978), pp. 212–26.

Ménard, Jacques E., 'L'Evangile selon Philippe et l'Exégèse de l'Ame', in Ménard (ed.), *Les textes de Nag Hammadi*, pp. 56–67.

—*L'Evangile selon Thomas*, Nag Hammadi Studies 5 (Leiden: E.J. Brill, 1975).

Ménard, Jacques É. (ed.), *Les textes de Nag Hammadi: Colloque du Centre d'Histoire des Religions (Strasbourg, 23–25 octobre 1974)* Nag Hammadi Studies 7 (Leiden: E.J. Brill, 1975).

Meyer, Marvin, 'Making Mary Male: The Categories "Male" and "Female" in the Gospel of Thomas', *NTS* 31 (1985), pp. 554–70.

Mitchell, Margaret M., *Paul and the Rhetoric of Reconciliation: An Exegetical Investigation of the Language and Composition of 1 Corinthians* (Tübingen: J.C.B. Mohr [Paul Siebeck], 1991).

Moore, Stephen D., *God's Gym: Divine Male Bodies of the Bible* (New York and London: Routledge, 1996).

Moule, C.F.D., *An Idiom Book of New Testament Greek*, 2nd edn (Cambridge: Cambridge University Press, 1959).

Murphy-O'Connor, Jerome, '1 Corinthians 11.2–16 Once Again', *CBQ* 50 (1988), pp. 265–74.

—'The Non-Pauline Character of 1 Corinthians 11.2–16?', *JBL* 95 (1976), pp. 615–21.

—'Sex and Logic in 1 Corinthians 11.2–16', *CBQ* 42 (1980), pp. 482–500.

Musurillo, Herbert, *The Acts of the Christian Martyrs* (Oxford: Clarendon Press, 1972).

Niccum, Curt, 'The Voice of the Manuscripts on the Silence of Women: The External Evidence for 1 Corinthians 14.34–35', *NTS* 43 (1997), pp. 242–55.

Orr, William F., and Walther, James Arthur, *1 Corinthians*, AB 32 (Garden City, NY: Doubleday, 1976).

Osiek, Carolyn, and Balch, David L., *Families in the New Testament World: Households and House Churches* (Louisville, Ky.: Westminster/John Knox, 1997).

Oster, Richard, 'When Men Wore Veils to Worship: The Historical Content of 1 Corinthians 11.4', *NTS* 34 (1988), pp. 481–505.

Padgett, Alan, 'Paul on Women in the Church: The Contradiction of Coiffure in 1 Corinthians 11.2–16', *JSNT* 20 (1984), pp. 69–86.

Pagels, Elaine, *Adam, Eve, and the Serpent* (London: Weidenfeld & Nicolson, 1988).

—'Exegesis and Exposition of the Genesis Creation Accounts in Selected Texts from Nag Hammadi', in Hedrick and Hodgson (eds), *Nag Hammadi, Gnosticism, and Early Christianity*, pp. 257–85.

—'Exegesis of Genesis 1 in the Gospels of Thomas and John', *JBL* 118 (1999), pp. 477–96.

—*The Gnostic Gospels* (Harmondsworth: Penguin, 1990 [1979]).

—*The Gnostic Paul: Gnostic Exegesis of the Pauline Letters* (Valley Forge, Pa.: Trinity Press International, 1975).

—'The "Mystery of Marriage" in the *Gospel of Philip* Revisited', in Birger A. Pearson (ed.), *The Future of Early Christianity* (Minneapolis: Fortress Press, 1991), pp. 442–54.

—'Pursuing the Spiritual Eve: Imagery and Hermeneutics in the *Hypostasis of the Archons* and the *Gospel of Philip*', in King (ed.), *Images of the Feminine in Gnosticism*, pp. 187–206.

—'Ritual in the *Gospel of Philip*', in Turner and McGuire (eds), *The Nag Hammadi Library after Fifty Years*, pp. 280–91.

Painchaud, Louis, 'The Use of Scripture in Gnostic Literature', *JECS* 4 (1996), pp. 129–46.

Payne, Philip B., 'Fuldensis, Sigla for Variants in Vaticanus, and 1 Corinthians 14.34–35', *NTS* 41 (1995), pp. 240–62.

Pearson, Birger A., 'Revisiting Norea', in King (ed.), *Images of the Feminine in Gnosticism*, pp. 265–75.

—'Some Observations on Gnostic Hermeneutics', in Wendy Doniger O'Flaherty (ed.), *The Critical Study of Sacred Texts* (Berkeley: Graduate Theological Union, 1979), pp. 243–56.

Perkins, Pheme, 'Irenaeus and the Gnostics: Rhetoric and Composition in *Adversus Haereses* Book One', *VC* 30 (1976), pp. 193–200.

Pétrement, Simone, *A Separate God: The Christian Origins of Gnosticism*, tr. Carol Harrison (New York: HarperCollins, 1990).

Poirier, John C., and Frankovich, Joseph, 'Celibacy and Charism in 1 Corinthians 7.5–7', *HTR* 89 (1996), pp. 1–18.

Pomeroy, Sarah B., *Goddesses, Whores, Wives, and Slaves: Women in Classical Antiquity* (London: Robert Hale, 1975).

Porter, Stanley E., *Idioms of the Greek New Testament*, 2nd edn, Biblical Languages: Greek, 2 (Sheffield: Sheffield Academic Press, 1994).

—'What Does it Mean to be "Saved by Childbirth" (1 Timothy 2.15)?', *JSNT* 49 (1993), pp. 87–102.

Quispel, Gilles, 'The *Gospel of Thomas* Revisited', in Bernard Barc (ed.), *Colloque Internationale sur les Textes de Nag Hammadi (Québec, 22–25 août 1978)*, Bibliothèque Copte de Nag Hammadi Etudes 1 (Quebec: Les Presses de l'Université Laval/Louvain: Editions Peeters, 1981), pp. 218–66.

Radcliffe, Timothy, 'Paul and Sexual Identity: 1 Corinthians 11.2–16', in Janet Martin Soskice (ed.), *After Eve: Women, Theology and the Christian Tradition* (London: Marshall Pickering, 1990), pp. 62–72.

Robinson, James M. (ed.), *The Nag Hammadi Library in English*, 3rd edn (New York: HarperCollins, 1988).

Robinson, William C., 'The Exegesis on the Soul', *NovT* 12 (1970), pp. 102–17.

—'Introduction' to the *Exegesis on the Soul*, in Layton (ed.), *Nag Hammadi Codex II, 2–7*, ii, pp. 136–41.

Rorty, Richard, *Consequences of Pragmatism* (Minneapolis: University of Minnesota Press, 1982).

—*Contingency, Irony, and Solidarity* (Cambridge: Cambridge University Press, 1989).

—*Objectivity, Relativism, and Truth: Philosophical Papers, Volume 1* (Cambridge: Cambridge University Press, 1991).

—*Philosophy and the Mirror of Nature* (Oxford: Blackwell, 1980).

—*Philosophy and Social Hope* (Harmondsworth: Penguin, 1999).

Rouselle, Aline, *Porneia: On Desire and the Body in Antiquity*, tr. Felicia Pheasant (Oxford: Basil Blackwell, 1988).

Rudolph, K., *Gnosis: The Nature and History of Gnosticism*, tr. R.McL. Wilson (San Francisco: Harper & Row, 1987).

de Saussure, Ferdinand, *Course in General Linguistics*, ed. and tr. Roy Harris (London: Duckworth, 1983).

Schmithals, Walter, *Gnosticism in Corinth: An Investigation of the Letters to the Corinthians*, tr. John E. Steely (Nashville and New York: Abingdon, 1971).

Schnackenburg, Rudolf, *Ephesians: A Commentary*, tr. Helen Heron (Edinburgh: T&T Clark, 1991).

Scholer, David M. (ed.), *Gnosticism in the Early Church*, Studies in Early Christianity 5 (New York and London: Garland, 1993).

Schottroff, Louise, *Lydia's Impatient Sisters: A Feminist Social History of Early Christianity* (London: SCM Press, 1995).

Schüssler Fiorenza, Elisabeth, *In Memory of Her: A Feminist Theological Reconstruction of Christian Origins* (London: SCM Press, 1983).

Schütz, John H., *Paul and the Anatomy of Apostolic Authority*, SNTSMS 26 (Cambridge: Cambridge University Press, 1975).

Schweizer, Eduard, *The Letter to the Colossians: A Commentary*, tr. Andrew Chester (London: SPCK, 1982).

Scott, E.F., *The Pastoral Epistles* (London: Hodder & Stoughton, 1936).

Searle, John R., *Speech Acts: An Essay in the Philosophy of Language* (Cambridge: Cambridge University Press, 1969).

Seim, Turid Karlsen, 'A Superior Minority? The Problem of Men's Headship in Ephesians 5', in David Hellholm, Halvor Moxnes and Turid Karlsen Seim (eds.), *Mighty Minorities? Minorities in Early Christianity – Positions and Strategies* (Oslo *et al.*: Scandinavian University Press, 1995), pp. 167–81.

Smith, Morton, 'The History of the Term Gnostikos', in Bentley Layton (ed.), *The Rediscovery of Gnosticism*, ii: *Sethian Gnosticism* (Leiden: E.J. Brill, 1981), pp. 796–807.

Spark, Muriel, *The Mandelbaum Gate* (Harmondsworth: Penguin, 1967).

—*The Prime of Miss Jean Brodie* (Harmondsworth: Penguin, 1965).

Spicq, C., *Les Epitres pastorales*, 4th edn, 2 vols (Paris: Gabalda, 1969).

Spivak, Gayatri Chakravorty, 'Translator's Preface' to Jacques Derrida, *Of Grammatology* (Baltimore and London: Johns Hopkins University Press, 1976).

Staley, Jeffrey L., 'What is Critical about Autobiographical (Biblical) Criticism?', in Kitzberger (ed.), *Autobiographical Biblical Criticism*, pp. 12–33.

Steiner, George, *Real Presences: Is There Anything in What We Say?* (London: Faber & Faber, 1989).

Stout, Jeffrey, 'What is the Meaning of a Text?', *New Literary History* 14 (1982), pp. 1–12.

Tajfel, Henri, *Differentiation between Social Groups* (London: Academic Press, 1978).

Theissen, Gerd, *The Social Setting of Pauline Christianity*, ed. and tr. John H. Schütz (Edinburgh: T. & T. Clark, 1982).

Thiselton, Anthony C., *The First Epistle to the Corinthians: A Commentary on the Greek Text*, NIGTC (Grand Rapids and Cambridge: Eerdmans/Carlisle: Paternoster, 2000).

Thomassen, Einar, 'How Valentinian is *The Gospel of Philip*?', in Turner and McGuire (eds), *The Nag Hammadi Library after Fifty Years*, pp. 251–79.

Towner, Philip H., *The Goal of our Instruction: The Structure of Theology and Ethics in the Pastoral Epistles*, JSNTSup 34 (Sheffield: Sheffield Academic Press, 1989).

Trompf, G.W., 'On Attitudes toward Women in Paul and Paulinist Literature: 1 Corinthians 11.3–16 and its Context', *CBQ* 42 (1980), pp. 196–215.

Turner, John D., and McGuire, Anne (eds), *The Nag Hammadi Library after Fifty Years: Proceedings of the 1995 Society of Biblical Literature Commemoration* (Leiden: E.J. Brill, 1997).

Uro, Risto, 'Is *Thomas* an Encratite Gospel?', in Uro (ed.), *Thomas at the Crossroads*, pp. 140–62.

Uro, Risto (ed.), *Thomas at the Crossroads: Essays on the Gospel of Thomas* (Edinburgh: T&T Clark, 1998).

Vaage, Leif E., and Wimbush, Vincent L., 'Introduction', in Leif E. Vaage and Vincent L. Wimbush (eds), *Asceticism and the New Testament* (New York and London: Routledge, 1999), pp. 1–7.

Valantasis, Richard, *The Gospel of Thomas* (London and New York: Routledge, 1997).

—'Is the Gospel of Thomas Ascetical? Revisiting an Old Problem with a New Theory', *JECS* 7 (1999), pp. 55–81.

Vallée, Gérard, *A Study in Anti-Gnostic Polemics: Irenaeus, Hippolytus, and Epiphanius*, Studies in Christianity and Judaism 1 (Waterloo, Ont.: Wilfrid Laurier University Press, 1981).

Vermes, Geza, *Jesus the Jew: A Historian's Reading of the Gospels* (London: Fontana/Collins, 1973).

Verner, David C., *The Household of God: The Social World of the Pastoral Epistles*, SBLDS 71 (Chico, Calif.: Scholars Press, 1983).

Waldstein, Michael, 'Hans Jonas' Construct "Gnosticism": Analysis and Critique', *JECS* 8 (2000), pp. 341–72.

Walker, William O., '1 Corinthians 11.2–16 and Paul's Views Regarding Women', *JBL* 94 (1975), pp. 94–110.

Wenham, J.W., *The Elements of New Testament Greek* (Cambridge: Cambridge University Press, 1991).

Williams, Michael A., 'Interpreting the Nag Hammadi Library as "Collection(s)" in the History of "Gnosticism(s)" ', in Louis Painchaud and Anne Pasquier (eds), *Les textes de Nag Hammadi et le problème de leur classification: Actes du colloque tenu à Québec du 15 au 19 septembre 1993*, Bibliothèque Copte de Nag Hammadi Etudes 3 (Quebec: Les Presses de l'Université Laval/Louvain: Editions Peeters, 1995), pp. 3–50.

—*Rethinking 'Gnosticism': An Argument for Dismantling a Dubious Category* (Princeton: Princeton University Press, 1996).

—'Variety in Gnostic Perspectives on Gender', in King (ed.), *Images of the Feminine in Gnosticism*, pp. 2–22.

Wilson, R. McL., 'Gnosis at Corinth', in M.D. Hooker and S.G. Wilson (eds), *Paul and Paulinism: Essays in Honour of C.K. Barrett* (London: SPCK, 1982), pp. 102–14.

—'How Gnostic Were the Corinthians?', *NTS* 19 (1972/73), pp. 65–74.

—'The New Testament in the Nag Hammadi Gospel of Philip', *NTS* 9 (1962/63), pp. 291–94.

—'Old Testament Exegesis in the Gnostic Exegesis on the Soul', in Martin Krause (ed.), *Essays on the Nag Hammadi Texts in Honour of Pahor Labib* (Leiden: E.J. Brill, 1975), pp. 217–24.

Winter, Bruce W., *After Paul Left Corinth: The Influence of Secular Ethics and Social Change* (Grand Rapids and Cambridge: Eerdmans, 2001).

Wire, Antoinette Clark, *The Corinthian Women Prophets: A Reconstruction through Paul's Rhetoric* (Minneapolis: Fortress Press, 1990).

Wisse, Frederik, 'The Nag Hammadi Library and the Heresiologists', *VC* 25 (1971), pp. 205–23.

—'On Exegeting "The Exegesis on the Soul" ', in Ménard (ed.), *Les Textes de Nag Hammadi*, pp. 68–81.

—'Prolegomena to the Study of the New Testament and Gnosis', in A.H.B. Logan and A.J.M. Wedderburn (eds), *The New Testament and Gnosis: Essays in Honour of Robert McL. Wilson* (Edinburgh: T. & T. Clark, 1983), pp. 138–45.

—'The Use of Early Christian Literature as Evidence for Inner Diversity and Conflict', in Hedrick and Hodgson (eds), *Nag Hammadi, Gnosticism, and Early Christianity*, pp. 177–90.

Witherington, Ben, *Conflict and Community in Corinth: A Socio-Rhetorical Commentary on 1 and 2 Corinthians* (Grand Rapids: Eerdmans/Carlisle: Paternoster, 1995).

Yates, Roy, 'Colossians and Gnosis', *JSNT* 27 (1986), pp. 49–68.

Young, Frances, 'The Pastoral Epistles and the Ethics of Reading', *JSNT* 45 (1992), pp. 105–20.

INDEX OF AUTHORS